Christmas 2005.   Dear

I hope you enjoy the
addition to your G·S works
with all my love
Steve

'A Wand'ring Minstrel, I'

'A Wand'ring Minstrel, I'

THE AUTOBIOGRAPHY OF THOMAS ROUND

CARNEGIE PUBLISHING LTD

First published in 2002
by Carnegie Publishing Ltd
Carnegie House, Chatsworth Road
Lancaster LAI 4SL
publishing website: www.carnegiepub.co.uk
book production website: www.wooof.net

British Library Cataloguing-in-Publication data
A CIP record for this book is available from the British Library

ISBN 1-85936-095-5

Designed and typeset by Carnegie Publishing
Printed and bound in the UK by
The Cromwell Press, Trowbridge, Wilts

Contents

FOR MY WIFE ALICE
For her love and support and encouragement
through the sixty-four years of our marriage
which has enabled me to achieve some
measure of success in my chosen career.
And for my son, Ellis.

Acknowledgements

I WISH TO THANK Ian Birnie who read the first draft of this book and encouraged me to carry on with it and who researched various publishers, including Carnegie.

And Susan Walsh for re-typing my original manuscript.

Also the many friends and devotees of Gilbert & Sullivan who have persistently requested that I write my life story.

The author and publishers have made extensive efforts to trace copyright owners of photographs reproduced in this book. Most of the photographs were presented to the author many years ago and in some cases it has been difficult or impossible to trace whether copyright clearance was required or not. If there have been any omissions in acknowledgement, we apologise to those concerned.

Prologue

WHAT ARE THE REASONS for wanting to put down in writing one's life story?

I suppose my reply is that over the past few years, many people have said, 'What an interesting life you have had – you should write a book.'

This set me thinking; not that I thought that anyone would be interested in reading my story, but for my own interest in later years I'd like to remember as much as I can, while I can.

For me, my life has been a fascinating one, from my early years in my home town of Barrow-in-Furness, my time in the Lancaster City police force, through the war years and my career as a professional singer. It is my hope that my son, Ellis, my grandchildren, Mark and Susannah, will be interested enough to want to remember me!

The process, however, has taken a long time to assume any practical form, with stops and starts over many years. I think it is finally in some sort of chronological order, although it could never be complete. Memories constantly come back to me, all of which are dear to me, but I had to stop somewhere and this is it!

CHAPTER ONE

Tom Round's Schooldays

The Cemetery Cottages, Barrow-in-Furness, Cumbria – three rows of them, Lime Street, Beech Street and Maple Street – were built on a fairly steep bank and facing east and west, bordered on the east side by Elm Road and on the west side by Oak Road. I was born in the middle row at 32 Beech Street.

The eastern end of the cottages was only separated from the cemetery by garden allotments; my father rented two of them.

I agree that my address sounds like something from a Hammer Horror Film, but as a boy I used to think it was a beautiful piece of countryside to have as a cemetery. Large plots of ground were literally bulldozed through forests of large trees – oak, ash, larch, beech, elm and maple – how else did our streets derive their names?

I'm not too old to remember that although my childhood was hard, I found it all very exciting; except school of course, which interrupted our very special evening games. We were generally a happy family and if I remember correctly, approximately six years separated each of the offspring, my elder brother William Joseph, my sister Ethel, myself and my younger brother Fred.

32 Beech Street, the Cemetery Cottages, where I was born.

My father was a strongly built, broad-shouldered 5ft 8in blast-furnaceman, employed by the Barrow Haematite Steel Company, and my mother a very handsome lady, about the same height as father.

His work of loading the great metal containers with iron ore to be cranked a hundred feet up a sloping gantry and then tipped into the enormous blast furnaces, was hard physical labour. Every day, when he arrived home at the end of his shift, covered with the fine red dust of the iron ore, he would strip and wash completely before touching any food. I remember even then admiring his strong body and his head of curly black hair, which was washed with carbolic soap every day of his life, and always hoping that I would grow up to be as strong and as good-looking as he. I took after my mother in both looks and being tall, as did my elder brother. My sister, who should have had mother's looks and build, took after my father and remained strong and stocky. Two of his descriptions of me, when I decided to try and build some muscles, were, 'that I looked like a freshly skinned rabbit' or 'a well-scraped matchstick'.

I think I could write a book just about my father and I'm sure he will turn up several times during these scribblings. I must give you a clearer idea of the type of man he was before I go any further. Apart from the last two years of his working life – he retired at sixty-five – he worked at the blast furnaces seven days a week. I only remember him being off ill once, when he had to go into hospital for a mastoid operation. He worked shifts – 6 a.m. to 2 p.m., 2 p.m. to 10 p.m. and 10 p.m. to 6 a.m. Every third Sunday two shifts came together so that he started at 6 a.m., and worked through until 10 p.m. It was one of my jobs to take his lunch to him at 1 p.m. – a walk of at least a mile and a half – race back home in time for Sunday School and then take his tea at 5 p.m. I liked to sit with him and his workmates in his cabin while they hurriedly ate their pies or sandwiches in the half-hour allotted to them. He would arrive home about 10.30 p.m., go through his washing routine and then settle down to a hearty supper. One of his favourite meals was what we called a suet pudding. It consisted of a lining of suet pastry in a basin, filled with chunks of beef, which I think had been pre-cooked, then boiled. It was my favourite meal too, and I'm afraid I used to will him not to feel too hungry so that he would at least leave a little. He was then free until his next shift of that week which would be 2 p.m. to 10 p.m.

I remarked earlier that he ran two allotments, but not only did he grow all the vegetables we ever needed, he also had a large hen run with a flock of Rhode Island Red hens which supplied us with eggs.

He also had a pigeon loft with some of the finest racers in the area. I spent many Saturday afternoons shaking a biscuit tin half full of corn to attract the racers into the loft so that Dad could remove the rings and run to the time clock held by the referee.

Apart from these activities, we also had a stable that housed, to me, the finest pony in the world. Joey was his name and his job in life was to transport the whole family in a highly polished and beautifully painted pony trap to weekend picnics. Even through the summertime I would run out of school at 4 p.m. to find Mother and Dad waiting at the school gates with Joey and trap and we would go a few miles along the lanes and find a nice place for a picnic.

Of course, my proudest job was to take Joey out to pasture, when I would spend the whole evening watching him eat the green grass before taking him back to his stable and a quick rub down. How my father managed all this on top of his eight-hour shift each day, I cannot imagine. I know our cottage was the smartest in Beech Street. He re-roofed it with heavy Lakeland slates. We were the first to have electricity installed in place of gas, and he did all the wiring himself, after reading all the books. He turned part of our back kitchen into a bathroom and built a wash house in the back yard.

When Joey became too old to transport us any more, he was put to sleep. Dad promptly built a garage and bought a giant motorcycle and sidecar. I remember it was a BSA twin cylinder model and carried five of us with ease – three in the sidecar, which had a dickie seat, one on the pillion seat and Dad driving. I longed for the time when I would be old enough to ride on the pillion seat. During the four or five years we had the motorcycle, we explored every lane and byway and every lake throughout the Lake District, and of course, our after-school picnics took us many more miles further afield than we could ever accomplish with the pony and trap.

I don't ever remember the motorcycle going into a garage for any repair. Dad bought and studied books on motorcycle engines and when we finally sold it, it looked as if we had just bought it brand-new.

Dad had decided that we all needed more exercise, so after the sale of the BSA, we were all supplied with bicycles. Where Dad found all the energy for all these activities, I shall never know.

He didn't drink or smoke and yet he told me that until the age of nineteen he did both, and then decided to stop. I never ever saw him with a cigarette or a drink in his hand.

We lived in a hard-drinking community – work at the blast furnaces was desperately hard and hot – and the management of the works supplied a keg of beer for each shift working on the pig beds. They knew the men were always thirsty and to drink water all the time and

All aboard for another drive: Father, Mother, Fred and me.

to be bent over, working with a shovel, gave them stomach cramps. They thought beer was a better substitute, but unfortunately it gave the men a liking for it, and I'm afraid I witnessed a lot of drunkenness and unhappiness and poverty caused by drinking.

Dad did not actually work on the pig beds; as I said before, he helped to supply the iron ore mixtures to feed the furnaces, so perhaps that was the reason he was able to give up drinking. To me, he was a man apart from the rest and I was proud that he didn't spend his spare time in the pubs. I remember ruining a party with our many hard-drinking Scottish relatives by going into hysterics because I saw my father with what I thought was a glass of beer in his hand. Even when I tasted it and knew that it was sarsparilla, I couldn't be consoled, because he had a beer glass in his hand and it didn't look right. Poor Dad, he had to put it down, or take me home to bed. We had lots of relations – I had five uncles living in the same row of cottages – all with largeish families and all of them drinkers. You can imagine the parties we had, and the marvellous picnics at the seaside, which was less than two miles from our doorstep. I never really knew our Scottish relatives, but I do know they descended on us once every year and all our houses seemed to be full of strange-talking people. The parties

'A Wand'ring Minstrel, I'

With Dad in front of his budgerigar aviary.

4

seemed to me to be endless, and among my father's accomplishments was his ability to sing comic songs – several of which I can remember to this day. We had one of the first gramophones in the area and we had nearly all the records made by Billy Williams and George Formby senior – such songs as 'The Inquisitive Kid' and 'What a Little Short Shirt You've Got' were great favourites of mine.

I seem to have given the impression that my father was larger than life, but to me he was larger than life and if I may jump a few years into my teenage years, I can add another star to his crown. My girlfriend Alice York (actually, we had known each other since we were about three or four years old), taught him simple algebra (it was never simple to me) and the basic rules of bookkeeping. He had been appointed Secretary and Treasurer of the newly formed 'Cemetery Cottages Working Men's Club'.

He was an avid reader and we had full sets of the *Encyclopaedia Britannica*, which he read from cover to cover. My annual Christmas present to him was a *Readers Digest* yearly subscription.

Even though I admired him so much, and loved to be in his company, he was a very strict head of the house. If he found out that I had had a caning at school for some misdemeanour, then I would receive another one from him when I got home.

What about my mother? Well, of course I was spoiled by her. She was quite tall and, I realise now, must have been quite good looking in her youth.

She had a very hard task in those days, as did all the wives of the furnace and steel men – cooking, washing, mending, eking out the meagre wages. She had a sweet soprano voice, but was very shy to use it. I think I was about six years old, so my sister would be about eleven or twelve, and my brother about seventeen or eighteen, when I was brought in from fishing in the local reservoir to be told some momentous news. I was completely mystified and more so when I was led upstairs into my mother's bedroom which seemed to be full of uncles and aunts. My first surprise was to see mother in bed – she wasn't ill when I left to go fishing after tea – and my attention was directed to what I would have said now was a medium-sized cantaloupe melon. But, never having heard or seen such things, I merely blurted out that it was the biggest pink orange that I had ever seen. Of course, it was the head of my newly born brother Fred, who had just arrived to complete our family of three boys and a girl. I had no idea where they had found him, but after being shown that he wasn't really an orange, I managed to escape to resume my fishing.

My elder brother and sister and I all attended the same school, but my brother had already left school when I started. He ignored the Iron and Steel Works and opted for life as a farm labourer, and the

The former Hawcoat School, now
a private residence.

first Hiring Fair that took place in the town of Ulverston every year
found him parading before the hiring farmers, alongside other young
men. Being tall and strong, he was quickly snapped up and offered
the usual thirty shillings plus food and lodgings. Shortly after this,
my sister also left school and went, as did all the girls of our class,
into domestic service to some large house or hotel in the Lake District.

Our school was called Hawcoat School, and that was in another
small village about one mile further into the country from us. Our
little group of cottages was about two miles outside the main town
of Barrow, whose population was around the seventy or eighty thou-
sand mark.

The school building was set in a narrow lane completely surrounded
on all sides by fields and woods. Half a mile away towered the cliffs
of the sandstone quarries, from which came the stone for the Town
Hall and the main buildings of Barrow, including endless terraces of
apartment buildings housing the Vickers Armstrong shipbuilding
workers. But the house that was a mystery to all us boys and girls
was about fifty yards from the school, hidden by tall trees at the end
of a long driveway. The home of Romney, the famous artist; I don't
remember seeing any member of his family, and we were far too
scared to venture down the driveway.

Before I go on, I must write again about my father. Our rows of
cottages contributed their quota of young men for the 1914–1918 Great
War, and I learned by chance that my father was the instigator and
organiser of the small War Memorial erected at the western end of

Tom Round's Schooldays

Beech Street. I was named after my uncle, who was killed only two months before the war ended.

Back to my schooldays. I was never very bright; at least I can't remember being bright, I only remember that I seemed to be kept in after school for an extra fifteen minutes for some prank or other. I never minded this too much, because although I was rather frightened of our headmaster, he never allowed me to walk home the one mile on my own. He owned a motorcycle, which I can see clearly in my mind's eye to this day. It was a make known as a Sparkbrook, and it was painted green. Well, by the time I had completed my punishment task, he was usually ready to go home himself, and he never failed to give me a ride on the back of his motorcycle. I was usually home before any of my schoolmates.

I remember one occasion when I wasn't offered a ride home. I set off on my lonely walk and I happened to be passing a bus stop and the local bus pulled up beside me. Having no money to pay my fare, I waited until the bus started to move and then jumped on to the step of the emergency door at the rear. I grabbed the emergency door handle and hung on for dear life. There was no other bus stop between Hawcoat and the Cottages, and it never failed to stop there – at least until this day. Obviously no one was waiting at the stop and to my horror, the bus went on past the stop. I knew I would be spotted as we got nearer to the town so I let go of the handle and took a wild leap on to the road. It doesn't take much imagination to picture the action of the next few seconds. I suppose the bus was travelling at about 20 mph, and when I hit the road I somersaulted, rolled over and finally lay still. I climbed to my feet and staggered to the roadside, and lay there for what seemed like ages before I was able to attempt to walk. Apart from a few tears in my jacket, I seemed to be all right. Miraculously, no one had seen what had happened and apart from the buses and a few bicycles, there was little or no traffic on our roads. I managed to walk home to find that some of my school mates had already told my parents that I had been kept in school, so my father was waiting for me with his belt already off. He didn't notice my torn jacket, but immediately proceeded to give me another punishment and sent me straight off to bed, which was what I wanted more than anything. I was still in a daze after my fall, and I don't think I remember him hitting me at all. Next morning, however, I was so stiff and sore that I couldn't get up from my bed, and of course, the rest of the awful story came out. I couldn't go to school because I was too sore to move, but I didn't get any sympathy either.

As the demands for the pig iron and Bessemer steel fluctuated, so did the workers' employment, and although I was very young, I soon

The War Memorial.

learned that when I heard my father say the words, 'the furnaces will be damped down for four weeks', I knew that he would be at home and spending more time in the garden. Groups of men would spend hours standing about on the 'bottom green' playing cards or just talking. It was during these times that some of the men found other ways to earn some money and extra food. We lived two miles from the sea and at the north end of Walney Island, where the channel known as Scarfe Hole opened on to the Irish Sea, quite a number of men owned fishing boats of various sizes. Line fishing and draw fishing on the ebb and flow of the tide was quite profitable. Line fishing consisted of a line of anything up to 500 feet in length being staked out along the sand about six inches high. From this line, at intervals of approximately a foot, short lines were hung on which were fastened fishhooks. The tide flowed in over these lines and when the ebb tide cleared them again, the men went out and lifted the line at one end and, with luck, there would be quite a few fish, mainly fluke, dangling from the hooks.

Draw fishing was performed with a long fishing net, probably about 200 yards in length and up to approximately 20 feet in width. Several men stayed on the shore holding one end of the net, whilst the rest was paid off the stern end of a boat being rowed in a wide arc, and returning to the shore about 50 or 60 yards further along the shore. The net was then pulled in evenly by both teams, closing in on each other, as the net became shorter. Sometimes there would be hardly anything caught in the net, but at others there would be a splendid mixture of crabs, eels, codling and fluke. This fishing procedure always took place when the tide was ebbing or flowing, to catch the fish coming in from the open sea through the narrow channel of Scarfe Hole. Apart from helping with this way of fishing, I also had a long throw-out line with which I could do very well at times.

On the edge of the sand dunes at Scarfe, the men had built cabins of various sizes which would be called now, I suppose, holiday chalets. The cabins were built mainly of rough planking with tin roofs, and some of course, were much better than others. During the school summer holidays, we spent most of our time there. Sleeping bunks were fitted so that we could spend days there and some of my happiest childhood days were spent at the cabins.

The 1921–22 General Strike brought great hardship to all the country, but as a six year old boy, I was only concerned with the way it affected our own little community. Free meals were provided at our schools, but some families were too proud to accept charity of this kind. Our family had to accept them on two or three days in each week. Unfortunately, the meals were not provided at Hawcoat School, so I had to run and walk a distance of two miles to Oxford Street School

'A Wand'ring Minstrel, I'

The cabins at Scarfe Hole. Blackcombe Mountain is in the background but is completely obliterated by mist.

for my free lunch, and then make my way back to my own school for the afternoon classes.

Also at this time, bakeries were provided to bake bread free of charge because there was little or no fuel to light the fires under our own ovens at home. So, once every week, not on a day when I was racing for my free lunch, I would run home from school, quickly eat my meal and then trot off with a barrow loaded with dough in bread tins, carefully covered, to our nearest bakery. I would leave the bread with the baker, all carefully marked with our own brand, trot back home and then on to school. After school, I would again collect the barrow, hurry down to the bakery, and collect the dozen or so now lovely brown loaves and deliver them to my mother.

At one period during the Strike, the beautiful Sowerby Woods started to be cut down to provide fuel for the various industries in the town. Our fathers were allowed to chop down the smaller trees for home fuel, but also to dig out the roots of the larger trees after they had been felled. They would be carried home in all sorts of transport and thrown into our coal sheds to dry and then to be used for our own fires. These were great and exciting days for us boys and girls, to be among the sawing and the chopping. I suppose we helped in some way or another, but it was just another picnic when our mothers arrived with thick slices of bread and jam and flapjacks. Most of those beautiful forests were ruined by this treatment, but many acres still remained for us children to roam in.

I can always remember one thing about those tree roots. I remember going into our coal shed to collect some wood for our fire one dark evening and when I stepped inside, I was confronted by patches of a weird greenish light. I was scared out of my wits and ran into the house for my father, who told me it was a phosphorous glow caused by the rotting tree roots. Many a night I took a piece of this rotting wood to bed with me to stare at under the bedclothes. Strange, I have never seen any from that day to this.

We were never bored as children – the games we played and invented were numerous, and when the big boys were not playing football on the 'bottom green', we would play there.

Saturday afternoons would see gangs of us going to the local cinema, namely 'The Electric', to watch our heroes in silent films. Our heroes at that time were Tom Mix, Hoot Gibson, Buck Jones and Elmo Lincoln. I didn't bother about the female heroines at that time. One of the most exciting films I can ever remember seeing during those early years was 'Ben Hur'.

Of course, I started paying attention to girls at a very early age, and my threepence a week pocket money usually went like this: a penny for the cinema, a penny for a hair slide or a comb for the girl and a penny split in two for two separate ha'p'orths of sweets. The girl herself paid to go into the pictures.

The one girl who could never be persuaded to go out with that terrible Tom Round was Alice York, snooty 'Yorky' from 6 Lime Street. Her brother Bernard and I were great friends. Bribes were useless, my other girl friends used to knock on her house door to see if she would come out to play with them and Tom Round, only to have the door slammed in their faces. There was no doubt at all; I had an awful reputation!

Of course, the more she refused, the more determined I was to make her walk out with me. Even her mother used to chase me off with a rolling pin if she saw me hanging around at the bottom of their street. If only I could have attended the same school, I might have stood a better chance, but the bitterest pill she had to swallow, was the fact that I went to the lowly Hawcoat School, and Alice attended the new Victoria High School. I'm sure she never knew what it was to be kept in after school hours for some prank or other, and although she told me in later years that she was never very bright, and had to work hard to keep up, she nevertheless became Head Girl and Head of Games. Why I was bothering to persuade such an egghead to go out with me, I'll never know, because I certainly wasn't short of girls. It seems as though destiny was already taking its hold on my life.

I wish I could remember how and when we went on our first date, but I know that by the time I was fourteen, the names of Tom and Alice were linked together by all the kids in the cottages.

The only dangers I ran in our relationship were purely physical, both from her parents and her uncle Sam, who made it quite public that he would skin me alive if he ever caught me with his niece. I

'A Wand'ring Minstrel, I'

can never think how our families reacted to each other over this, because they were always on speaking terms as far as I can remember.

I can imagine my own mother thinking that at last Tom was going out with a decent girl, whilst Alice's parents thought that their daughter had got the worst in the neighbourhood. I think Alice must have been very brave to put up with the troubles she must have had at home over me. Strange that my father should have been one of the most respected men in our area. I wasn't a real bad boy, just high-spirited. No, I was an angel compared to lots of the lads. Some of them were never out of the hands of the police for various offences.

At twelve years of age, I was transferred to Holker Street School, virtually in the heart of the town. A few months later, I passed the entrance examination to the Barrow Technical College. I was one of two boys who lived in the cottages to attend this College at that time, the other being Fred Morgan, and we felt very proud to be the only boys who wore an official school uniform. Fred's parents ran the local off licence, and he was to become a well-known local tenor, and much in demand as a soloist in the Barrow churches. The Americans and Russians have at last reached the moon, but I don't know why it has taken them so long, because Fred Morgan and I were drawing up plans to do just that when we were twelve years old. I was always in favour of waiting until the moon was just above the horizon because then we wouldn't have to fly so high. Anyway, I'm glad someone has at last made it.

My ambition at this time was to join the Royal Air Force and Alice York and I (we had become steady sweethearts now) spent hours talking about this. I also became very keen on swimming, not an unnatural thing, considering that we lived so near to the sea, had two fairly clean reservoirs and a very good public baths. I managed to get into the school team, but I lived in a town that seemed to breed speed swimmers. One of Alice's cousins was to become the schoolboy champion of England, and another cousin was a local champion. I also played football and rugby league, but not very well.

CHAPTER TWO

'A Hammer Came Up and Drove Them Home'

$\mathcal{A}$T FIFTEEN AND A HALF, my father decided that my education had gone far enough – I think mother influenced him in this – and I was taken from school and placed in the steel works as an apprentice joiner, the one subject at which I was completely hopeless!

Use is everything of course, and it didn't take too long before I could drive a nail into a floorboard without leaving too many 'shillings' on the wood (hammer indentations). I started to attend evening classes at my old Technical College, studying building science and construction, practical geometry and joinery. There was a fee for this, which my parents willingly paid; I believe it was only twelve shillings a term, but to pay anything at all for education seemed crazy. Still, I learned more at night school in three years than I did in all my previous schooling. I even managed to pass my exams each year with a Distinction, which entitled me to free tuition each following term, thus relieving my parents of the twelve-shilling fee.

It was about this time, when I was sixteen or seventeen, that singing started to come into my life. I had already won sixpence for singing

The former Barrow Technical College. It is now the Nan Tate Centre.

'A Hammer Came up . . .'

St Paul's Church Mission, now the headquarters of the local Multiple Sclerosis Society.

at a local Band of Hope concert – I think the song was 'Me and Jane in a Plane', but I thought singing was for sissies!

My elder brother and my sister were members of our Mission Church choir, he a tenor and my sister a contralto. My girlfriend Alice was also a contralto in the choir. I realise now that there was some very good talent in the thirty or so members, in all the five voices – soprano, contralto, tenor, baritone and basses. The organist was a Mr Tomkins, and we were trained by a very good tenor, Lawrence Sidaway.

I attended the Sunday School and the Sunday evening service of course, but my biggest contribution to the Mission was when they acquired a new organ. I was given the job of building an organ loft for it. Very much assisted by my boss, Arthur Heaton, I accomplished this: nothing very elaborate, it was only a small three manual organ, but everyone seemed pleased with the result. I seemed to be becoming more and more involved at the Mission, mainly, as I have said before, because Alice was a member of the choir and I had to sit in the vestry twiddling my thumbs, waiting for her after choir practice or a service. One Sunday evening that I shall never forget, after helping to put out the hymn books in the choir stalls, I found myself not yet finished when the choir started to file in and Mr Tomkins took his place at the organ. Too late to get off the platform, I sat down, much to everyone's amusement, in the bass section. I'm convinced that the whole thing was a set-up, but strangely enough after the first shock had passed and the opening hymn had been sung, I found myself enjoying the experience. From then on, I became one of the choir's keenest members, and a few weeks later I stood up to sing my first solo, 'Flow Softly Flow' in a very breathy baritone voice. I enjoyed learning 'Stainer's Crucifixion' and 'The Messiah', and to this day I can still read the bass line in those works easier than I can the tenor line. I still love singing 'Stainer's Crucifixion', especially the tenor and baritone duets.

Now, of course, I was completely committed to the Mission activities: we had a football team, a well-fitted gymnasium, an excellent concert party – 'The Merrymakers' – and of course, the choir.

It was during this period that I became a real fanatic on physical culture; I sent off for several courses on weightlifting and bodybuilding, Charles Atlas's among them. I saved my pocket money and bought barbells, chest expanders etc., and turned our small back bedroom into a private gym. I also thought it was time I started to shave, and my father jokingly suggested that the easiest way would be to put some milk on my face, and then let the cat lick my whiskers off, or better still, stand in a doorway and he would blow them off with the draught when he slammed it shut!

Let me tell you something of my life as an apprentice joiner. At first I used to envy the pattern makers at the far end of our large workshop. They, of course, made the wooden patterns that formed the moulds in the moulding sand, for the metal to be poured into. Weird and wonderful shapes came from their special chisels and saws, all made from yellow pine, soft and free from knots and so easy to work with. The maintenance work that we did only called for common or garden spruce, with knots every six inches or so, also the tough elm and occasionally, oak.

Most of our work was very rough, from repairing crane cabins to laying railway level crossings, erecting telephone poles, and I think I became one of the best wheelbarrow makers in the area (just my joke!). I made enormous barrows for carrying coke, shallow ones for carrying cement and any other design that was demanded. It was wonderful for me when alterations were required at the company offices, or repairs to the company houses, when we would be involved in real joinery work. I envied my friends at night school, most of whom were serving their apprenticeship at the Vickers Armstrong Shipyard. They had all the modern woodworking machines you could wish for, in making the bulkheads, cabins and furniture for the luxurious P & O Liners, which were built there. I really felt like the village carpenter compared to them. They actually wore proper joiners' aprons whilst I wore ordinary workman's overalls which were usually covered in dirt and grease by the middle of each week. But, and this consoles me, working with machines that took in a piece of timber at one end and sent out window frames at the other, which just had to be assembled, didn't teach the apprentices how to use their tools. We had a circular saw, a band saw, a lathe and a hand-operated morticing machine. The rest of the work was by hand and I can honestly say that I can handle all the joiner's tools. I never failed to get a Distinction in the woodwork classes but, at the same time, I didn't feel that I was getting a thorough enough training to send me out amongst the clever joiners on the building sites. I could only assemble roofs with ridges and valleys in theory; I had never had the experience of building an actual house. Yes, I had worked on the roofs of large workshops, but it wasn't the same.

When the furnaces were damped down and the works empty, only the foremen and the apprentices of each department were kept on, and we were hard put to keep occupied. I spent many weeks assisting the wagon builders. When it was decided to re-line one of the furnaces with a three-foot-thick lining of fire bricks, I would be helping to erect the scaffolding that the bricklayers worked from, and which had to be raised three or four feet, as the enormous bricks were laid. To walk across a couple of planks fifty feet up inside the furnace and saw a piece off one end, was a physical challenge.

By the way, I started my apprenticeship at the princely wage of seven and sixpence a week.

I had earned money before this though; I started work at twelve years old, delivering milk from 7.30 a.m. until school time and also on Saturday and Sunday mornings. When I asked permission from my parents to do this job, my mother was convinced it would be the death of me because, according to our doctor, I was growing too fast and was outgrowing my strength! As usual, Dad thought it would do me good. He was proved right, because from the day I started work with William Penny, delivering milk, my general health improved immediately and I started to put on weight. I drank all the milk I wanted; in winter it was made into delicious cocoa, and in summer just lovely cool milk. The milk wasn't delivered in bottles of course, but in cans slung on the handlebars of the bicycle Mr Penny provided. I would ride along the streets to the various houses and pour the gill, pint or quart into the waiting covered jug left on the doorstep, or brought to the door by the lady of the house.

I would ride behind Wm. Penny's milk float, one of the smartest in town, and he would shout to his many friends, what better recommendation for Penny's milk than round Tom Round's legs? I wore the shortest of short pants until I was nearly sixteen and my legs were strong and brown.

I wonder how many develop a dislike for a certain food in childhood which stays with them through their life. I remember attending one of the Mission Church's Christmas parties at the age of seven or eight, and choosing an attractive looking cake. I took one bite and within seconds I had to rush out to be violently sick. The cake was made with almond essence, and to this day I have an intense dislike for this flavour. Unfortunately, I cannot always tell which cakes contain this essence and Alice often stops me when she sees me reaching for a cake that she knows contains it. Strangely enough, I am attracted by the colour. Some cherries have this flavour, so I always have to check before tasting a cherry on top of ice cream etc.

During my joinery period, I had an accident which curtailed my athletics and also kept me off work for three months. I was keen on wrestling, and at camp one weekend I was involved in a match which resulted in a very bad dislocation of my left elbow. We were miles away from a hospital and after one or two amateurs had tried to put the bone back and I had fainted once or twice, I was finally stretched out in a cart, kindly loaned by a farmer, and transported to a hospital in Barrow, a distance of approximately ten miles.

Even this upset had its compensations; everyone spoiled me, not least Alice and, of course not being at work meant we could spend more time together. I had already started a correspondence course to improve my prospects – more about that in a moment – and so I was able to make great strides with my lessons. Sheaves of papers were continually passing back and forth between myself and the British Tutorial Institute in London.

Alice's parents had been won over by this time, but I could never, at any time, visualise myself working as a full-time journeyman. The men I worked with were excellent joiners and marvellous characters in themselves; Bill Pennington, Bill Rawlinson and Amos Spry. I remember, one day, asking Amos when he might retire and his reply shocked me: 'When I drop dead at this bench', he said. That reply really set me thinking, and I finally came up with the idea that I must find an occupation that not only carried security, but also a pension at the end of it. I had seen too much poverty and families living off the dole.

After long talks with Alice, we decided that I should try to join a police force.

The entrance examinations were rather important in those days, so I started on a correspondence course in mathematics, general knowledge, geography and history. This idea was much to my mother's disgust, as she couldn't see any advantage in all this book learning.

Dad as always encouraged me and even helped to pay for the course. He had already paid out considerable sums to fit me out with a set of joiner's tools, many of which I still have to this day, but if he thought I was improving myself, then he was all for it.

At the age of nineteen, I started to apply to various police forces, and I remember setting out for Sheffield for interviews and exams. This was the furthest I had ever travelled in my life, and as the train approached this vast city, slowly crawling through mile after mile of towering steel furnaces, I wanted to catch the next train back home. The feeling didn't improve when I walked out of the station on to the streets. Where was the sky? How did people live in this dark atmosphere? I had no desire to pass the tests, and was very apprehensive when I was shortlisted to the last six, that I might be chosen; they only required two out of the six.

I was half an inch short of their require height of six feet in my stockinged feet so, apart from the natural disappointment of having to tell Alice and all at home that I had failed, I was secretly very glad to be back on the train, heading for the other side of the Pennines, where I could once more see the sky and the sea.

I then applied to Southport and Lancaster forces, and was finally accepted for Lancaster Borough police force, whose full strength at that time was fifty constables plus officers. I became Police Constable No. 51.

It was a sad day when I cleaned off my bench for the last time, packed my tool box and said goodbye to my three journeyman mates, the pattern makers and the wagon builders in the workshop below.

CHAPTER THREE

'A Policeman's Lot is Not a Happy One'

THE DAY I LEFT HOME to join the Lancaster police force was a black day at 32 Beech Street; I might have been leaving for darkest Africa instead of just across Morecambe Bay.

There was a great wailing and crying from my mother and sister, and the whole street seemed to be out to see me off on my journey. Alice said goodbye to me at the station and this was the hardest wrench of all. I had become used to seeing her every day, and now it would be at least a week before we met again.

My life as an apprentice joiner had ended (except as a hobby), and my new life as a police constable had begun. I'm sure there was never a more baby-faced rookie PC than I. I reported to the police station under the Town Hall in Dalton Square, Lancaster and was immediately sent to the clothing stores to be fitted out with my uniform. After lots of form-filling and other settling-in paper work, I was told that I had been placed in lodgings with a Mrs Bennett, Regents Point, Regent Street. I was taken there with my one suitcase and duly introduced, and shown to my room. I was told to report to the police station the following morning. Left to myself, I sat on the bed and started to plan how I could call the whole thing off, and catch the next train home – I was filled with self-pity. A warm, friendly Lancashire voice called me downstairs to have a meal and I was introduced to Nellie Clark (Mrs Bennett's daughter), and her husband, who were to become my dearest friends for many years.

I reported as ordered, at nine o'clock the following morning, and was handed the largest pile of clothing I had ever seen – two tunics, two pairs of trousers, two helmets, two greatcoats and two capes. One truncheon, one pair of handcuffs and several pairs of gloves also. We had to buy our own boots, for which we were given an allowance. I changed into my uniform and was immediately photographed for my warrant card.

I couldn't have joined the force at a more busy or exciting time. The police station, the town and even the whole country was buzzing with a morbid excitement over the now infamous Dr Buck Ruxton murders that had taken place in the good doctor's house across the

1936, when I first joined the force – the 'L' is for Lancaster, not learner!

Lancaster Castle, where I lived and trained for three months.

square from the police station. The house remained empty for many years after the murders were solved.

The crime had already been solved prior to my arrival, so my obvious talent for crime detection was not required on this occasion. I was given the grisly task of helping to pack various bloodstained exhibits which were to be sent to the Assize Court in Manchester. Exhibits such as stained stair treads and floorboards that bore poor Mary Rogerson's (the housemaid) blood, as she tried to stagger to the front door, before the panic-stricken doctor caught her, and committed his second murder within minutes – his poor wife already lying dead upstairs. I also helped crate the bath where both bodies were bled and dismembered, as only a surgeon could do it. He then transported them to Scotland where the remains were hidden in a ravine.

The case was a triumph for our Chief Constable, H. J. Vann, and in later months we constables were to be shown films and given lectures on how the case against Dr Ruxton was built up. Later still, one could buy a paperback book of famous murders, in which the Buck Ruxton murders were featured.

That was the Lancaster police force's hour of glory in the big crime league – nothing ever happened again in my time with the force to approach that grisly episode.

The following day I was sent to Lancaster Castle, which was the Police Training School for the whole of Lancashire County. The course was to last three months.

The castle was the home of John o'Gaunt in bygone days; needless to say, we were not housed in that part of the castle, but in the then unused prison section. I was allotted a whole cell to myself, which was to be my home for the following three months. I forget the number of police recruits that were starting their training that day, but they were from police forces all over Lancashire and the men themselves were from all over the country. I can honestly say that my training and life in Lancaster Prison was the happiest and most interesting period of my years on the force. I revelled in the hard physical training and found the study of Common, Criminal and Statute Law, fascinating.

Each weekend, I headed for Barrow and Alice, and each Sunday night saw me racing from the railway station, up the steep cobbled Castle Hill to ring the bell on the giant castle doors, just in time to sign in at 10 p.m.

Towards the end of our training, we were all sent with a squad of experienced police officers on our first official duty to the Grand National racecourse at Aintree. A sweepstake was organised on the train journey down to Aintree, and I drew 'Reynoldstown' – the winner that year! I was posted to patrol along the rail at Bechers Brook, and I'm happy to say that not one horse fell at that jump on either circuit. This was the first time I had faced the public in my uniform, and I felt that everyone along the rails knew that I was a new, raw copper and that they were not even interested in the horses, but only in my baby face, half hidden by my helmet. I felt they were all wondering what the country was coming to, if such kids like me had to try to keep Liverpudlians in order! I dreaded anyone speaking to me, even to ask the time, because I'm sure I wouldn't have been able to reply, my mouth was as dry as a bone with nerves.

The three months came to an end and we were all dispatched to our various forces – no one had a shorter journey than I did. I was to meet some of those men again in very different circumstances, but that dark time was still three years away. Less than five minutes' journey from the castle, and I was safely in my digs.

I reported for official duty at 2 p.m. the next day, for the late day shift of 2 p.m. to 10 p.m., and I was given an area to patrol, which included my digs. Less than three hours later I was back in my digs, telling Mrs Bennett that I had made a big mistake – I could never be a policeman, I didn't want to be a policeman and that I was going straight back to the police station to tell them so, and then I was back off to Barrow as soon as possible. I'm sure I would have tried to do this if Mrs Bennett and Nellie hadn't persuaded me that I was being very foolish, which of course I was, and that I had to give the job a fair trial. I just don't know what came over me in those first few hours alone on the streets of Lancaster. I think I must have expected that crime would be breaking out all over, and that I would be engaged in arresting robbers, rapists and all manner of lawbreakers almost at once.

'A Policeman's Lot . . .'

No one even spoke to me in those first three hours, and I couldn't stand it. I was soon to learn that the only real friends a policeman can have are other policemen. People spoke to you with a guarded friendliness and sometimes I would spend an eight-hour tour of duty, having passed the time of day with perhaps half a dozen people.

I realised that one of the first jobs was to memorise all the streets in the town, and where they were, and generally stock myself up with a general knowledge of the market town of Lancaster. No one seemed to want to commit crime of any sort and I began to wonder why I had worked so hard at those complicated law books, when all I had to do was endless hours of traffic point duty – there were no traffic lights then, and the main A6 trunk road ran through the heart of Lancaster. I also had to prevent cars from causing an obstruction in our narrow streets, and help people find the places they were looking for.

Life in the force soon developed into a pattern. We were a happy force of fifty-one constables plus sergeants and inspectors; there were some wonderful characters I shall never forget.

PC Eddie Thacker, newly joined from the Coldstream Guards, soon joined me at my digs and we were to become great friends. We requested, and were granted, the same tours of duty, so that we could spend our free time together. We became known as the Terrible Twins of the force. No one looked smarter than we two did, in our uniforms and the Lancaster Borough fireman-type police helmets never shone brighter than ours.

Our Chief Constable, H. J. Vann, realised the narrow social life we had, and he encouraged all sorts of sports. We had our own football and cricket fields, bowling green, tennis court and badminton court. We took possession of the local swimming baths every Friday afternoon. We had a very good male voice choir, and a concert party. We gave concerts and entertainments for children, old people's homes and for all sorts of charities.

Eddie and I were fairly prominent in all the sports activities, but we spent most of our time on the tennis courts, and we were hard to beat locally as a doubles team. My years of swimming paid off, and I soon established myself as the local police champion, which title I was to hold all the time I was in the force.

After two years in the force, we were allowed to marry – if any girl was foolish enough to want to marry a policeman! In August 1938 Alice and I did marry. Eddie was my best man and we moved into our first home, a detached, flat-roofed house on the Scale Hall estate, 6 Penrhyn Road. I was given two days off to marry and move into our new home. Our honeymoon came later when my annual leave came round. My Chief Inspector thought it was a great joke to put me on night duty for the first two weeks of our married life, and to

Police Constable Thomas Round, PC 36, of Lancaster City Police.

Lancaster Borough Police Football
Team, 1938.
Standing, left to right: R. Ayrton,
R. Carmichael, E. Thacker,
G. Knowles, W. R. Parkinson,
W. Alston, T. Round,
C. Eastwood, T. Shaw.

Seated, left to right: J. Cookson,
N. Wilson, J. Smith, F. Eccles,
W. Mackenzie.

have my leg pulled unmercifully throughout the whole fortnight's tour of duty.

I was not a good policeman in the true sense of the word. The small misdeeds of the public didn't interest me. Instead of reporting some harassed housewife for allowing her chimney to catch fire, I would help her to put it out. A car without lights was usually an oversight, so what was the point in spoiling a family's evening out, by booking the husband for the offence? An obstructing car was easier to move than to cause more obstruction by taking time to book the driver. I was a popular policeman, all right, but not in the eyes of my Sergeant or Inspector.

There was a large floating population of Irish labourers in the town, working on the new ICI works at the Heysham Docks, and their favourite sport at the weekend was to get drunk on 'Red Biddy', a mixture of red wine and methylated spirit, and cause general havoc by fighting amongst themselves. The trouble was that as we went to the assistance of the underdog, he would set upon us himself. I soon learned that although the people around the fight were shouting for me to go in and stop two men trying to kill each other, the best way was to let them knock each other about a bit. It was then easier to pack them into a police car, which I had had the foresight to call for, and then get them to the cells for the night, without even disturbing my helmet. It didn't always happen that way of course, and a hard Irish head has butted me on more than one occasion. Still a trip to Walton Jail with two or three prisoners, sentenced to seven days' detention for being drunk and disorderly, was a welcome break in the daily routine.

Alice and I were very happy building our life together; after all we had talked about it since we were kids, and she proved to be a wonderful housekeeper and a marvellous cook. My weekly wage of £3 15s., including wife allowance, was dutifully handed over to Alice, and our little household ran like clockwork. I had 2s. 6d. a week

'A Policeman's Lot ...'

Leighton Hall near Carnforth, home of my friends, the Gillows, who were unaware that their family had been immortalised by G & S:
'Rich oriental rugs, luxurious sofa pillows
And everything
that isn't old from Gillows'
(Act II, 'HMS Pinafore').

pocket money, out of which I paid the instalment on a £9 Echo radio. We went to the cinema once a week, always leaving my seat number with the box office and having told my Inspector where I was going, and generally lived it up!

I built myself a workshop in the back garden and Alice presented me with a list of joinery jobs she wanted doing. Cupboards here, shelves there, a meat safe, doors to open the other way, etc, etc.

At long last we did make some civilian friends, the Smith family – Gertie and George, with their three daughters Phyll, Eileen and Vera. Also the Porter family who owned one of the most popular fish and chip shops in Lancaster, and who also ran a very busy general grocery store. The elder daughter Winnie was a very fine soprano, and for many years before we met, had been the principal soprano of LADOS (the Lancaster Amateur Dramatic and Operatic Society). This cemented the bond between us.

We also often went on walks around the Warton and Silverdale areas, when we explored Warton Crag, the Fairy Steps and Arnside Knot, walking and singing our way through the woods. One walk I remember very clearly; it was a beautiful day and, together with the Smith family, Winnie Porter and her friend Margaret Whiteside, we wandered through the woods in Yealand. Breaking out of the trees we found ourselves looking down on Leighton Hall, the home of the Gillow family, who were responsible for importing mahogany into this country and whose world-famous furniture workshops were based in Lancaster.

We sat down to rest and refresh ourselves and one of the group suggested it would be a great place to sing a song. Of course I was always ready to oblige and I started to sing 'Your Tiny Hand is Frozen' from the Puccini Opera 'La Boheme'. My voice seemed to echo all around the valley in front of us and presently we noticed a group of people leave the front entrance of the hall and remain standing on the forecourt. At the end of my aria Winnie Porter joined me in singing the duet 'Lovely Maid in the Moonlight' from the same opera. A few seconds after our duet had ended a soprano voice floated up the hill towards us, singing another aria. We all listened with amazement and when the song had ended a man left the group and started to walk up the hill towards us. We didn't know whether to disappear into the woods or stand our ground, thinking that we were trespassing. We all stood to meet him and were astounded when he said how much they had enjoyed our singing, that it was his wife Helen who had responded and would we all like to come down to the hall to meet her and her mother Mrs Gillow. He introduced himself as Major Jimmy Reynolds. Of course we were delighted to accept and we spent a wonderful hour or so in their music room where Mrs Gillow accompanied us on their beautiful Steinway grand piano in an impromptu concert. We became good friends of the family and although Mrs Gillow, Major Jimmy and Helen have died, Alice and I are always welcomed at the hall by Major Jimmy's son, Richard, and his wife, Susie. Susie Reynolds is a staunch supporter of the Bolton-le-Sands branch of the NSPCC and I have presented a number of concerts in aid of their funds, several of which have been in the Music Room at Leighton Hall.

From then on our lives became one round of music. It became purely incidental that I had to go out on police duty eight hours of every day or night. One evening each week, we had a musical evening – one week at the Smiths', one at the Porters' and one at our house.

I arrived in Lancaster still a baritone, and I decided to enter the Morecambe Musical Festival to see what I could do. I obtained the songs for the baritone class and having heard of a singing teacher in Lancaster called Robert Sewell, I decided to go to him for some lessons and to learn the songs. I remember our first meeting so well. He asked me to sing for him so that he could judge my voice. I forget

Lancaster Music Festival adjudication.

what I sang, but it was definitely a baritone song, and when I had sung the last note, there was quite a long pause before he said, 'I'm afraid you have entered the wrong class, you should be in the tenor class'. I know that I had always had a tendency to want to sing in a higher key than the normal baritone key, but to be told that I was a tenor was rather like an insult, which proved my lack of musical knowledge. I thanked Mr Sewell and wished him a very good morning. I discussed this problem with Alice and we decided that there could be no harm in me looking at the tenor songs. Two weeks later I was back in Mr Sewell's studio, starting work on my new voice.

I remember that the adjudicator was Leslie Woodgate of BBC fame, and out of about twenty entries I miraculously came second. Mr Woodgate described me as 'this tenor with the baritone quality.' I had only been singing as a tenor for less than seven weeks. I entered one other Festival a year later and it took place in Lancaster. The adjudicator was a Mr Harold Dawber, a well-known organist from Manchester. If my memory serves me correctly, there were only six entries in the tenor class. I took first prize, which was ten shillings and a certificate. I think I was the best of a bad bunch, because in his adjudication, I was given a very severe lecture indeed, and he admitted that he really didn't feel that he could award the first prize to any, but had finally decided to award it to me. I remember being very incensed at being spoken about in this way in front of a couple of hundred people, and I marched myself round to the Festival Office to return the cash and the certificate and to state that I wouldn't be entering any more Musical Festivals.

I did keep the cash and the certificate, but I gave up singing in Festivals – not because I couldn't take criticism, but because there was an atmosphere of competition in them that I didn't care for. What I mean is, that there seemed to be a class of singer or instrumentalist who made a hobby of competing in Festivals and consequently knew all the angles. Still, those two Festivals put me on the map locally and I was soon in demand, as an amateur of course, to sing in the local churches and various functions in Lancaster and Morecambe. Naturally enough, I became known as 'The Singing Bobby'.

I joined LADOS Company, but as they already had a very good team of principals, I had to be content with small parts. It was very difficult for me to fit in the rehearsals while having to work shifts, and the week of the performances at the Grand Theatre was always a marathon for me. The only way I could be available for the shows was to be on night duty – 10 p.m. to 6 a.m. I would arrive at the theatre at 6 p.m. in uniform, change and make up, perform the show, change back into uniform, and report for duty, usually about fifteen minutes late, for which I was forgiven. I would fall into bed at about seven o'clock next morning, and sleep until the middle of the afternoon.

Lancaster Music Festival
certificate for first prize.

"VIKTORIA AND HER HUSSAR."

Amateur Dramatic and Operatic Society Score Another Success.

Principals and Chorus Share Honours in Sparkling Show.

Snappy Danc...   Striking En... ...eature.

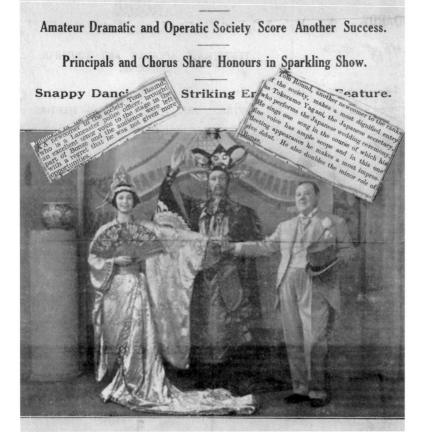

members of the cast. Tom Round, brought of the society, police officer, brought who is a Lancaster police officer, the an excellent tenor voice to the were left part of Bonze, and the audience were not given more with a regret that he was not given opportunities.

Tom Round, another newcomer to the ranks of the society, as Tokeramo Yagani, the Japanese secretary, makes a most dignified entry. He performs the Japanese wedding ceremony. He sings one song in the course of which his fine voice has ample scope and in this one fleeting appearance he makes a most impressive debut. He also doubles the minor role of Bonze.

My first venture with an amateur
society.

It was all very well worthwhile, and already I had the feeling that it would be marvellous if I could ever become a professional singer.

Dreams of a professional career seemed crazy, but they persisted, and when the war started in 1939, and a fit-up Sadler's Wells Opera Company visited the Ashton Hall in Lancaster, I sat, entranced, through performances of 'La Traviata' and 'Rigoletto'.

It was about this time that an American film of 'The Mikado' came to town and I remember sitting through it twice without leaving the cinema. I knew 'A Wand'ring Minstrel', but had no idea of its origin.

Apart from keeping up with my singing lessons and local singing, I had little time to think of the future. We were now on twelve-hour tours of duty and on call for the other twelve. My friend Eddie Thacker was in the Army Reserve, and he was recalled to the Guards in quick time. I approached my Chief Constable, who was now W. Thompson,

Here are my first ever reviews:

'Viktoria and Her Hussar': The Lancaster Amateur Dramatic and Operatic Society score another success ... a newcomer to the Society, Tom Round ... brought an excellent Tenor voice to the stage in the part of Bonze and the audience were left with a regret that he was not given more opportunities.' *Lancaster and Morecambe Observer*, 1937

'Victoria and Her Hussar': LADOS. Tom Round, another newcomer to the ranks of the Society, makes a most dignified entry as Tokeramo Yagani, the Japanese Secretary. He sings one song, in the course of which his fine voice has ample scope and in this one fleeting appearance he makes a most impressive debut.' *Lancaster Guardian*, 1937.

Hymn of Praise – Choir Festival at Sandylands. Mr Thomas Round of Lancaster made a very great impression. He is a rising young tenor of great promise and has a remarkably good voice of surprising range and power. He also possesses that rare gift of interpretation and his rendering of the recits. and air 'The Sorrows of Death' was unusually impressive. *Morecambe Observer*, 1940

Lancaster Amateurs Jubilee ... highlight of the performance was the striking finale featuring the Home Guard. This included a song 'The Holy War' composed by Dr J. H. Dixon FRCQ. The soloist, Tom Round, was in officer's uniform. Mr Round's singing was an outstanding feature and he well deserved the enthusiastic ovations accorded him on his many appearances during the performance. *Lancaster Guardian*, 1941.

to allow me to volunteer for the Navy, but was told that the police forces were now a reserved occupation, and could not join the armed services.

The country was now under heavy bombing attacks and the Barrow Shipyard and Iron and Steel works were prime targets. Even the army barracks at Bowerham in Lancaster were attacked with incendiary bombs.

After one particularly heavy raid on Barrow, Alice and I decided to drive there (I had acquired a small 250cc motorcycle) to see if our parents were all right. We were not on the telephone. We were soon in Barrow, to find that my parents were OK, but Alice's parents' house had suffered some damage. Fortunately, they had taken cover in their air raid shelter and there were no injuries. We gave all the help we could before it was time for us to return home. I was due on duty at 10 p.m. that night.

We set off in heavy rain, and when we were driving along the Levens Flats, the engine cut out. I knew very little about the mechanics, but when I tried to start it again, after a few minutes it broke into life and we got on our way. A couple of miles further along we stopped again. The only way we could start again was for Alice to push me until the engine fired up again. Another couple of miles and another stop, and so it went on until we reached Carnforth, when we were both pretty well exhausted, especially Alice. Fortunately, this time, we were near a garage and I asked a mechanic to have a look at the engine. I told him I was a policeman and that I was due on duty in a few minutes. He quickly solved the problem – it was water in the carburettor. We had kept going by the carburettor filling up with petrol every time we stopped; this floated the water to the top of the carburettor housing and the engine would start again. This kept it running until the water reached the intake pipe again, and cut out the engine.

We raced home – by this time the sirens were sounding – I threw on my greatcoat and helmet, grabbed my bicycle and dashed to the nearest police telephone and reported for duty, just as the Town Hall clock was striking 10 p.m. I then raced home, put on my full uniform and resumed my duty, which on that night was patrolling Skerton Bridge that spans the River Lune. Other nights I guarded and patrolled the gas works, the electricity works or Carlisle Bridge, which carried the railway over the river. We were virtually waiting for the Germans to arrive in Lancaster!

The Battle of Britain in 1941, when we lost so many fighter and bomber pilots, changed the Government's policy, and it was announced that the police could now volunteer as pilots or navigators in the RAF. I didn't waste a moment, and was given the necessary three days to report to RAF Cardington for medical and written tests. Our new Chief Constable, who had never looked kindly on my singing activities or my police activities either, scoffed at the idea that Round was intelligent enough to pass an RAF pilots' test. Nevertheless, I did pass, and now there was nothing to stop me from doing a bit more in the war than keeping guard on power stations etc.

CHAPTER FOUR

'Up in the Air, Sky High, Sky High'

*I*T WAS NOW THE LATE SUMMER of 1941 and I was due to be called for training in September, when Alice broke the news that she was pregnant. My first reaction was to try to get my call up cancelled, but the wheels had started to turn and nothing could be done. Our last week together was heartbreaking, and I left for London convinced I would never see her again. My instructions were to report to Lords Cricket Ground and before I was over the shock of my first sight of London, I was milling about with hundreds of other young men, waiting to be told what to do next. This was to be the pattern of my next three weeks in the Air Force – waiting to be fed, to be jabbed, to be medically inspected, or fitted out with uniforms. Being well down alphabetically didn't help either. I began to wish that I was called Aaron; at least I would be first in line for everything.

We were first formed into large sections, again alphabetically, so I didn't have the opportunity to meet anyone whose surname began with A, B or C etc. However, on that first day, I did meet three young men who were to stay with me for over a year and one for nearly four years – Jim Simpson (a Wigan policeman), Mickey Shelton and Collyn Warren (both only nineteen and fresh from university). We became very good friends and fortunately, we were billeted in the same block of luxury flats, newly requisitioned by the Armed Services – Viceroy Court, Regents Park. I think they had only been recently completed, because there was no sign of any previous occupation. We slept on the floor, on three-foot square 'biscuits'. We queued for everything and by the time we four had reached the Regents Park Zoo Restaurant – it had been turned into a mess hall – for our breakfast, marched back to Viceroy Court, washed our knives, forks and spoons, and tidied our rooms, it was nearly time to start queuing for our mid-day meal. I can never walk or drive along Regents Park Road, leading to the Zoo entrance, without visualising the long queues of men slowly moving along in three ranks, waiting to be fed to the accompaniment of the whooping calls of the apes in the nearby cages.

A few men became so homesick in those first few weeks that they went AWOL and hitched rides in cars or lorries back to their families for a few days. After one particularly harrowing telephone call to Alice one evening, I was preparing to do the same, and was only prevented at the last moment by the good sense of Collyn Warren. He was lucky though; his home was on the luxurious estate of Moor Park, on the outskirts of London, and he was able to visit his parents practically every evening, if he wanted to. On this depressing evening, I was invited by his mother to accompany Collyn to their friend's home on Hamilton Terrace, St John's Wood. Their friend was Beverley Baxter, MP and theatre critic. Mr and Mrs Baxter were on holiday in Canada. I had never seen such a splendid house and I sat, open mouthed, as Collyn's mother opened a food hamper and laid out a super meal. After a couple of weeks of RAF food, I couldn't believe my good fortune. Before we were allowed to eat we were sent upstairs to have a bath. What a wonderful evening that was; Mrs Warren was a charming person born in Cologne, and she had married a soldier in the First World War. He was now an officer in the Royal Navy Reserve and had duly reported for duty.

She was also a very good pianist and we sat and listened while she played to us on a beautiful grand piano. Of course it wasn't long before she was playing melodies I knew and when I joined in, and she had got over the surprise of hearing me sing, we had a wonderful evening. It was the start of a deep and lasting friendship, which lasted to the end of their lives.

One evening Collyn suggested that we should see a show in the West End. I left all the arrangements to him; after all, London was his hometown and he was used to what was to me a very sophisticated way of life.

We first went into a Quality Inn restaurant in Leicester Square, where I sampled my first taste of waffles, covered with butter and maple syrup – delicious. We then went to the Piccadilly Theatre, where a new show called 'Strike a New Note' had recently opened, starring Sid Fields. He was a marvellously funny man who had me rocking with laughter throughout the whole show. Jerry Desmond was his straight man and Sid Fields became my favourite comedian for many years – I still tell and act out several of his sketches. My first-ever digs in Liverpool were where Sid Fields stayed when he played the Liverpool Empire and the landlady had lots of photographs on display around the house.

I was very fortunate in having Collyn for a friend; he certainly helped me through those homesick few weeks.

I was posted to Newquay in Cornwall for initial training, which not only involved studying navigation and other subjects to do with flying, but also hours of drill or 'square bashing' as we called it. I was billeted in the Coniston Hotel on the sea front from December 1941 until the middle of March 1942. It was a particularly cold winter, but no matter what the weather, the physical training took place every morning on the cliff tops opposite the hotel.

Flight Lieutenant Stephens, our Adjutant, heard me singing to the boys one evening in the hotel and he invited me to visit some friends of his in Newquay. He proved to be an accomplished pianist and we had a splendid musical evening – the first of many during my stay in Newquay.

I was then invited to sing at the Sunday morning church parade, and each continuing Sunday found me singing a solo in either the Church of England, the Methodist or Baptist Churches. I soon realised that singing was proving to be an open sesame to meeting people, and also offering me one or two perks, in that I didn't have to march down to the churches at 140 paces to the minute when I was singing, because it would have made me a bit breathless. Instead, I was able to walk down at my own speed.

I was caught climbing through a toilet window of the hotel one evening about fifteen minutes after lights out, and I was put on a 'charge', and confined to barracks for seven days, scrubbing floors, cleaning latrines and other unpleasant jobs. After about a couple of nights of this, it was discovered that I was due to sing at a camp concert that weekend and I was involved in several rehearsals. I was promptly released from my punishment.

Flight Lieutenant Stephens was a tall slender man, a typical aristocratic looking Englishman, ideally suited to be an Administrative Adjutant and I was very sorry to have to say goodbye to him when our initial training was over. I often wonder what became of him during and after the war years, and if he ever remembered playing for me at various churches in Newquay.

Later on, I was to meet another Flight Lieutenant Adjutant in Texas who was also a brilliant pianist, and was also a tall elegant man, but more of that later.

Also in Newquay, I was introduced to Cornish cream teas, in the various homes to which Flight Lieutenant Stephens and I were invited. I was also still in close contact with Jimmy, Micky and Collyn who often accompanied me to various functions and homes. I was fast beginning to find out how other people lived, compared to my life in Barrow and Lancaster.

At Newquay we were also fitted out with our flying clothes and at the end of the course, we were posted to a flying field at Cliffe Pypard, near Swindon. The next three weeks were to be crucial for all of us – we were due for a crash course in flying the Tiger Moths, which had to result in flying solo at the end of the three weeks. Those who failed that test would be eliminated from the flying course and posted

A Tiger Moth – memories of my first solo flight.

to another branch of the service. I thought I had reached the end of the line in my RAF career, because although I hadn't mentioned it to any RAF doctor, I used to be sick merely looking at a fairground roundabout, so I couldn't see me surviving even my first flight in an aeroplane.

I was fortunate in my flying instructor, an ex-Schneider Cup racing pilot, who put me completely as my ease, and I believe I was so interested in all about me on that first flight in an open-cockpit aircraft that I didn't have a twinge of sickness, either then or at any time during my five years in the RAF.

A rookie pilot.

I soloed after 10 hours 35 minutes' dual instruction, which made Micky Shelton mad, because I beat him to it by 35 minutes. He considered that I was too old at twenty-four to be flying at all. He was nineteen! What a thrill that first solo was – never quite the same again. Once off the ground on my first circuit of the airfield, my instructor having kittens watching me, I was singing songs from 'Rose Marie' and I was still singing when I hit the ground, rather hard on my first landing. Now I was all set for a posting overseas to continue my training as a pilot.

Fortunately, all my pals made it – some of the others fell by the wayside in this first test, either through airsickness or the sheer inability to cope with flying.

From Cliffe Pypard, we were posted to Heaton Park near Manchester, to await transport to Canada. We were all billeted in private homes and again I was fortunate in that Mr and Mrs Kay were very keen on music, and I spent a very happy three weeks with them. I remained friends with Ethel and Bill Kay for many years after the war, and often stayed with them when I was on tour with the D'Oyly Carte and Sadler's Wells Company, when we played the Opera House in Manchester.

Alice was fast approaching the time when our baby would be born, and it was while I was at Heaton Park that it was discovered that she would have to undergo a caesarean operation and I had to give my permission for the operation to take place. On 22 April, I obtained a seventy-two hour compassionate leave to enable me to go home and take Alice to the hospital. Thomas Ellis was born on 24 April 1942. I had just enough time to see her come round from the operation, and take a quick look at my son, before I had to dash to catch the train back to Manchester.

The date was now set for our departure to Gourock, Scotland. Alice was in hospital about ten days I think, and I was just able to see her and baby Ellis back in our home at 6 Penrhyn Road. Our parting was even more harrowing then than at our first good-bye, and this time it was to be two years before I was to see her and my son again.

We travelled to Gourock and boarded a Polish ship called *The Batory*, of about 19,000 tons. We zigzagged our way over the Atlantic taking nine days, during which time the Polish crew went on strike because the Captain banned them any alcohol during the voyage. We RAF men were then ordered to take on the jobs of collecting food from the ship's stores for the cooks, various cleaning jobs and generally maintaining the running of the ship. Fortunately, the strike didn't involve the engineers or the officers. We finally docked in Halifax, Nova Scotia.

We were immediately loaded onto a train, which took us to Moncton, New Brunswick, where we were to stay for about a month waiting to be posted to one of the airfields throughout Canada and America to start our flight training. Once again, we were playing the waiting game, but the weather was marvellous, which helped enormously. We were issued with little handbooks and seemingly endless lectures on how to conduct ourselves on meeting our Canadian and American cousins.

One afternoon we were packed by the hundred into a cinema to await the arrival of a Group Captain who was going to tell us once again about the dangers of 'VD'. Fifteen minutes after his appointed arrival time, there was still no sign of the Group Captain, and we were all sweltering in the hot cinema and getting very restive. I had the bright idea that some community singing might help. I ran down the aisle and onto the stage, and in no time at all we were having an impromptu concert.

My efforts that afternoon had not gone unnoticed, because a few days later I was invited to sing on the local radio station by a young

With Mickey Shelton (right) and
our Moncton, New Brunswick,
host, Jack Armstrong.

man called Jack Armstrong. My first-ever broadcast was quite successful and Jack invited me to his home to meet his parents. I said I had two special friends, and could they be included – no problem at all – and from then on our stay in Moncton became a delight. Again, the Armstrong family became firm friends and I was to see them several times in future years on my concert tours of Canada and the USA.

The day came in mid June when we were all paraded to hear our destiny and destination in either Canada or America. Forty or fifty names would be called, and then unheard-of town names and states – Medicine Hat, Manitoba, Pensicola, Florida etc. We had heard rumours of the qualities of the various airfields, and when Jimmy, Micky, Collyn and myself were again called out in the same batch of fifty, we were completely baffled by the name of our destination – Terrell, Texas.

It wasn't until a few hours later that we had news from a chap who had been eliminated from a flying course for some reason, that Terrell was one of the most popular of the airfields being leased to the RAF throughout Canada and the USA.

Reviewers at the time wrote:

The regular Friday evening broadcast was one of the best yet held ... an outstanding English vocalist sang two numbers and won applause as one of the best singers to appear in Moncton for some years. The vocalist, LAC Round, will sing again next week.

Talented RAF artists in variety show ... LAC Round of the RAF and a favourite English tenor sang several selections. Round has only been in Moncton for a short time, but his appearance in similar programmes has won him great popularity. *Moncton Daily Times*, June 1942.

' *Up in the Air, Sky High* '

We said goodbye to our friends in Moncton and after a three-day two-night journey in an air-conditioned train, we arrived at the smallest country railway station I had ever seen, and we looked at each other in disbelief. That clot in Moncton had really fooled us with his glowing account of Terrell, Texas. I jumped down on to the track and nearly fainted in the wave of heat that hit me. I pushed past Collyn back on to our air-conditioned train, to collect my wits. Texas temperatures are well into the eighties in the middle of June.

We were finally formed up into columns of three ranks, and to the cheers of a few locals, we were marched off to the Kaufman County Airport. We didn't even see the town of Terrell, because the airfield was on the outskirts of town, through the black shanty town – on the 'wrong side of the track'. To say that we were depressed at the sight of our future home was putting it mildly. Within a few minutes we were at boiling point under our heavy packs. Fortunately, we had been ordered to change into our tropical kit before leaving the train, but the khaki cotton drill was black with sweat before we had marched a mile.

We brightened up considerably at the first sight of the airfield. By this time, we were marching down a narrow dirt lane on the blackest soil I had ever seen and the long, low, white barrack blocks looked really inviting.

When we were finally marched into our barrack room it looked like a country club room, compared to what we had been used to in England and Canada; wide, soft double-tiered bunks, comfortable chairs and tables and air-conditioned. The mess hall was a dream – the food was served cafeteria style and would have put some of our

Our first sight of the barrack blocks of Kaufman County Airport, Texas.

present motorway restaurants to shame. After two years of food rationing in England, it was to be expected that half of us went down with stomach upsets within a week, due to the unaccustomed richness of the food.

We were designated No. 10 course, BFTS (British Flying Training School), Kaufman County Airport, Terrell, Texas. This flying training programme was known as 'The Arnold Training Scheme', and was formed while America was still a neutral country. An agreement was arranged that America would supply us with food and other essentials and also allow us to lease private airfields and to employ private flying instructors to teach RAF personnel, in return for payment, of course. It was known as the Lend Lease Scheme and was started in 1941. When the first contingent arrived in America, they wore civilian clothes and were trained by non-military personnel, but when the USA entered the war after the bombing of Pearl Harbour in May 1941, the RAF wore military uniforms. Courses 1–6 were trained as civilians and subsequent courses were trained as RAF personnel. In England at that time, because of the bombing, the blackout and the RAF casualties, there was neither the time, airfields or instructors available, to train new pilots. Alice was to say later that America sent us 'Spam' to eat and I was sent to the USA in exchange.

Life now became one round of study and flying. The Primary Course flying was accomplished with a Stearman Biplane, rather more powerful and larger than a Tiger Moth. I have omitted to say that there were quite a number of policemen in the hundreds who sailed over on *The Batory* who, obviously like myself, had volunteered as soon as we were released by the Government, and we were a few years older than most of the others. I was then twenty-four, and Micky and Collyn were not yet twenty. I am telling you this because being those few years older, I felt I had to strive harder to keep my end up, also because Micky Shelton was always calling me 'old Tom'. As a result of this, I was determined to be one of the first to solo in our flight, and definitely had to be ahead of Micky.

I persuaded my instructor to let me solo after nine hours and he reluctantly agreed. I did a perfect take-off, a good circuit of the airfield and a reasonable landing. I must tell you that the Tiger Moth has a tail skid at the rear end which merely slides along the ground after landing, but the Stearman has a free running small wheel about three inches in diameter, which is completely directional.

As I said, I did a reasonable landing and I was so delighted at being the first in the flight to solo, that I'm afraid I relaxed while the aircraft was still running at a fair speed across the grass field. Instead of concentrating on keeping the plane in a straight line, I allowed it to veer slightly, and before I could straighten it out, the little rear wheel

'A Wand'ring Minstrel, I'

OPPOSITE

Posing with our instructor;

Ready for take off in an A.T.6 Harvard;

Climbing into a Stearman Primary Trainer;

No.1 British Flying Training School, No. 10 course.

No 1 British Flying Training School   No 10 Course

Anglis Keane Belton Chambers K. Chambers G. Crabtree Croft Ballaway Day Drew Crime Hall Hathwell

Hardy Harris Henfrey Hunter Hussey Ingram Kerr Kilner Larder Moore H. Moore A. Noldrett O'Hagan Orr

Patterson Peck Richards Ringrose Round Sandifer Shelton Simpson Smith Stevenson Stones Summers Tattle

Taylor K. Taylor W. Thomson Todd Travers Troop Walgate Ward Warner Warren Wheeler Wolff Wright turned sharply at right angles and sent me into what is known as a 'ground loop'. The plane merely turns round and round in a circle. After the second or so turn, the plane started to keel over and there was a horrible ripping and grinding noise as the lower wing tip dragged along the ground, tearing off about a foot or so. The engine stalled and I was stranded in the middle of the field in the loudest silence I've ever heard.

A figure left the flight hut and started to walk towards me – my instructor. By the time he reached the Stearman, he seemed to be about ten feet tall and I felt that I had shrunk to about ten inches tall. I sat in the cockpit and for the next few minutes I was treated to a comprehensive sample of American swear words that I have never heard equalled. I sat dazed and miserable, but when I heard him say that I would be eliminated from the flying course that very day, I came to life. How I persuaded him to retract his threat I'll never know, but I did. It proves how critical the programme was – that one slip was enough to send a chap home. I was very grateful for his decision and two weeks later I was shocked to learn that he had been killed when his plane blew up in the air.

At the end of our first week in Terrell, we were all wondering how we could get to Dallas, or 'Big D' as it was known, which was about thirty miles away. When we were dismissed on the Saturday mid-day, we made for the main gates and the black dirt road we had recently marched along, and we were surprised to see a long line of cars waiting. Some of the boys from the 7, 8 and 9 courses made straight for cars that they obviously recognised, and were driven away. We had been told of the Texas hospitality and that we may be invited to a home for the weekend, but neither Collyn, Micky or myself had received any invitations, so we walked on down the road past the waiting cars. We had nearly reached the end of the line, when we were stopped by a very quietly spoken man, who said that if we had no definite plans, he would be delighted if we would accept an invitation to visit his family in Dallas for the weekend. We looked at each other and the same thought must have crossed our minds; we wanted to get to Dallas anyway, so there could be no harm in accepting the lift.

We couldn't have made a wiser choice because William Mottram Preston, a bachelor, living with his mother and sister at 4712 Eastside Avenue, Dallas, became one of our greatest friends in Texas, and we were to spend many weekends with them. His mother was English and came to Dallas with her husband, in its early days. He had become the City Civil Engineer. Before his death, he was responsible for bringing the first electric street tram cars to Dallas, and his last project had been a giant new reservoir.

'A Wand'ring Minstrel, I'

William Mottram Preston, a real Texas friend.

That weekend, I sampled my first Southern fried chicken and it is still one of my favourite dishes whenever I visit the USA.

One evening during the following week, I was invited, and I cannot remember how I received the invitation, to the home of Mr and Mrs Arthur Boyd, one of the town's bank managers. During the evening meal the subject of music came up and I remarked that I was an amateur singer and a tenor. They inquired if I had met Flight Lieutenant Palmer, the Field Adjutant, who was a brilliant pianist. I said that I hadn't met socially, as I was only an LAC (Leading Aircraft Cadet). A couple of days later I was again invited to the Boyds', together with Flight Lieutenant Palmer and I was officially introduced. I remember thinking how like the Adjutant in Newquay in Cornwall he looked – at least six foot three inches tall, thin and aesthetic looking. After supper he played the piano and I sang, which started a ball rolling that has never stopped since.

Bill Palmer became a good friend to me during my stay in Texas. He was also a good organist and he usually played the organ at the Sunday morning church parades. I was invited to sing a solo the following Sunday and I don't think I passed more than half a dozen Sundays during my many months in Texas without singing at some church or other in the state. In later months, when I had gained my Pilot's Wings, I was able to fly to various towns, not only in Texas, but also in other states, to sing at 11 a.m. Sunday services.

How I completed my studies I'll never know, because I wasn't very bright and I had to struggle to keep up with boys like Collyn and Micky anyway, and because I was dragged from classes, even by the Wing Commander to accompany him to some function or other in Dallas to sing. When I timidly objected, because of getting behind with my work, I was told it was all part of good International Relations. I was soon in great demand and both the Dallas and Terrell papers were talking about this pilot who could sing. I did several broadcasts with Bill Palmer and he composed a patter song entitled 'We're the Boys of No. 1 BFTS', which I broadcast on a few occasions.

My 'fame' spread even into New Mexico, because a family, who had heard me on the air, invited me to spend my first leave with them. Collyn Warren was off to visit friends in Tucson, Arizona, so I accepted, and had a wonderful holiday on a real working ranch near the town of Clayton, New Mexico. From there I took a Greyhound bus trip to Albuquerque, Taos and Santa Fe. I also sang and gave a talk at the local college.

At this time, I was wearing my RAF blue uniform because, even though the sun shone every day it remained quite cool. Clayton was about 4,000 feet above sea level. Of course the blue uniform created quite a bit of curiosity. I remember standing on the wooden sidewalk

THE BOYS OF No. 1 B.F.T.S.

We're the boys of No. 1 B.F.T.S.,
To our country's call we bravely answered "yes";
Crossing oceans at our peril, we have landed here in Terrell
And what we think of Terrell you can try to guess!
And though flying is the thing we're here to do,
We don't forget we're propaganda too;
So 'neath starry spangled banners we're so careful of our manners
We're the boys of No. 1 B.F.T.S.,
            Oh yes!
The British Boys of 1 B.F.T.S.

We're the Boys of No. 1 B.F.T.S.,
And the Kaufman County Airport's our address;
It's a quiet little spot on down amongst the fields of cotton
But we're never quite forgotten by the public or the Press;
And when we're tired of doing rolls and Cuban eights
We tramp into the town and look for "dates";
And if girls are coy or callous, well, we thumb our way to Dallas,
We're the Boys of No. 1 B.F.T.S.
            Oh yes!
The British Boys of 1 B.F.T.S.

We're the boys of No. 1 B.F.T.S.
And we're always very natty in our dress;
We polish ev'ry button till we shine like Barbara Hutton,
But there's no roast beef or mutton, and it's hard you must confess;
We've had the barbecues, the gumbo, and the grits;
The Pabst and the Budweiser and Schlitz;
But our craving is most vocal
For a bitter at the Local
For the Boys of No. 1 B.F.T.S.
            Oh yes!
The British Boys of 1 B.F.T.S.

We're the boys of No. 1 B.F.T.S.,
And our very grateful thanks we must express;
For though we're now in clover it will very soon be over,
We shall see the Cliffs of Dover, and be clearing up the mess;
But when we've finished off the War and seen it through
We shall think of Terrell, Texas, and of you;
And though sea and sky may hide you,
They never can divide you
From the Boys of No. 1 B.F.T.S.,
            Oh yes!
The British Boys of 1 B.F.T.S.

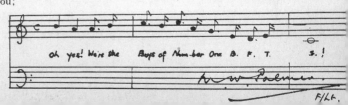

oh yes! We're the Boys of Number One B. F. T. s.!

F/Lt.

'Up in the Air, Sky High'

in a small town called Dumas, and being asked by one of the locals, 'What the hell is that uniform you are wearing?' Fortunately, I remembered the advice we had been given in Moncton and politely replied that I was in the British Royal Air Force. He replied, 'Is that some sort of flying club?' I won't tell you my reply to that remark, but thinking about it afterwards, I realised that in the middle of America, it was difficult to appreciate that there was a war going on in Europe between the British and Germans.

Having completed our Primary Flying Training, we moved to the basic flying course, which meant flying a low-winged monoplane called a Vultee Valiant. This aircraft was nearly twice the size of the Stearman, and much more powerful. Our ranks were becoming thinner; some had already been eliminated from the course for reasons of air ability, airsickness and even failing the theory exams. We weren't as relaxed as we had been and things were getting tougher. I seemed to be attending funerals every other week as some unlucky chap crashed attempting some new manoeuvre. Old courses moved out, new courses moved in – every few weeks a Flight would complete their training and after a Wings presentation, would take the train north back to Canada and wait for transport to the UK and the War.

Number 10 Course proceeded to the advanced flying course, and we were the senior course on the field. We were now flying the AT6 Harvard, a low-winged aircraft, with a 650HP Pratt & Whitney in-line engine.

Things were also changing on the field – a new form of discipline was put into operation. Kaufman Airfield was a private airfield and all

---

The Kaufman newspaper wrote:

Finest musical talent heard on Sunday at the Afternoon Program sponsored by the Kaufman Music Study Club ... The auditorium was not filled to capacity, but the audience was made up of appreciative music lovers who were thrilled by the songs sung by Cadet Round. (Kaufman, Texas, 1942)

Programme from the Rotary Club, Clayton, 1942:

SPECIAL – we are proud to have as guest today, Cadet Tom Round of the RAF from Lancaster, England. Tom Round is a very fine singer and an interesting speaker.

Lancashire Daily Post, 1943:

From Dallas, Texas, I have received news of a former Lancaster Police Constable, now Pilot Officer Tom Round who is training at Terrell, Texas. Mrs Blant Burford, Chairman of the Texas Federation of Music Clubs, writes that she and her husband have become good friends with Tom. A tenor of ability, Mr Round has taken part in musical services at Haskell Methodist Church, Dallas, where Mrs Burford directs the choir and last June he took the solo lead in a special programme of thanksgiving. A cutting from the *Dallas News* says that he was principal soloist at a Christmas Vesper Service at the Hockaday Institute of Music, Dallas.

The B.T. 13 Vultee Valiant, our
basic trainer.

the instructors were civilians. The only RAF personnel were a Wing
Commander, a Squadron Leader, a Flight Lieutenant, a Warrant Officer,
a Sergeant and a Corporal. This was a heavy burden for a few officers
and NCOs to carry, so, under instructions from Washington, a system
was devised whereby the discipline of the field was placed in the hands
of the cadets. I had always been (for some reason beyond me) our
Flight Leader, as far back as Newquay, and now I was appointed Cadet
Wing Commander, answerable only to Wing Commander Moxham
(also my family name on my mother's side), the Senior Officer. Cadet
Squadron Leaders and Flight Lieutenants were appointed, together with
cadet NCOs, and we became completely self-run. This allowed the real
officers and NCOs to attend more important duties, although I cannot
think what those duties might have been!

BELOW LEFT: the advanced
trainer A.T.6 Harvard.
BELOW RIGHT: newly appointed
Cadet Wing Commander.

Taken on my return from the USA – Ellis was two years old and Alice is wearing my US Air Force wings.

I did not want the Wing Commander's job, I can tell you, and I was having enough trouble staying on the course without adding to my worries. The flying part of the programme was mainly physical and as long as I kept my head, I felt I could handle it, but the classes were another matter and I spent many extra hours of study just to keep up. I was also doing quite a log of singing and I was not allowed to refuse any request for my services, in case it upset our American hosts. Whether I liked it or not, I was becoming quite well known locally and, as I said to Flight Lieutenant Palmer, I would look and feel very foolish if I didn't gain my Pilot's Wings. I felt I would not only let myself down, but also the whole flying school, as I was now virtually running it.

Alice had to leave our house in Lancaster and return to her home in Barrow – she was still very weak after her operation and little Ellis was proving a handful to manage. We rented our Lancaster house on a short lease and I felt much better knowing that she was with her parents. Our letters flew back and forth and I soon received the first snapshots of our little son, which were duly shown to everyone I met. Friends in Terrell sent off parcels of clothing to Ellis and everyone

My first real sight of Thomas
Ellis with Alice, received in Texas.

took a great interest in his progress. They had great difficulty in doing otherwise, because I never stopped talking about Alice and Ellis.

Our circle of friends had grown, but still the Prestons in Dallas, the Basses and Boyds in Terrell were our favourites, together with a couple called John and Faye Griffith who lived in the small town of Kaufman nearby, and the Birdsongs who lived in Longview, about sixty miles away.

Collyn, Micky and myself passed through our basic training course (sadly Jim Simpson was eliminated and returned to Moncton to be re-allocated), and we moved on to the Advanced course, which involved flying the Harvard AT6 Radial Engined Monoplane. Our ranks were thinned still more and Number 10 course looked sadly depleted with eliminations and accidents. One sad morning I lost two pilots, one a policeman who I had appointed a Cadet Flight Lieutenant that day.

They had crashed together while flying in formation. I was now automatically in charge of funeral parades and I dread to think of the number of slow marches I did to our little war cemetery.

Number 10 course's great day arrived and for some reason this Wings Parade was to be something different. Apart from worrying myself sick that I would never pass the final exams, I was involved in meetings and rehearsals for the Parade. I was to run it and give a demonstration of Squadron Drill before a specially invited audience. I spent hours memorising the orders I would have to give over loudspeakers to move the Squadron. I begged my superiors to release me from the job if I failed my exams, but was merely told to obey orders and anyway, no one would know who had passed until the names were called out and each man had marched out to receive his coveted wings from top brass officers from Washington. Perhaps you can imagine the tension, when I tell you that more than one chap threatened suicide if they failed, and had to return home to England without his Pilot's Wings. I cannot express my own feelings – I felt I had taken too much on with my singing and also as Senior Cadet Officer. I just felt that I had failed and that when the ceremony was over and my name hadn't been called, I would try and slip quietly away and disappear.

I had drilled the Squadrons and everything had gone smoothly, and I stepped down from the rostrum and took my place with my colleagues and tried to look as though I hadn't a care in the world. My name was called out, but I can't remember marching out to have my Wings pinned on.

After the ceremony and while we were all congratulating each other, I will always remember Flight Lieutenant Palmer saying in quite a

Myself, Micky Shelton (left) and Collyn Warden (right) were the inseparable trio.

loud voice that he thought Round would have been placed higher in the marks list. The marks were out of 1,000 and I had got just over 600, in other words sixty per cent, which I thought was great, but Palmer thought it was a poor show.

We were all automatically promoted to Sergeant, but there was a shock in store for half a dozen of us. We were called to the Wing Commander's office and calmly told that we would not be returning to England with the rest of the flight – instead we were to take the train to Toronto, Canada, where we would be commissioned as Pilot Officers, and spend two weeks being fitted out with officers' uniforms, including tropical kit. We were then to travel down to San Antonio, Texas, and report to the Kelly Field Air Force Base, where we would be seconded into the American Air Force. We would undergo a month's intensive flying course with an American Squadron and, if successful, we would be posted somewhere in the Gulf Coast Training Command as flying instructors in the US Air Force. We would, of course, be paid the same as American officers. There was no time limit put on our stay, but it would be approximately one year.

I was completely stunned by this news – as were my colleagues – and when I finally found my voice I raised all sorts of objections as to why I could not a) accept a Commission and b) stay on in the USA. The main reason, of course, was that I wanted to get back home to Alice and my son.

Predictably, my objections were brushed aside, those were my orders and nothing could be done to alter them. I did extract a vague promise that everything would be done to get my wife and son over to join me. It remained a vague promise. I sent a cable to Alice, followed by an airmail letter, explaining this new situation and generally tried to

Christmas Day in Dallas, me with Collyn Warren and Mickey Shelton.

'Up in the Air, Sky High'

Proudly displaying our newly won wings and sergeants' stripes, waiting to board the train to Toronto to receive our commissions. Left to right: myself, Collyn, Gerry Smith, Hussey and Sgt Sam Walgate.

reconcile myself to this new situation. Micky Shelton was not included in this group, and only Collyn was left of our close group. It was further explained to us that the American Air Force was desperately short of flying instructors and this was a way of repaying them for the use of their skies etc. I suppose it was something of an honour to be chosen for this assignment, but how they came to choose me, I'll never know. This is where Alice's remark comes in, in reply to my cable: 'The Americans are sending us Spam to eat, so it's only fair they should have something in return.' I still think the Spam-eaters had the better part of the bargain!

I must say that Alice was very brave about it and very sensibly added that I would be safer in the US than joining a Fighter Squadron in England. She was to be proved so right, because Micky Shelton and a few others of the Number 10 course were soon to be shot down, some only a few weeks after operation training.

After the end-of-course celebrations, we few took the train to Toronto from Terrell Station, and what a send-off we had. I can't remember much about our two weeks in Toronto, except that in the first day or so we all received our commissions, and after only several days as a Sergeant, I was now Pilot Officer T. Round, No. 150002.

Having also received our clothing allowance, Collyn and I went off into the city to visit one of the recommended tailors to have our uniforms made. After looking at the regulation cloth, the tailor showed us what quality we could have for just a few dollars more. We didn't hesitate and gladly paid the extra cash, and we never regretted the decision, because our uniforms, especially the tropical outfit, became the envy of even the odd Air Vice Marshall in the months to come.

It was obvious why we were to be in Toronto for two weeks: not only for the official paperwork and travel arrangements, but also to have our uniforms made. Collyn and I had chosen our tailor well and in just over a week, we were beautifully kitted out and, with time on our hands, we went skating and skiing. We had travelled from the warmth of Texas to the Canadian winter. I wasn't any good at either

'A Wand'ring Minstrel, I'

With my grandmother Plumb in London, Ontario, in 1943.

'Up in the Air, Sky High'

My big day at our 'Wings parade'. After drilling, the cadets witness No. 10 course receiving their Pilots' Wings.

skating or skiing, but Collyn was quite brilliant at both sports having spent most of his winter holidays since childhood in Austria.

However, a letter from my parents quickly changed my plans. It seemed I was within a hundred miles of my grandmother (on my father's side), and her family, who had emigrated to Canada many years previously. In fact, my father was the only one of the family who decided not to emigrate. I can imagine it was my mother who talked him out of it, not wanting to leave her side of the family, all of whom lived in or near 'The Cottages'. That's how close I was to becoming a Canadian. This news from home sent me off to London, Ontario, to be reunited with my eighty-three year old grandmother – I was a mere toddler when they left England. I spent a very happy three days visiting various members of my father's family, before returning to Toronto, and then travelling to San Antonio to our posting at Kelly Field.

The United States Air Force (USAF) were certainly in a hurry to qualify us as instructors, and I seemed to spend more time in the air than on the ground. It seemed to me that although I had gained my Pilot's Wings, I was only just beginning to learn how to fly. Our instructors drove us hard – so hard that I decided I couldn't take any more. My own instructor was a fine pilot and I felt I couldn't meet his standards. After all, one degree out in a 180-degree, 45-degree-banked turn didn't appear to me to be too bad, but it wasn't good enough for him and his screaming down the intercom was completely tying me up. After one particularly nerve-racking flight, I climbed out of the aircraft and told him I wanted to pack the course in and return to England. I can't remember his exact words in reply to my request, and I certainly couldn't repeat them here. I was so blazing mad by the time he had finished that I couldn't wait to get back in the air to show him that I wasn't as big a fool as he obviously thought me. From then on I relaxed and started to make real progress – our row had done the trick. He was not only a good instructor, but a good psychologist as well.

I never did like air shows, and I always dreaded the news that some General or big-shot politician was to visit the airfield, and we were ordered to put on an air display. It happened several times in my RAF career, and I always felt the same. If I was killed or injured during my ordinary duties – OK, but to have an accident while showing off, was to me a complete waste of a pilot and an aircraft. Still, as a prospective fighter pilot, I wasn't supposed to be cautious, and in a typical reverse fashion, I used to try to go slightly better than anyone else. I dared not speak about my feelings because being a few years older than the majority of my flight, I knew I would have difficulty getting into fighters at all, and would have to go into Bomber Command when we finally got back to England. Strangely, Collyn, who was four years younger, wanted to go into multi-engined aircraft, but I didn't feel they were my cup of tea.

Our social life during this high-pressure five weeks or so was practically nil, but I remember one evening I was invited to a concert to hear the 'Von Trapp Family Singers'. I enjoyed the concert very much and even though my taxi driver broke all the speed regulations, I arrived at the gates of Randolph Field about ten minutes after lights out. I decided that the safest way was to pay off the taxi at the gate and walk to my barrack block. All went well, and I was within a hundred yards of my room, when a car drove around the corner of the building and I was caught in the headlight beam. Of course it had to be the Colonel of the field and I was ordered to report to him the following morning. This I did, and was ordered to be confined to barracks for a couple of nights. No great hardship really, we were living in luxury at Randolph, but I was surprised to receive a telephone call from my Colonel asking me to join him in the bowling alleys at 7 o'clock that evening. I never enjoyed a 'jankers' so much in those two nights confined to barracks.

I don't know how many hours I spent in the air, during that period (my logbook will tell me), but I certainly learnt my trade as an instructor – aerobatics, spinning, stalling, instrument flying, night flying, spot landings etc.

I was even more proud at the end of the course when I was presented with a certificate and had USAF Wings pinned on under my RAF Wings on Graduation Day. We were now available to be posted any-where in the Gulf Coast Training Command, and Collyn and I immediately put in a request to be posted as near to Dallas and Terrell

'A Wand'ring Minstrel, I'

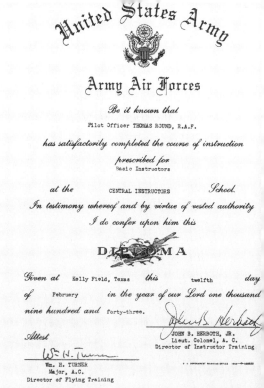

Not only commissioned but seconded to the USA Army Air Force.

as possible. We were delighted when we were told that we would be attached to Majors Field, Greenville which was thirty miles from Terrell and fifty miles from Dallas.

We duly arrived in Greenville, right in the heart of the cotton and onion growing country. A permanent banner across the High Street proclaimed 'The Blackest Land and the Whitest People'.

After the comparative luxury of Terrell and San Antonio, it was a bit of a shock to see the ten-foot square space that was allotted to me in a partitioned-off, wooden barrack hut, with not even a ceiling to give some degree of privacy. Still, I was getting used to the lack of privacy in the ablution department of the US Forces, because when I first arrived in Terrell and went to the 'bathroom' area, I was horrified to see no fewer than twenty-four very smart toilets about eighteen inches apart, facing twenty-four washbasins. I decided I would rather die of constipation in the first couple of weeks than use these very public conveniences! The course of nature soon got rid of my prudery.

I certainly felt more confident about my flying, but now I had to teach other men. Cadets came to Greenville for their basic training, after having completed the Primary Course, so all of them had logged quite a few flying hours. My job was to teach them to handle a heavier and much faster aircraft such as the Vultee Valiant. Apart from flying with six cadets every day, I was expected to log so many hours in the link trainer, callisthenics, lectures and also – and I think this latter was to prevent us becoming bored with instructing – we were expected to complete a schedule of cross-country flights on our free days.

As far as possible, I tried to arrange my own flights to fit in with my social and singing engagements. For instance, if I was due to sing in the downtown Baptist Church in Dallas at the Sunday morning service, I would set off on Saturday morning and fly to, say, Memphis, Tennessee, to log the necessary flying time, stay the night and then take off on Sunday morning for Love Fields, Dallas. I would park the plane, and ring my friends, who would collect me and deliver me to the church in time for the 11 a.m. service. I applied this system to quite a few towns – Waco, San Antonio, Terrell etc.

It was after a Sunday morning service at the Southern Methodist Church in Dallas, that I was introduced to a Miss Doris Comstock. She was the assistant and accompanist to the Principal of the Hockaday School of Music in Dallas. She was invited to join us for lunch, during the course of which she said that she would like to introduce me to the Principal of the school, Ivan Dneprov.

My next free day found me meeting the man who was to become my teacher and friend during my stay in Texas. After I had sung a couple of songs for him, I asked if he would agree to give me a series of lessons on voice production to which he agreed. I had to choose my lesson times very carefully because flying with six cadets every day and talking endlessly over the intercom made my voice very tired for singing. At the same time, having an outside interest prevented me from having a nervous breakdown. It is amazing how quickly you can forget your own learning days and begin to think that anyone who cannot perform an Immerlman or recover from a three turn spin perfectly, or execute a barrel roll, must be a complete imbecile. It took quite a lot of courage on my part to ask a cadet, who I wasn't very sure of, to spin a Vultee from 8,000 feet and recover at 4,000 feet, after completing two and a half turns.

In the Vultee, the instructor sat in the rear cockpit and the procedure was to ask the cadet to climb to 8,000 feet and then spin the aircraft to the right or to the left, and to recover when I gave the order over the intercom.

The spin was accomplished by catching the aircraft on the point of stalling, by closing the engine throttle, pulling the joystick right back and kicking in full right rudder. The right wing would drop and the plane would go into a bone-shaking spin to the right, in a virtual nosedive. If you were lucky, recovery was accomplished by sharply applying full opposite rudder and violently pushing the joystick fully forward. After what seemed an age, the plane would pull out of the spin into a steep dive, which would be corrected by easing back on the stick, and slowly opening the throttle. The hardest thing for me was to keep my hands off the controls and allow the cadet to execute the manoeuvre himself. The control movements had to be violent or they would have no effect at all on the Vultee.

One cadet gave me the fright of my life. We had climbed to 8,000 feet and I told him to spin to the right and to recover after two and a half turns. I knew, as soon as he had pushed in the rudder and the stick, that the movements hadn't been violent enough and the plane continued to spin. I ordered him to release the controls to me but he had frozen hard on both the rudder and the stick and I could not move them. We were diving towards the ground very fast and I really thought we would crash. I literally screamed down the intercom, which must have nearly burst his eardrums. His hands and feet flew off the controls and I put them back in the spinning position and repeated the recovery movements with all my strength. Nothing seemed to happen, except for an increase in the juddering and the trees becoming sickenly closer. I could only sit and wait for the crash which seemed inevitable, when I realised that we were pulling out of the spin and were in a near vertical dive. I wasn't conscious of pulling the stick back, but soon we were flying straight and level at less than 500 feet above the ground. I eased on the throttle and started to climb again. My thoughts were to return to the airfield, land and give up for the day, but I realised that if I did, I would probably never want to fly with another cadet, and also that the cadet sitting in front of me would never fly again.

I can honestly say that I have done one brave thing in my life – I spoke as quietly and calmly as I could and told him to climb back to

My first group of cadets as a basic training instructor.

8,000 feet and do me a three turn spin to the left. He did it correctly; we then returned to base and I gave the rest of my group instructions for solo manoeuvres for the rest of that afternoon, and then I went to my room and to bed.

There were only two RAF instructors to each US Squadron and we soon found ourselves in demand. In some way, our reputation as instructors became known and we found cadets from each new course practically drawing lots for our attention. Just for the record, this wasn't because we were outstanding as instructors – at least I wasn't – but because we were not as tough on the cadets as the US instructors were; although I had to go along with most of the US Army rules, life with Collyn and myself was a bit easier than with our US counterparts.

The basic course lasted seven weeks and I don't remember having to fail or eliminate one cadet, and they all passed the Chief Flying Instructor's final test. They were not all good, natural pilots, but I was prepared to work harder with the slow ones. I did not want them to fail because I was too tired or irritable to take the trouble.

The most nerve-wracking part of the course was the night flying and to sit quietly in the rear cockpit and let your student perform his first night landing took a large amount of willpower. I was lucky – whenever any of my students had accidents, I was never in the aircraft at the time. Fortunately, the accidents were not serious – one merely landed in the field before the runway and dragged a hundred yards of wire fencing down, with very little damage to the aircraft. Another landed with his wheel brakes already on – this was at night-time on a strange grass field and I could understand his panic – but the plane stood beautifully on its nose.

However, other instructors and cadets were not so lucky and a notice was issued to all the airfields in the Gulf Training Command that more instructors and cadets were being killed or injured than in the operational squadrons at that time.

One weekend, Collyn and I decided to make a flight to Oklahoma City, spend some hours there and then fly back to Greenville at night in order to log some night flying hours. The pilots always posted their weekend destinations on the flight room notice board and if any of the ground crew – mechanics, electricians etc., lived in or near the town to which we were flying, then they could apply to accompany us as a passenger. Both Collyn and I had passengers that weekend, both of whom lived in Oklahoma City.

We arrived safely at the Oklahoma Air Base and told our passengers that we would take off again at 10 o'clock that evening. We took off again according to plan, and climbed into a beautiful star lit sky and set course for Paris, Texas. After about an hour's flying time, I signalled to Collyn that he seemed to be drifting off course, but he didn't agree. We drifted further and further apart until I lost sight of him against the stars. We were running short of aviation fuel at Majors Field, and we had been instructed to fill the tanks at Paris before flying on to Greenville. I soon realised I had missed the Paris airfield when my ETA (estimated time of arrival) passed. Fifteen minutes later I was hopelessly lost and my fuel tank was approaching the danger mark. Fortunately, a glow of light appeared ahead and I was soon over quite a large town. I spotted an airfield on the outskirts and decided to land without asking permission – I would accept the consequences as long as I was down safely. I was on my approach leg and virtually over the end of the runway, when two brilliant lights suddenly blinded me. They were the lights of a commercial airliner taking off straight towards me, and I was attempting to land downwind. I pushed the throttle full on and banked sharply away and roared over the buildings of the town, hoping that no one in the control tower had been able to identify my aircraft. If they had, then I was in serious trouble. Suddenly, I saw a brilliant Red Horse, revolving on top of a tall building and immediately recognised it as 'Pegasus', the large Red Horse on top of the Magnolia Building in downtown Dallas. I knew the course to fly to Greenville like the back of my hand and in a few minutes, I had covered the fifty miles between the two towns and the lights of Majors Field came into view.'Pegasus' had saved my life and I landed safely; my passenger thanked me for a safe flight!

I had to explain to the Flight Officer that I had failed to land at Paris to refuel and had headed straight for Greenville. I made no mention of my escapade over Dallas, and hoped that they had not

The flying red horse, Pegasus, on top of the Magnolia Building in Dallas (now dwarfed by much taller skyscrapers). I was lost in the night sky over Texas and Pegasus guided my plane safely home.

been contacted. Nothing was said, but I lived in dread for the next few days. After a week, nothing had happened and I was able to relax.

The Flying Horse had truly saved my life and I enclose photographs of it. On one of my later visits to Dallas, a friend (Overton Shelmire – more of him later) obtained permission to enter the now deserted Magnolia Building and take me to the top. We climbed on to the scaffolding surrounding the structure and took these pictures.

In recent months, the Magnolia Building has been beautifully restored and the Red Horse is once more circling the top, lit up at night with hundreds of red lights.

In 1943, the Magnolia was the highest building in Dallas, but it is now dwarfed by the dozens of towering skyscrapers, some built almost entirely of glass, that have since been built. The Red Horse is difficult to find in this maze of high rise blocks, but in the 1940s it served as a beacon for pilots flying in the Dallas area.

I'm sure my singing kept me sane because, apart from the strains of flying, it was becoming clear that I was not going to be able to have Alice with me, which depressed us both. At least twice a week I presented myself at Hockaday and I could tell I was making progress – so much so that I was thrilled to learn that Ivan was planning an open air production of Leon Cavallo's 'I Pagliacci', and he wanted me to sing the role of Canio. The rest of the cast was to be from the school except for the part of Tonio who was a professional, engaged for the production.

Dneprov really worked hard with me and I enjoyed every minute of it. The opera was a success and the critics were very kind to me. After all, my voice was never a Canio voice. We made a lot of dollars for the American Red Cross.

Flight Lieutenant Palmer didn't like what was happening to my

Ivan Dneprov rehearsing Lieutenant Joesph N. Kotzin, left, in the fiendish interest he, as Tonio, should show when Pilot Officer Tom Round, as Canio, kills Dorothy Durand, the fickle Nedda.

'Up in the Air, Sky High'

voice; he thought I was not singing with my heart any more, but with my head! I told him that as soon as I had mastered the voice techniques with my head, then I would bring my heart and head together. Several years later, when he heard me with the Sadler's Wells Opera Company in various operas, I think he approved. He attained the exalted rank of Air Vice-Marshall. He followed my career until he died.

My reputation as a singer was growing fast and every Sunday morning would find me in a church in some part of the State of Texas singing 'The Holy City', 'The Ninety and Nine', 'The Lord's Prayer', 'The Prayer Perfect', 'King Ever Glorious' and the like.

I met hundreds of wonderful people at the end of every concert or church service; I shook hands with every member of the audience or congregation. Dallas became like my home town, and when the time came for me to be posted back to the UK, certain dignitaries of Dallas wanted to send a petition to Buckingham Palace requesting that I be allowed to stay in Texas. They felt I was doing more good for international relations with my singing than I could ever do as a pilot. The idea was never allowed to get off the ground, but it was a wonderful feeling to be wanted in that way. I had already stated that Dallas had

Here are just some of the reviews from the *Dallas Morning News* at the time:

DNEPROV TO GIVE PAGLIACCI WITH RAF PILOT AT THE CASINO. Ivan Dneprov, Executive Director of the Hockaday Institute of Music, has announced the production of Leoncavallo's 'I Pagliacci' for late May.

In the role of Canio will be Pilot Officer Tom Round, RAF. When he was sent to Terrell last fall for RAF training, he heard Dneprov was in Dallas and utilized his first leave to see him. He sang for the maestro who agreed to give him lessons. 'His progress has been amazing,' Mr Dneprov said. 'He has a God-given voice, a good ear and keen musical aptitude; he will be a magnificent Canio'.

HOCKADAY'S PAGLIACCI IS AL FRESCO DELIGHT. It was in the spirit of 'Ham' that RAF Pilot Officer Tom Round gave his wide, high and handsome delineation and played vengeance to the hilt. He also gave the role a fluent tenor voice. His training has been under Mr Dneprov who has developed his innate tastefulness and the natural and expressive beauty of his voice to such a degree that the lapses from finished musical punctuation were negligible, and his mastery of his two big arias was notable.

From *Opera in Review*, Dallas:

The leading role of Canio was taken by RAF Pilot Officer Tom Round. This young Englishman had never sung professionally before coming to this country and Monday night's appearance was his first on an opera stage. The part of Canio has its advantages and disadvantages as a debut role. Musically it is demanding and in this category Tom Round's naturally magnificent tenor voice and clean intonation served him well. His interpretation of 'Vesti la Giubba' drew continued applause and he built his feverishly emotional climax skilfully in the last Act.

There is no doubt but that he has a musical future when the business of war is done.

given me the courage that, should I survive the war, I would try to become a professional singer.

It was to be 1970 before I returned to Dallas, to sing at the Southern Methodist University, and to have the *Dallas Morning News* welcome me back as a 'Dallasonian'.

My life now revolved around flying and singing – in that order. I became known as 'The Singing Ambassador of Goodwill' because I never refused to sing at any worthwhile function and although naturally I didn't receive any fees, I am sure that my efforts in Texas gave me the confidence to turn professional.

Finally the day came when I was due to leave for the UK. It was with very mixed emotions indeed because, on the one hand, I had reached the end of my tether as an instructor – the sight of an AT6 Harvard or a Vultee Valiant gave me the shakes. The RAF and the USAF were wise in limiting the time a pilot could be an efficient instructor. At the end of my last flying period, I threw my parachute into my locker and walked to my quarters and never gave a backward glance to the runways and flight huts that had been my home for over a year.

On the other hand, I was very sad indeed to be leaving all my Texas friends in Dallas, Terrell, Waco, San Antonio, Longview, Tyler and a host of other towns. They all held some special memory for me and I wished with all my heart that I would be able to return some day.

That wish has been granted time and time again.

I was thrilled to be going home to my wife and son. Alice and I had kept up virtually a daily correspondence and she sent me lots of photographs to remind me that I also had a son.

It was also very sad to say goodbye to the Preston family – Gran Preston, her daughter Hannah, her granddaughter Genevieve and of course Bill Preston. Bill was the personal secretary to a Mr Pettit. I never knew what his business was, but I do know he was a very wealthy Texan who owned a very large ranch called 'Flat Top Ranch' near Walnut Creek, between Dallas and Fort Worth.

Collyn, Mick and I sent a very happy weekend there and very much admired his herd of Hereford cattle and especially his champion Hereford bull, called C. P. Tone.

Bill was very proud of the progress I had made with my voice studies and especially of the performance of 'I Pagliacci'. He presented me with an album of a recording of the opera issued by Victor Records, together with a Texas belt with a silver and gold buckle, with my initials carved in gold, and also a pair of hand-made Texas cowboy boots, made in Fort Worth.

I also have a silver and gold tie clip which Genevieve gave me after Bill, Hannah and I had driven from Dallas to Oklahoma City, arriving

'Up in the Air, Sky High'

at 1.30 a.m. to sing at her wedding at the home of her husband-to-be. I remember I sang 'At Dawning', and 'I'll Walk Beside You'.

Collyn had become engaged to a Terrell girl called Peggy Bass. Her family owned a large drugstore and café in Terrell. Every new course that arrived in Terrell was invited to the Bass drugstore, where they were treated to a real Texas hamburger with a coca-cola as a welcome to the town.

I have stayed with Peggy and her husband on several occasions when on my various concert tours. Sadly Collyn was killed when his Wellington Bomber crashed and Peggy later married her girlhood sweetheart.

We had been given a three-week leave before we had, once again, to reach our starting point at Moncton, New Brunswick. Collyn and I had temporarily parted company, and made our own plans for our last three weeks in America.

My last goodbyes were said – it was saddest of all to leave Ivan Dneprov and Hockaday – and I headed for New York, determined to see as many performances of opera as I could in the ten days I had allotted myself in New York.

I had a letter of introduction to the Principal of the Julliard School of Music in New York, where I was offered a scholarship to study singing, after the war had ended.

Finally, I returned to Moncton and renewed my friendships there; I had left as a lowly LAC, and returned as a Flying Officer which was the cause of much celebration. We embarked on the *Mauritania* and had a wonderful crossing, zigzagging all the way to avoid trouble.

I went on immediate leave and wasted no time at all in getting home to Alice and Ellis. My leave was extended twice – we seemed to have a surplus of pilots at that time – before I was finally posted to an orientation course to familiarise myself with flying conditions in England. It was very strange indeed for me to have an instructor behind me telling me what to do, instead of vice-versa. I soon realised that I needed him for a while because I became hopelessly lost on my first cross-country flight. I had been used to wide open spaces and CAVU (ceiling and visibility unlimited). When I say that my first solo flight was around the Derby area, where the visibility was decidedly limited and hardly any country at all, perhaps I could be forgiven for putting down at a private airfield to ask the way back to Derby.

I kept insisting that I wanted to be posted to a Fighter Squadron and would settle for nothing less and as replacements were not needed as fast as they were earlier in the war, my posting was delayed. Collyn, on the other hand, wanted bombers and he was soon on his way. We really parted company after a wonderful night out at 'The Trocadero' in London, where Micky Shelton, who had left us in Texas, and was now a veteran fighter pilot, joined us. He roared with laughter to think that 'Old Tom' was still insisting on joining Fighter Command.

The last I saw of Micky was a very handsome face grinning from the cockpit of a red MG sports car as he roared down Piccadilly. Two days later, he was shot down during a sortie in France. Collyn and I parted company, he to an operation bomber training field, and me to await my posting to Fighter Command.

Collyn had finished his operational training in Wellingtons and I was still at Derby when one black day I was called from a flight and handed a telegram from Alice that my younger brother Fred had been killed. I was given immediate leave to go home for seventy-two hours. As in my case, my mother had done everything she could to stop Fred from going into the services. He was a valued electrician with Vickers Armstrong's of Barrow and was an expert on gun firing installations on warships – and he had no need to join up. Mother hid letters, tore them up, burned them, but he finally made it as First Electrician in the Merchant Navy. Three months later he was blown up by an anti-personnel mine while walking on the beach at Bayeaux

Me with my instructor, relaxing back in England on the wings of a Miles Master.

With my favourite Spitfire.

while his ship was off-loaded. Seven days later I had another telegram telling me that Collyn Warren had been killed while on his first flight in a Wellington Bomber.

After one or two extended leaves, during which I gave several concerts, including one at Barrow-in-Furness, and sang at one or two church services, I was at last posted to Tern Hill to do a course on Miles Masters, prior to operational training. From Tern Hill I was posted to Hawarden on the Wirral, where I converted to Hurricanes and then to Spitfires. From Hawarden I transferred to Chilbolton, where I started operational training in earnest. I was able to rent a bungalow on the outskirts of the airfield and Alice and Ellis joined me. It was just like going to work every day and we enjoyed it. Two and a half year old Ellis became the Mascot of our flight and he would spend his days on the airfield with us and there cannot be many

In 1944 the *North Western Evening Mail* in Barrow wrote:

MUSICAL TREAT AT BARROW. Much interest was aroused in the appearance of Flying Officer Tom Round, a tenor of undoubted ability and with a bright future before him. His first song was 'Your Tiny Hand is Frozen' from 'La Boheme' and for this he was accorded well-merited applause. He responded with a fine song by Carl Bohm, 'Calm is the Night' and made a deep impression on the audience ... Flying Officer Tom Round was a joy to listen to. His interpretation and phrasing, backed by cleanness of diction were very evident.

children who have been photographed sitting in the cockpit of a Spitfire Mark 5. This is where his interest in aeroplanes began and grew.

From Chilbolton, I was posted to Lasham, only twenty-five miles away. Alice went back home. The war was nearly over and it looked as though I would never become fully operational – we were merely filling in time.

I made frequent trips to London and often stayed with Collyn's parents at Moor Park. We had become firm and fast friends. I also visited Beverly Baxter at his home on Hamilton Terrace. I had told him of my musical activities in Texas and that I had decided to try to become a professional singer. A few days later he told me that he had written to Joan Cross (the artistic administrator with the Sadler's Wells Opera Company), requesting that they grant me an audition.

I had been waiting about three weeks to hear from Sadler's Wells, and I was once again in London for the day, when I chanced to see a poster while going down an escalator in the Piccadilly tube station. It advertised the fact that the D'Oyly Carte Opera Company were performing a 'Season of Gilbert & Sullivan' operas at the Kings Theatre, Hammersmith. I had never heard of the D'Oyly Carte Opera Company and the only Gilbert & Sullivan Opera I had seen, was a film version of 'The Mikado' in about 1938 at the Lancaster Odeon Cinema, and of course I knew the song 'A Wand'ring Minstrel, I'.

The poster stated that there was a matinée that day, Thursday, at 2.30 p.m., so purely out of curiosity, I decided to go and see the

Young Thomas Ellis – now the squadron mascot – in the cockpit (right) and posing with Robin Elverson and George Cook (left).

'Up in the Air, Sky High'

performance. I found my way out to Hammersmith and to the Kings Theatre, paid for my ticket and found my seat – little knowing the emotional shock that was waiting for me.

The opera was 'The Mikado' and after the brilliant Overture, the curtain rose and within minutes I was completely enthralled by the lovely music, the witty dialogue, the colourful costumes and scenery and the talented cast. Halfway through the first act, I had mentally replaced the tenor singing the part of Nanki-Poo with myself.

By the time of the interval, I knew what I must do – I went straight to the box office and asked if I could please speak to the company manager. After a short while, a tall-distinguished man confronted me with a shock of snow-white hair and bristling eyebrows – Mr Hugh Jones. I told him that I was watching the performance and how much I was enjoying it and in the same breath I told him that I sang as a tenor and could I please audition for the company. He was taken aback by my sudden request, but told me that the usual procedure was to write to the D'Oyly Carte Office at No. 1 Savoy Hill, and they would contact me when they were arranging future auditions. I told him that as a pilot in the RAF, I never knew where I was going to be from day to day, and that I might never be in London again, so I would have to sing for them that day. I have never had the same courage again.

Finally, and I'm sure that it was my uniform which won him over, he asked me to see him again after the performance. By the end of the second act, I was more convinced than ever that I had reached a turning point in my life.

When the final curtain came down, I again presented myself at the front of the house and when Mr Jones came, I was taken to the Circle bar, where there was a piano. After a few minutes, a red-haired gentleman came in and I was introduced to Isidore Godfrey, the musical director of the company, who was conducting that afternoon and who wasn't very pleased at having his between-shows break interfered with by a service man who thought he could sing. He asked me what I would like to sing and could he see the music. I explained that, not knowing I was going to sing for anyone, I had not got any music with me. Mr Godfrey firmly stated that he could not possibly play any songs without the music, and was about to leave the room, when Mr Jones said that Richard Walker could play the piano by ear and that he would ask him to join us. Very soon, a man in a multi-coloured dressing gown came in, still in his make-up (he had played Pooh-Bah that afternoon). After a short discussion he said he would try to 'busk' his way through 'O Maiden My Maiden' from Franz Lehar's operetta 'Frederica'. After the song both Mr Godfrey and Mr Jones said that they liked my voice and that they would inform Mr Rupert D'Oyly Carte. They would contact me to arrange an audition as soon as possible. I gave then the address of the airfield, which was near the town made famous by W. S. Gilbert in the opera 'Ruddigore' – yes – 'Basingstoke' it is!

I really didn't expect to hear anything, but a few days later I received a letter asking me to present myself at the Savoy Theatre, The Strand, London, to audition before Mr Rupert D'Oyly Carte. Naturally, I was thrilled and on the appointed day I walked into the stage door of the Savoy Theatre, and joined about a dozen more people, also due to audition. Amongst them were Peter Pratt and Sybil Ghilchick who were both successful that afternoon.

This time, of course, I did have my music and when my turn came, I walked out on to the stage and put the aria 'Your Tiny Hand is Frozen' from 'La Boheme' in front of the pianist – a little old lady. She took one look at the aria and said, 'I hope you're not going to sing all this'. I replied that I would keep going until someone told me to stop. In the event, I was allowed to sing right through the aria and a Mr Richard Collet – Mr Carte's general manager – walked down the stalls and asked me to sing the song I had sung for Mr Godfrey. I then repeated 'O Maiden My Maiden'. Afterwards, I was asked to meet Mr Carte, and he told me that he had liked my singing and asked when I would be available to join his company.

I replied that I had no idea when I would be released from the Air Force, but when I was I would have to return to the police force in Lancaster City. He asked me to write to him when I had obtained my release and he would arrange to hear me again. To say that I was thrilled with the result of the audition was putting it mildly, and I wrote off to Alice to tell her the news.

In the meantime, I went back to my flying – the war had ended and I knew now that I should never get on Operations. In fact, our training programme was practically at a standstill.

I was airborne in a Spitfire Mk 14 at 3 p.m. on 7 May, when I received a call ordering all planes to return to base and land imme-diately. We had been expecting that the Prime Minister would be announcing the end of hostilities that day, and I knew this was it. It was a strange feeling to know that all our work and training for war, was at an end and that there was suddenly no purpose for it. I don't know what the other pilots felt who were airborne at that time, but I couldn't wait to get that Spitfire safely back on the ground. I was quite wrong in thinking that I wouldn't have to fly again, though.

About twenty of us decided to celebrate VE Night in Winchester, which we did. I can't remember what time we got back to our Nissen huts, but I know that I had just settled down on my camp bed when we were told that we wouldn't be required for flying duties the next day. We all piled out of bed and fifteen minutes later, two carloads of us were on our way to London to see what was happening there on this historic night. It was strange, in the following weeks, to realise that there may be another life waiting for me – after nearly five years of sleeping and waking flying, I really started to think of the future. Sometimes I was excited at the thought of a new career and sometimes scared that I would soon be back in competition with civilians. Some of my colleagues decided to sign up for a two- or three-year commission – having no real job to go back to – so I felt very lucky indeed with virtually two careers waiting for me. One I didn't want and intended to get out of as soon as possible, and one that was completely unknown to me, but one that I wanted to try more than anything I had ever known.

All flying training ceased and our time was taken up ferrying new aircraft, which kept arriving at our base, to storage fields in the Midlands. The war was over, but the factories couldn't stop turning out the guns and planes immediately. I hadn't minded flying while the war was still on and there was a purpose, but now that it was all over, I began to get jittery that I would have a bad crash and kill myself. I even started to avoid flying duties as much as I could, especially when I lost two other friends just on practice flights.

We had been grounded for nearly a couple of weeks because of bad weather, but eventually the weather lifted and the cloud ceiling was about 1,000 feet. George Cook volunteered to take off to check the denseness of the cloud cover. I remember he borrowed my rather battered flying cap. He became disorientated in the clouds and went into a spin, from which he couldn't recover. Alan McCartney, an Australian pilot, crashed into the Welsh hills near Shrewsbury when the cloud bases dropped to around 500 feet. I had anguished letters from his father in Australia as he couldn't come to terms with the fact that his son had been killed after the war had ended.

None of us knew how long it would be before we were de-mobbed, so I welcomed a posting to Hanover as an assistant Law Officer. I rang Alice and she came down to Alton and we took a room at the Swan Hotel to spend a few days together before I flew off to Hanover. The morning of my departure came and I was due to take off in an Anson Aircraft at 8 a.m. I had left Alice at the hotel and she was going to keep a lookout for my plane as I flew over. I was having a quick breakfast in the Mess, when I received a message to report immediately to the Adjutant. I was received with a broad smile and a handshake and the news that my posting had been cancelled and instead, I was being de-mobbed under Class B Regulations which applied to personnel in reserved occupations. I left the office in a complete daze, but I lost no time in telephoning Alice and giving her the fantastic news. We spent the day just walking and talking and trying to make plans. I simply couldn't take it in that I had made it in one piece – I was even scared to cross the road in case I had an accident.

Alice left for home the next day and two weeks later I joined her at No. 6 Penrhyn Road, where five years earlier I had left her in such sad circumstances. I had a couple of weeks before I was due to report for police duty and they were spent in trying to adjust to being Mr Round or PC 36 Round as opposed to Flight Lieutenant Round, and to being a husband and father.

Boarding the AT6 Harvard.

CHAPTER FIVE

'Life's a Pudding
Full of Plums'

*M*Y OLD POLICE FRIEND, Eddie Thacker, had been demobbed at the same time, as had all service police officers. He had become a Captain in the Coldstream Guards. I shall never forget the day, or rather evening, that we reported for our first tour of duty. We stood in Dalton Square, outside the police station, and we looked at each other and our thoughts were just the same – what had happened in the last five years and had we really been away? The fact that our first two weeks were spent on night duty didn't help us to feel kindly towards our superior officers. Perhaps they had thought that the sooner we were brought down to earth, the better.

I was demobbed in October 1945, and after a couple of months I knew that I couldn't continue in the police force. I wrote to the D'Oyly Carte Offices to inform Mr Carte that I had been released from the Air Force and was now back in the police force – was he still interested in me joining his opera company?

Mr Carte's reply invited me to the Royal Court Theatre, Liverpool, on a date in November when the company would be playing there, for a further audition. Enclosed with the letter was a vocal score and a libretto of 'The Yeomen of the Guard' with instructions to learn the dialogue between Colonel Fairfax and Elsie Maynard in Act 2, beginning with 'Mistress Elsie – so thou leavest us tonight'. Also, to learn the songs 'Is life a boon?' and 'Free from his fetters grim'. Events were starting to move – but they were also starting to move in the police force. For some unknown reason, I was transferred into the Detective Department and I was sent off on a course to the Police College in Wakefield for four weeks. It was just like being back in the Air Force, and I enjoyed it very much.

Returning to Lancaster, the day came in November for me to travel to Liverpool. I had managed to arrange my weekly rest day to coincide with the audition date and I duly presented myself at the stage door of the Royal Court Theatre.

I was told that I would be playing the scene with the principal soprano understudy – a young lady called Ann Nicholson. I sang the song 'Is life a boon' first and received a thumbs-up sign from the

D'OYLY CARTE OPERA COMPANY

Telegrams
SAVOYARD, LONDON.
Telephone
TEMPLE BAR 4343.

SAVOY HOTEL,
LONDON, W.C.2.

Office Entrance
EMBANKMENT
GARDENS.

23rd January, 1946.

Dear Mr. Round,

I acknowledge receipt of your
telegram and letter addressed to Mr. Collet.

Mr. Collet has been ordered
away for a month's complete rest and I am not
able to get hold of him at the moment. It is
alright, however, for you to start on February 4th
and, unless I hear from you to the contrary, I shall
expect you at this Office at 10 o'clock on that
morning.

Yours truly,

Stanley Parker

TREASURER.

Thos. Round, Esq.,
6, Penrhyn Road,
LANCASTER.

D'OYLY CARTE OPERA COMPANY

Telegrams
SAVOYARD, LONDON.
Telephone
TEMPLE BAR 4343.

SAVOY HOTEL,
LONDON, W.C.2.

Office Entrance
EMBANKMENT
GARDENS.

6th July, 1945.

Dear Sir,

I understand you sang to my Stage
Manager at the King's Theatre, Hammersmith,
on June 30th.

I am hearing a few people sing on
Tuesday afternoon next, July 10th, at the
Savoy Theatre and would like to hear you
myself if you can attend.

If you can, please come to the Stage
Door of the Savoy Theatre at 3.30 p.m. and bring
a bright English song with you.

Please let me know if you can keep
this appointment.

Yours faithfully,

R. D'Oyly Carte

F/Lt. T. Round,
Officers Mess.
84. G.S.V.
R.A.F. Lasham.
Nr. Alton, Hants.

D'OYLY CARTE OPERA COMPANY

Telegrams
SAVOYARD, LONDON.
Telephone
TEMPLE BAR 4343.

SAVOY HOTEL,
LONDON, W.C.2.

Office Entrance
EMBANKMENT
GARDENS.

12th July, 1945.

Dear Mr. Round,

Further to the audition that you
had yesterday with Mr. D'Oyly Carte, I would be
glad if, when you are in this vicinity, you would
call in and see me, that is, if you are interested
later on in joining the Company. It is quite possible
that we might get your demobilization earlier than
Group 32.

Yours sincerely,

R. D'OYLY CARTE,

Richard Collet

General Manager.

F/Lt. T. Round,
Officers Mess.
84. G.S.V.
R.A.F. Lasham,
Nr. Alton, Hants.

THE D'OYLY CARTE OPERA COMPANY LTD

Telegrams: Savoyard, London   1, SAVOY HILL, LONDON, W.C.2   Telephone: Temple Bar 1533

29th November, 1957.

Dear Mr. Round,

I herewith offer you a contract with my
Company to begin on or about the 1st August 1958,
for a period of five years, at a salary of £50.0.0.
(Fifty Pounds) per week, plus £10.0.0. (Ten Pounds)
per week expenses.

The form of official contract to be
subsequently agreed.

Yours sincerely,

Bridget D'Oyly Carte

Thomas Round, Esq.,
203, Hambermill Lane,
Oxhey,
Herts.

I agree to the above.

DIRECTORS: BRIDGET D'OYLY CARTE · HUGH WONTNER, M.V.O. · A.F. MOIR · WALTER HORE stage manager and then went straight into the dialogue. I had no idea of the moves, but I remember that Miss Nicholson moved around me, which must have put some life into the scene. I then sang 'Free from his fetters grim', and was called off stage to await Mr Carte in one of the dressing rooms. The stage manager whispered that I had nothing to worry about. Another person who informed me that he was the principal comic in the company also approached me. He said he had heard the audition from the back of the circle, and that I would definitely be offered a contact. His name was Graham Clifford. Obviously word had spread around the company that this was a special audition. This was all very encouraging but I still had to meet the great man himself.

Mr Carte turned out to be a man of medium height, slim and dark-haired with a soft speaking voice, and I shall never forget his first words to me. 'Mr Round', he said, 'I cannot see any good reason why Colonel Fairfax shouldn't have been a North Country gentleman, but in the Gilbert and Sullivan operas, I like my artists to speak with a neutral accent.' My Lancashire dialect must have stood out like a sore thumb. However, Mr Carte went on to say that he had no doubt that I would be able to overcome that small obstacle and he would like to offer me a contract with his company, and to eventually become a principal tenor. I was absolutely delighted, and said that I would first have to obtain my release from the police force and that I would let him know when this could be done. I left the theatre walking on air.

Now had to come the big decision. It was all very well talking about a singing career, but in the few months that I had been back in the force, I had begun to have that feeling of security once again.

Alice and I spent long hours talking over the problems that would arise if I decided to end my career in the force. Finally, we could see that unless I tried, I would never know whether or not I could have made a success of singing and I would always resent not having given it a try, especially when things were not going well for me as a policeman.

I wrote out my letter of resignation asking to be released at the end of the official month's notice and giving my reasons. I was quite unprepared for the bombshell that followed. Chief Constable Thompson had never had any great liking for me even before I went into the RAF and now, to want to leave his force for a career in the theatre, seemed to him the height of foolishness and he made no bones about telling me so. He also stated that he would feel it his duty to inform the Ministry of Labour that I had been especially released from the RAF on Class B to return to the police, and that he recommended that I be recalled to the RAF to await my Class A release.

Morally, I suppose he was right, but if he felt it was his duty to do this, then the letter could have been written in such a way as to show

City Police Office, Lancaster

This is to Certify

That P C 36 *Thomas Round*

served in LANCASTER CITY POLICE FORCE

from *31st January 1936* to *20th January 1946*

Cause of leaving *Resigned*

His conduct was *Exemplary*

Personal description: Age *30 years* Height *5' 10½"*

Eyes *Blue* Hair *Brown* Complexion *Fresh*

W Thompson.
————————————Chief Constable.

20th January 1946.

My certificate of resignation from
the Lancaster Police.

that I was trying to improve my career prospects. I knew he wouldn't do this, but I didn't think the Ministry would take any action. How wrong I was. I worked out my notice, most of it on night duty as a last parting shot from my Chief. When I arrived home after my last tour of duty, I felt like a ship without a rudder. I had always been in employment and still had the northerner's fear of unemployment. For the first time, I felt really scared at what I was doing. I was more scared still the following morning when an official letter arrived for me. I opened it and was horrified to read that I had been recalled to the RAF and was to report to Fighter Command Headquarters, Stanmore, Middlesex on – would you believe it – the same day that I had been instructed to report to the D'Oyly Carte offices at the Savoy Hotel. My Chief had really done a good job; my boats were well and truly burned. I could only obey the Ministry order and report for duty at Stanmore and at the same time inform Mr Carte as to what had happened.

I packed my civilian clothes in a suitcase and wearing my RAF uniform once again stood on Lancaster Station, but this time, not knowing whether I was a civilian or an officer in the RAF.

On arrival in London I made my way out to Moor Park, where I had been invited to stay with Collyn Warren's parents, while I was studying and rehearsing at the Savoy. Mrs Warren was on holiday in Texas and after I had told Mr Warren my amazing tale, I made my way to Stanmore. I had no idea what action I could take, but I was determined to explore any and every angle to get me out of my mixed-up situation. Surely, no one else had had to face up to such a peculiar dilemma. Within an hour, I was once more absorbed into the armed services. Just a name and a number, and I couldn't see what I could do about it.

The last straw came when the Adjutant and the Officer in charge of flying, not having had to deal with my type of case before, and not knowing what to do with me, finally came up with the idea of posting me to a night fighter squadron. I immediately jumped in and said that as I had not flown for more than five months and had never been attached to a night fighter squadron anyway, I would kill myself in a week. After some persuasive talk, the Adjutant finally agreed to give me two weeks' compassionate leave in order to give me a chance to find a way out of my difficulty.

That evening, back at the Warrens' flat, we had a meal and sat down to talk about the problem. Out of the blue, Mr Warren said that in the flat above lived his good friend, a Group Captain who worked in the Air Ministry and who might be able to give me some advice. We went upstairs immediately and I was introduced to the Group Captain, who, when he had heard my story, said that he felt sure he could do something about it and the situation should never have arisen. The services were trying to get rid of personnel, not recruit them. His reply staggered me.

He said that he was in charge of promulgating release orders and if I would report to his office at 11 a.m. the following morning, he would have the solution to my problem.

I couldn't believe that I had been so fortunate to meet by chance, the one person in the RAF who could help me (thanks to John Warren). I told the Group Captain that I was also due at the Savoy Hotel the following morning at 10 a.m. for my first rehearsal in my new profession. He told me to report to his office nearer lunchtime to give him the opportunity to work things out.

The next morning I presented myself at the D'Oyly Carte offices in full uniform, not knowing whether I was starting my new life as a professional singer or resuming it as a pilot. The D'Oyly Carte staff were equally puzzled, but I assured them that everything would be put right that day. I didn't feel very confident, but I had to say so. I was then introduced to the pianist with whom I would be working for the next three months and she turned out to be the same lady who had played for my audition, Miss Maude Brown, known to her friends as 'Brownie'. We went to a room to start the process of teaching me the Gilbert & Sullivan operas and also started a friendship that was to last many years – she was then in her early seventies.

We worked for about two hours and then I said I would have to report to the Air Ministry and that I would be back for rehearsal after lunch.

It is difficult to imagine my feelings at this time – my head was spinning with my first two hours of G & S, and now I was walking along the Strand as an Officer in the RAF and being saluted by every non-commissioned man I met on my way to the Air Ministry.

I reported to the Group Captain and he informed me that I was to be placed on indefinite compassionate leave until my Class A release orders came through in the normal manner. This would enable me to carry on with my new career. My leave would be extended at the end of each month and a fresh supply of ration cards would be sent to me. I would receive my full pay as a Flight Lieutenant with full allowances for my wife and child. I couldn't believe my good fortune and couldn't begin to thank him for his help, but said that I couldn't accept my pay and allowances and asked that they be paid into the RAF Benevolent Fund. I was firmly told that this could not be done as I was officially in the Air Force awaiting demobilisation. He wished me luck in my chosen career and I left the Ministry and walked back to the Savoy – stopping en route for some lunch – unable to believe my incredible luck. I'd had visions of being back in the service cog-wheels and being lost for ever, and here I was virtually a free man once again. Of course, I lost no time in telling Alice the good news and I settled down to my new life as a singer.

I soon found out that Brownie lived only about a mile from the Warrens' flat and to save her the weary journey up to town every day, we arranged to meet at her house on Hampermill Lane, Oxhey. Seven years later I was to buy a house only a hundred yards from her.

'A Wand'ring Minstrel, I'

CHAPTER SIX

'Only in Theatrical Performances'

*I*T WAS IN APRIL THAT I LEFT LONDON for Leicester to join the company on tour, where I immediately started rehearsing the chorus business of several of the operas and soon made my first professional appearance in 'The Mikado'. This was a good idea, because I had never been on a professional stage before and it was a good experience for me. I started immediately to rehearse the roles of Nanki-Poo, Luiz, Ralph Rackstraw and Frederic. The idea was that I should give one or two performances of each of these roles before the end of the present tour and also to see if I could make the grade as a principal.

It was towards the end of May, and we were playing at the Royal Court Theatre, Liverpool (where I had auditioned), when I received a telegram instructing me, once again, to report to RAF Stanmore for my Class A release. I was given the necessary time off from the company and made my way to Mr and Mrs Warren's flat at Moor Park, where I had left my uniform. I reported to Stanmore and was immediately quartered in a very nice room and allocated a 'Batwoman'. This second demob took about three days. I had to go through the whole procedure – medical, stores, equipment etc. At last it was all over, but I had difficulty persuading stores that I really wasn't entitled to another demob suit of clothes, shirts and shoes etc. I returned once more to Moor Park, stayed the night and next day bade goodbye to the Warrens, packed my uniform and returned to Liverpool a real civilian at last.

My first principal role was Luiz in 'The Gondoliers', and this took place at the Theatre Royal, Birmingham. Of course Alice travelled down to see my début together with my son Ellis. I am told he caused quite a stir in the audience by crying for his daddy to 'get off there'. After the performance, when Alice took him round to the stage door, the doorman must have been a little difficult about letting them go to my dressing room, because I am told Ellis flatly stated, 'If I could see my daddy when he wasn't a King, I can see him now that he is a King.' No one could argue with that bit of logic.

Through the remainder of the 1947 tour, which finished at the end of July, I played performances of Nanki-Poo, Frederic, Ralph and Luiz. My first performance of Nanki-Poo was at the Kings Theatre, Hammersmith, where a year and a half previously I had seen my first stage performance of 'The Mikado' and had boldly asked for an audition.

These first few months on tour convinced me that I had made the right decision. Financially we were worse off. Mr Carte's £12 per week was not enough to keep me on tour and also run the Lancaster home, and we had to dip into our savings. I had never been happier and I thought that my first principal contract would solve our cash difficulties. I was due to take over from John Dean as one of the two principal tenors – the other being Herbert Garry – at the beginning of the next tour due to start at the beginning of September. I soon learned why Rupert D'Oyly Carte was a rich man. I left his office with my first principal contract in my hands and a salary of £15 per week. However, he had promised that if I proved satisfactory, he would increase it to £25 per week! It was difficult for me to believe that someone was paying me a weekly salary to sing – I was being paid for doing something I enjoyed.

I took over as a principal tenor at the beginning of the following tour on Monday 9 September 1946 at the Theatre Royal, Newcastle. I felt very proud to see my name on a professional playbill outside the theatre.

My first performance was Nanki-Poo in 'The Mikado' (just over a year after seeing my first-ever 'Mikado' on stage) followed on Tuesday and Wednesday by Luiz in 'The Gondoliers' and on Thursday by Frederic in 'The Pirates of Penzance'. Not bad for my first week as a professional and I was quite overawed by the cast: Darrel Fancourt, Graham Clifford, Helen Roberts, Margaret Mitchell, Ella Halman, Leslie Rands and Marjorie Eyre. The second week in Newcastle I played my fourth role in 'HMS Pinafore' as Ralph Rackstraw and also repeated my other three operas.

The tour finished at the end of July and the company disbanded for a four-week holiday. We were not paid for holidays in those days so the members of the company were really out of work for four weeks. We were called for rehearsals a week before the tour was due to start, and on Monday 9 September 1946, we opened at the Theatre Royal, Newcastle, with 'The Mikado'. As I waited in the wings to make my first entrance as Nanki-Poo at the end of the opening chorus, I began to realise the responsibility that rested on my shoulders. It was a different feeling entirely to the previous tour when I was going on for the odd show, and mistakes could be forgiven or even laughed about – now I was a principal and the management and the audience expected a certain standard, and the D'Oyly Carte standards were high.

I don't remember much, if anything, about that first performance.

'… in Theatrical Performances'

My first playbill.

THEATRE ROYAL
NEWCASTLE·upon·TYNE

LESSEES
Chairman & Managing Director - A. STEWART CRUIKSHANK. Assistant Manager - Fred Rumbell.
Manager & Licensee - WM. WHITEHEAD. Musical Adviser - Harrogan McLeod, Mus.Bac.
HOWARD & WYNDHAM LIMITED.

'PHONE:
BOX OFFICE—
22061

MONDAY, 9th SEPTEMBER, 1946. TWO WEEKS ONLY. Evenings at 7
MATINEE: Each Saturday at 2

THE
D'OYLY CARTE
OPERA COMPANY

INCLUDING

NANCY FISHER	ELLA HALMAN
	MARGARET MITCHELL
SYBIL GHILCHIK	HELEN ROBERTS
WYNN DYSON	C. WILLIAM MORGAN
DARRELL FANCOURT	LEONARD OSBORN
RADLEY FLYNN	LESLIE RANDS
MARTYN GREEN	THOMAS ROUND
HILTON LAYLAND	RICHARD WALKER

IN

GILBERT & SULLIVAN OPERAS

REPERTOIRE:

FIRST WEEK.	SECOND WEEK.
Mon., Sept 9th - - - The Mikado	Mon. Sept. 16th - The Yeomen of the Guard
Tues., Sept. 10th - - The Gondoliers	Tues. Sept. 17th - The Yeomen of the Guard
Wed., Sept. 11th - - The Gondoliers	Wed., Sept 18th - - - Iolanthe
Thur., Sept. 12th - The Pirates of Penzance	Thurs., Sept. 19th - - - Patience
Fri., Sept. 13th - - - Patience	Fri., Sept. 20th - - The Mikado
Sat. Mat., Sept. 14th - The Mikado	Sat. Mat., Sept. 21st - The Gondoliers
Sat. Eve., Sept. 14th - The Mikado	Sat. Eve., Sept. 21st - The Gondoliers

PRICES OF ADMISSION (Including Tax):—

PRIVATE BOXES £1 10s. AND 18s.	ORCHESTRA STALLS	GRAND CIRCLE	PIT STALLS	UPPER CIRCLE	AMPHI-THEATRE	GALLERY
	9/- & 7/6	9/-	4/6	4/-	1/9	1/-
ALL BOOKABLE IN ADVANCE					UNRESERVED	

BOX OFFICE OPEN DAILY AT THEATRE 10 to 7-30.

Station Hotel Private Line direct to Box Office. Box Plans open two weeks ahead for all attractions. Telephone Seats must be claimed by 12 NOON the day before the date of Performance. The Management reserve the right to make any alteration in the Cast owing to illness or other unavoidable circumstances. The Management reserve the right to refuse admission.

Week Commencing MONDAY, 23rd SEPTEMBER, 1946. EVENINGS at 7
MATINEES: Wednesday and Saturday at 2.
H. M. TENNENT, Ltd. (in association with BARRY O'BRIEN) presents

ALAN WEBB	HAZEL TERRY
ALLAN JEAYES	IN PATRICK CREAN

THE YEARS BETWEEN
By DAPHNE DU MAURIER
BETTER THAN "REBECCA"

I know that everyone was very kind and helpful and the good wishes from the whole company were ringing in my ears. My dressing room table was full of good wishes cards and telegrams.

One thing about working in a repertory company is that there is little or no opportunity to become too familiar or stale in a role. By the end of the first week of the tour, I had played three of the roles allotted to me; the fourth one came during the second week at Newcastle when I also repeated some of the other three.

During the next few months there were to be a number of changes in the company. It had been operating on a wartime footing; for instance, the average age of the chorus must have been at least sixty years, and one man was seventy-two years old. Gradually, new members were auditioned and brought in. Leonard Osborne, who had been a principal before the war, returned from the services to take his place as a principal tenor in the place of Herbert Garry. He took over the roles of Colonel Fairfax, Earl Tolloller, Dick Dauntless, Duke of Dunstable, The Defendant and Box. Graham Clifford, who played the comic roles throughout the war, was replaced when Martyn Green also returned from the services, to resume where he left off as the successor to Sir Henry Lytton.

By the summer of 1947 the company was in fine shape and our performances were acclaimed in every town. I, too, was holding my own among these well-established and well-loved exponents of the Gilbert & Sullivan operas. I soon learned that, as opposed to other theatrical companies, the Cartes were a law unto themselves and were ruled by the gentle but firm hand of Mr Carte. There was a tremendous feeling of tradition and history in everything the company did. The beautifully made costumes were by Victor Nathan in London – there were no hand-me-downs in the Cartes; each costume for principals and chorus alike was individually made of the very finest materials, made to last through the rigours of constantly being cleaned and packed. I spent many hours in the fitting rooms at Nathan's in Panton Street, London, while Victor slowly, methodically and painstakingly pinned on a new costume, as he talked of the artists for whom he had made costumes in the past.

Once the costumes were handed over to the touring wardrobe, they were in the charge of Cissie Blane and her staff who maintained them with the same loving care that Victor Nathan had taken in making them. What a wonderful sight it was, to see the girls in the opening chorus of 'The Gondoliers' with the white blouses and frills of the costumes starched and sparkling. How Cis Blane and her assistant kept this high standard in some of the dark and dingy wardrobe rooms, I shall never know.

The scenery also, under the strict supervision of Harry Haste, always

'A Wand'ring Minstrel, I'

looked spick and span. I know how scenery can get knocked about on tour, and how difficult it is to keep it in good repair, but Harry and his team played their part in upholding the D'Oyly Carte tradition.

The Sunday morning train calls were always a sight to see, and these were also organised according to rules of tradition. It was one of Hugh Jones's big moments of the week. Hugh was one of the Business Managers. At least two rail coaches were reserved for the company and compartments were allotted to the principals towards the front of the train, then the small part players, followed by the chorus, the wardrobe and stage staff and the orchestra. If your friend was a member of the chorus or orchestra, you could sit with them only when the train had left the station.

The train call was also an opportunity for the girls to show off their best dresses and they brightened many a dull railway station on a Sunday morning. That was another thing about belonging to the D'Oyly Carte Company. I have seen new girls arrive in the company who looked like little scared mice not rating a second glance, but after a few weeks they were beautifully groomed young ladies and a credit to the company.

I noticed that some of the luggage of the principals and some of the chorus included golf clubs, and I was soon informed that, apart from golf being a good form of exercise for singers, it was also a good thing socially to play the game. The company had its own golf club known as 'The D'Oyly Carte Golf Circle', and fixtures were arranged in a number of towns with either the press or at one of the local golf clubs, where we were usually made Honorary Members during our visit to the town.

I had never played golf in my life, but accompanied by Tom Hancock (the tenor understudy), I went along to a sports shop in Sauchiehall Street, Glasgow, the second town on this first tour, and bought a second-hand set of clubs and bag, and was duly initiated into the honourable and ancient game.

CHAPTER SEVEN

'All About Golf'

I WAS STILL VERY MUCH IN AWE of some of the older principals, such as Darrell Fancourt, Leslie Rands, Marjorie Eyre and Helen Roberts, and could not bring myself to call them by their first names, but golf was a great leveller. When I discovered that Darrell could pull or shank a shot just as badly as I did, I realised these great artists were only human after all.

Martyn Green was a very keen golfer and when he rejoined the company I think we could muster a team of at least twelve, ranging from mediocre to bad and very bad, but we all took the game very

Alan Styler, Thomas Round and
Donald Adams on the course at
Sale Golf Club.
(*Photograph courtesy of The
Manchester Daily Mail*)

go, he has high hopes. *Glorious, manly, British game!* and extracts from
(Art and Educational. the writings of Ian Hay, E. V. Lucas, Neville Cardus,
ok to read, but it has W. G. Grace and other giants.

SAVAGES AND OPERA KINGS : A cheerful gathering at Wimbledon Park Golf
Club when members of the D'Oyly Carte Opera Company met members
of the Savage Club, the latter winning by 4 games to 3. Front row, left to
right—Raymond Newell (Savage), Thomas Round (D'Oyly Carte), Charles
Downing (D'Oyly Carte), Martyn Green (D'Oyly Carte), Billy Lennard (Savage),
and Ian McLean (Savage). Back row—Julian Mitchell (Savage), Richard Walker
(D'Oyly Carte), Jerry Verno (Savage), Darrell Fancourt (D'Oyly Carte),
Trefor Jones (Savage), Hugh R. Jones (D'Oyly Carte), Harold Williams (Savage)

A golf match with 'The Savage Club' at Wimbledon Golf Club.

seriously, some more so than others. Martyn was one of the latter. I
always felt that he asked me to play with him because his regular
club member wasn't available. I don't think he ever noticed that I was
actually playing; he was so wrapped up in his own game. I'm sure
he felt it was an education for me to watch him addressing and hitting
the ball. Any bad shots were certainly not his fault.

I remember one Sunday morning on a course in Glasgow. It was
one of those still, sunny mornings when every sound seems magnified.
Martyn was addressing his ball, for the second shot on the fairway,
with his usual care and concentration. I was doing my best not to
breathe, when a snip, snapping sound travelled across the still air.
Martyn did his best to ignore it, but finally he looked around for the
source of the sound. When he had located it, without saying a word
to me, he strode off across the fairway towards some gardens that
backed on to the course. There an unsuspecting man was daring to
clip his privet hedge while Martyn was addressing his ball. I never
knew what Martyn said to the poor man, but all was quiet for the
time it took for him to hit his ball. Baaing sheep never seemed to
understand, no matter how hard Martyn stared at them.

The incident I shall never forget took place on the Hazelhead Course,
Aberdeen. Martyn, Leonard Osborne, Tom Hancock and myself were
playing a four ball game. It was quite a blustery morning and we
were preparing to drive off from the tee that was surrounded on three

sides by quite high trees. We were all obediently quiet as Martyn stood up to his ball to address it. The wind, however, decided not to be quiet and it blew quite strongly, causing the trees to sway about considerably, and for one old tree to creak and groan as though we were on board a ship. Martyn stared at the offending tree, but to no avail, when Tom Hancock ran across the tee, leapt into the air and flung his arms around the offending branch shouting 'Go on, Martyn, hit your ball, I've got it.' We all fell about laughing, including Martyn.

We had some wonderful mornings on golf courses all over England, Scotland and Ireland. If we were playing in towns for more than a week, towns such as Manchester, Liverpool, Bristol, Edinburgh etc., we would arrange matches with the golf course that was offering us hospitality, usually on a Sunday. We would play all day with a break for lunch, and then have dinner at the clubhouse. After dinner we would present a concert for the club members and their wives. Apart from the principals performing, members of the chorus were able to show off their talents. I always found this very interesting, because you never really had the chance to hear the voices of chorus members.

Being a member of the D'Oyly Carte Company was certainly an 'Open Sesame', and in some towns it became difficult to fit in all the invitations that were received. I quickly settled down into the routine of touring. I was still involved in lots of rehearsals, and I had a lot to learn about the parts I was playing; my dialogue for instance, though sincere, had lots of room for improvement. Paul Arnold, who was the Stage Director at that time, was a tremendous help to me, also in stage movement. Although I seemed to have a natural talent for walking on a stage, there were lots of rehearsals required to get the timing exactly right, especially working with great G & S artists like Martyn Green, who was a master of timing and inventive comedy.

Slowly, but surely, I began to be accepted by the company and also the audiences, as an artist in my own right.

During my first few months, I sensed a feeling of resentment from some members of the company because it was very unusual for Rupert D'Oyly Carte to make someone a principal without having first served a long apprenticeship in the chorus and as an understudy. I like to think that, for once in my life, I was in the right place at the right time at the Kings Theatre, Hammersmith.

Some members of the audience too, were reluctant to accept this new tenor who was daring to appear on the same stage as some of their long-established darlings.

I was even stopped on the station platform during one Sunday morning train call by a very forthright lady who informed me that John Dean was her favourite tenor and that I had a long way to go before I could match him. It must have been very hard for some

'A Wand'ring Minstrel, I'

G & S devotees to accept change. I also remember the producer, not Paul Arnold, but Anna Bethel, on my second tour, after a particularly good personal review in the Bournemouth papers, took me on one side just as I had started to make up for Nanki-Poo, to remind me that, although I had had a good write up in the press, Gilbert & Sullivan were the real stars and never to forget it – I didn't.

At the beginning of the second tour in 1947, Alice and Ellis joined me and you can imagine the amount of luggage we carried. I had acquired a large wardrobe trunk and together with Alice's cases and all the paraphernalia for a young baby, we presented a depressing picture for any taxi driver, who had the misfortune to pick us up at our digs on a wet Sunday morning. We couldn't have chosen a worse time for Alice to start touring. The winter of 1947 proved to be one of the worst in memory. I think the snow started to fall when we were playing York, but just before it did start, I remember one bitter frosty morning when I was playing golf with Darrell Fancourt. The ground was rock hard and I had just made a dreadful stroke with my five iron. I was so angry with myself that I flung my club high into the air – it landed on the corner of the blade and it snapped off on the hard ground, as clean as a whistle. Darrell roared with laughter and I felt extremely foolish. Later in the week, Martyn and I went out to play and we had reached the second green when the first snow started to fall. We agreed that it would be useless to continue and we turned back for the clubhouse. Within a few minutes we were in the middle of a raging blizzard and everything, including the clubhouse, completely disappeared. We had visions of wandering about for hours, but we finally made it back safely. A few days later and the whole country was under a blanket of snow. The company moved on to Sunderland for a two-week season, and it never stopped snowing.

Electricity was being cut off and we had to make up by candlelight at the Empire Theatre. It was bitterly cold the whole time, but it didn't seem to bother my two-year-old son who wanted to play snowmen from dawn to dusk.

Coal was in very short supply and our landlady told us that people were down on the beach searching for coal washed in by the strong wind and waves. Alice and I thought we would try it and each morning found us among the rocks and pools, battling the wind and snow. It was unbelievably cold, but we all three enjoyed it, especially Ellis, and returned to our digs at lunchtime carrying a small sack full of sea-smoothed pebbles of coal. What a grand addition to our meagre ration of fuel it was, and how cheery it made our fire – the salt in the coal made it crackle and spit and it gave off a blue and yellow flame.

From Sunderland we moved down to Huddersfield where the snow was banked five feet high along the pavements. The dressing rooms were bitterly cold and the girls suffered agonies in their flimsy costumes. Imagine singing in 'The Gondoliers', in the supposed hot sunshine of Venice, with our breath going out in white clouds.

It was very little different in our digs – even the beds seemed damp and the only places we were really warm was in the cafés and restaurants through the day, where we drank endless cups of coffee. I'm sure little Ellis was largely responsible for keeping up our spirits through that awful winter because he had to be kept amused and so compelled us to always be on the move.

From Huddersfield we went to Wolverhampton where we had awful digs – damp and cold. How we kept fit for singing and acting, I'll never know. Then on to Bristol and excellent digs I'm delighted to say. Our landlady had two organs and two pianos in the house, and so we had lots of music all day and every day.

I didn't play in the opera 'Patience', but I almost invariably watched the opera from the front and on one 'Patience' night at the Hippodrome, a real Gilbertian drama took place, which made the front pages of most of the national press.

The principal baritone, Charles Dorning, was taken ill and it was

'A Wand'ring Minstrel, I'

'The Pirates of Penzance'. From left to right: Nancy Fisher (Kate), Martyn Green (Major General), Helen Roberts – seated – (Mabel), Ella Halman (Ruth), Thomas Round (Frederic), Sybil Ghilchik (Edith).

82

RICHARD'S TROUSERS
AT HIPPODROME

"Alas, They Are Gone!"

THE performance of "Patience" by the D'Oyly Carte Opera Co. at Bristol Hippodrome last night was a collector's piece which will provide a theatrical anecdote for each member of the packed audience for many years to come.

Poor Richard Walker, as Gilbert's idyllic poet, had the misfortune to damage the seam of his trousers, and though we suffered for him it was impossible to restrain our laughter at the aptness of each line which followed.

His first lines after he finished the song where the accident occurred were, "Alas, they are gone"! and the others which followed, were equally appropriate. The embarrassment was overcome in the best possible spirit, and the company shared the joke.

The Artistry

The whole performance was up to the wonderfully high standard we have come to expect.

There are, indeed, times when the expert fooling and lovely singing are so smoothly blended, that the tendency is to forget the artistry which lies behind. It looks so very easy, when the result is obviously achieved only by hard work and skill.

Martyn Green, Margaret Mitchell, Ella Halman, and the chorus work were all delightful, but it must remain Mr. Walker's evening!
V. M.

EVEN GILBERT COULDN'T BEAT IT !

HALF-WAY through the second act of "Patience" at the Bristol Hippodrome, last night, the audience was helpless with laughter —at something which was not "in the script."

Portly Richard Walker, as the velvet-clad poet Archibald, was in the middle of a quartet when he rose from a tree-stump seat and walked to the back of the stage—and, oh horror ! his tailored breeches displayed a six-inch split. . . .

Every time he turned, the audience gasped with suspense or howled with wicked delight.

But the best was yet to come. Left to himself on the stage, the Idyllic Poet soliloquised on his loneliness and exclaimed: "ALAS, THEY ARE GONE ! "

The audience rocked. Puzzled, but unperturbed, the Poet faithfully delivered his next line—"WHAT IS THIS MYSTERIOUS FASCINATION THAT I HAVE ? "

The audience shrieked. Plainly alarmed now, but steadfast in the traditions of the Old Savoy, Archibald shot his parting bolt : "A CURSE ON MY FATAL BEAUTY !" The audience appeared to have hysterics.

Next time Mr Walker came on, his party pants had been repaired, but his equanimity remained, and he and Martyn Green gave an extra emphasis to a quip about a " back parting " for his hair.

Would Gilbert have turned in his grave ? No; he would surely have enjoyed it as much as we all enjoyed the whole superb production, which did credit even to the D'Oyly Carte Company. Martyn Green's Bunthorne was a personal triumph of parody, and Ella Halman was the best Lady Jane, in voice and comedy, that we have heard since Bertha Lewis.

decided to call in an ex-principal of the company to play the part of Grosvenor – his name was Richard Walker (who had played for my first audition). The dark green velvet costume fitted very neatly on Dick's plump frame and all went well through the first act but, in the second act, Grosvenor leads the lovesick maidens on stage and after a dialogue, he invites the girls to gather round him and he sits down on a low stump and sings the song 'The Magnet and the Churn'. After the song he gets up and, with his back to the audience, waves goodbye to the girls. The audience started to titter, because his trousers had split wide open, but Dick wasn't aware of this and he carried on with his dialogue, 'At last they are gone'. The audience yelled, but poor Dick still didn't know what had happened. He ploughed on with his next line, 'What is this mysterious fascination that I seem to exercise over all I come across?' The audience exploded, but Dick

'The Mikado' with Margaret
Mitchell as Yum Yum and myself
as Nanki-Poo.
(*Photograph courtesy of The
Scotsman Publications Ltd*)

carried on, 'A curse on my fatal beauty'. What a night – every line
was printed on the front pages of nearly every national newspaper.

I still couldn't believe that I was still not in the Air Force or the
police force, and that my life was now on the stage, singing. I expected
a letter every day calling me back to duty. It didn't seem quite right
that I should be allowed to wander about the country singing for a
living.

CHAPTER EIGHT

'He's Gone Abroad'

OWARDS THE END of 1947, news leaked out that the company was planning an American tour. I didn't know whether to be pleased or not. I had spent five years apart from my wife and now, after only a year or so together, we were to be parted again for a five-month season in the USA.

Alice and I talked over the situation and decided that it wasn't to be, and if Mr Carte wanted me to go to America, then I could only consider it if Alice and Ellis accompanied me.

When I was called to see Mr Carte to discuss my next contract, which included the US tour, I felt very apprehensive about my interview. I needn't have worried. Mr Carte was very understanding and suggested ways that he could help me with the very considerable fares involved. The tour was to consist of a four-month season at the Century Theatre, New York, followed by a month at the Schubert Theatre, Boston.

With my new contract in my pocket, including a US tour, I felt very grand indeed and our summer break and the autumn tour passed quickly by as we all looked forward to late December, when we would board the *Queen Mary* bound for New York.

Alice didn't accompany me on this second English tour, but stayed at home to make arrangements to let our house at 6 Penrhyn Road for the five months that we would be abroad. She found a short-term tenant and arranged to keep one room of our house for the storage of our furniture.

If I remember correctly, we had about a week's break to enable the company to prepare for the trip. It would have been an interesting exercise to find out what each member of the company had to do to enable them to leave home for five months. Not very difficult for a single person of course, but for wives leaving husbands and husbands leaving wives, this must have created some complex problems. Since 1948 I have left my wife on numerous occasions for overseas tours, and it had never become easier. Anyway, the problems of taking a wife and son abroad for five months and leaving a house in England were large enough, with Alice having to cope with the whole business while I was on tour.

The evening before our departure arrived and I finally went to bed about midnight, with Alice's promise to follow me shortly afterwards.

I set the electric alarm clock for 5 a.m., our taxi was due at 6 a.m., and the train for London was due to leave at 6.20 a.m. from the Morecambe Promenade Station. I learned later that Alice came to bed at 3 a.m., giving her only three hours' rest.

We were not awakened by the alarm but by a loud knocking on the front door – it was the taxi driver, and the time was 6 a.m. I hadn't pulled out the little knob on the alarm clock, which allows it to ring. I haven't lived that error down to this day! The following few minutes were a blur – I, at least, had to catch that train because we were due to attend an official farewell party at the Savoy Hotel. Alice raced downstairs and opened the door to allow the taxi driver to load our cases while I threw on my clothes, and without washing or shaving ran out to the car with Alice's shouts in my ear, that she would catch the next train to London. She also shouted other things and there was no doubt that I deserved them all!

That taxi driver was a marvel. Admittedly it was a virtual straight run into Morecambe, and we made it onto the platform just as the train was given the signal to move off. My cases were literally thrown on as the train was moving, and I fell in on top of them. The taxi driver shouted that he would go back to the house and help Alice to catch the next train and to load our large cabin trunk. I learnt that he had breakfast there as well. I couldn't believe I was on the train at all, and felt sure it was a nightmare and that the alarm would go off and waken us as planned.

What a horrible start to what should have been a happy morning; poor Alice had had weeks of planning and worry for the trip, and then I had to step in at the last moment and ruin the whole thing.

I duly arrived at Euston Station and took a taxi to the Savoy. I told my sad story to all who would listen, which seemed to be the whole company. The next train from Morecambe was due to arrive two hours later and I took a taxi back to Euston to await its arrival. The first to greet me on its arrival was little Ellis running down the platform towards me shouting in his high treble voice for all to hear – 'Come quickly, Mummy has been sick'. How right he was, the awful shock of the morning, followed by the preparation to catch the next train, with no super-efficient husband to help, and the long weary journey to London coping with a very excited Ellis had taken its toll.

I managed to get them and the luggage into a taxi and finally to the Savoy, after several stops on the way to allow Alice to be ill. Once inside the hotel Dr Charles Budd took charge of her and while we enjoyed a super reception, he battled to get Alice into a fit state to travel on to Southampton to board the *Queen Mary*.

Proof of all of this is in *The Tatler* magazine, which clearly shows an excellent photograph of members of the company and me with Ellis

Guests at the farewell party given at the Savoy to celebrate the D'Oyly Carte Opera Company's departure for an extended season at the Century Theatre, New York. From left: Darrell Fancourt, William Morgan, Mrs Fancourt, Dr C. Budd of Cambridge, Denise Findlay and Mr Alan Robin of *The Times*.

RIGHT: Martyn Green, who played the principal male roles.

LEFT: Thomas Round (tenor), Margaret Mitchell (soprano), Master Ellis Round, Joan Gillingham (soprano) and Thomas Hancock.

Mr Godfrey (conductor), Mrs Osborn, Leonard Osborn (tenor), Mrs Watson, Richard Watson (baritone), Charles Dorning (tenor) and Mrs Godfrey. In the first week's US booking over $100,000 were taken, and seats for the first seven weeks were sold out in a fortnight.

Radley Flyn, Mrs Grace Lovat Fraser (designer), Helen Roberts (soprano), Richard Walker (baritone) and Ella Halman (contralto).

87

on my knee, but no Alice. After the party, we were all put aboard the boat train for Southampton and the *Queen Mary*. Alice by this time was feeling better, weak and white, but better and she stood up to the journey quite well. I'm afraid the sea voyage didn't help her though – it was so rough, we could only walk about with the assistance of ropes, and many other passengers were confined to their cabins. Ellis had the time of his short life on board, and we hardly saw him except at meal times when he had to be literally dragged from the children's playroom. He was unwell only once, when he announced to the whole dining room in his distinctive treble voice, 'Mummy, I've been sick'.

We arrived in New York in four and a half days on Christmas Eve 1948, and we were driven to our hotel, the Churchill, on 76th Street. The company was spread about in various hotels but quite a number were staying at the Belvedere on 48th Street.

We had arranged to join the Belvedere group on Christmas Day, but we spent the remaining hours of Christmas Eve shopping for a Christmas tree, decorations and presents for Ellis. We had all been given an advance on our salaries because we were not due to open until Christmas week, so we were very wary of spending too many dollars; still we were able to give Ellis quite a nice Christmas.

We joined the group on Christmas Day and when we saw how large and well furnished their apartments were compared with the Churchill, we immediately booked one and arranged to move in on Boxing Day. We told our landlord that we realised we were too far away from the theatre and that the management had instructed us to move nearer. This was partly true, and the manager was quite good about it.

We repacked our trunks and arranged to move out after breakfast the next day. However, we awoke next morning to a fantastic sight – the city was buried under four feet of snow and it was still blizzarding. Parked cars were completely buried and no traffic was moving, except down Broadway. We decided to leave our big trunk and we struggled the few yards to Broadway and after what seemed ages, we managed to flag down a taxi to take us down town. It was to be nearly two weeks before we were able to collect our big trunk from up town, and even then it had to be dragged through thick snow and ice to where we could get a taxi.

I was really thrown in at the deep end at the Century Theatre. We opened with 'The Mikado' and as I was waiting in the wings to make my first entrance after the opening chorus, I wanted to rush out and bury myself in the snow. After only a year as a professional here I was making my début on Broadway. It seemed incredible, but the moment of truth arrived and I was on stage singing 'A Wand'ring Minstrel'. The opera went well and the press gave us rave reviews the next day.

'A Wand'ring Minstrel, I'

My own press reviews were very good after the opening of 'The Mikado', and they resulted in the film producer Hal Wallis, of Paramount Films, making contact and inviting me to meet him at his office. I duly kept the appointment to be told that his company were planning a production of 'The Vagabond King', and he would like to arrange some film tests in Hollywood, because he thought I was right for the leading role.

Of course I was amazed and flattered, but I had to inform him that I could not possibly ask the D'Oyly Carte Company to grant me time away from the company to travel to California so, reluctantly, I had to turn down the offer.

I think we had five operas with us on that tour – 'Mikado', 'Gondoliers', 'Pinafore', 'Pirates' and 'Iolanthe', and I was playing in four out of the five, so I was kept pretty busy. I think the greatest hazard I had to deal with was the central heating. The temperature outside was often well below zero, but in the hotel rooms it was in the eighties. We very rarely dressed before lunch, it was much more comfortable

'HMS Pinafore'. John Reed was Sir Joseph Porter, and yours truly played Ralph Rackstraw.

to attend to our various chores in pyjamas, but the heat all through the night was affecting my voice and we decided to turn it off in our bedroom and I immediately felt better. We had a large separate lounge, plus a bathroom and kitchen. Unfortunately, the coloured maid refused to make up the bed unless we turned the heat on each morning and we had to agree to this.

It became too cold to venture out in January and we only made quick visits to the food stores whenever necessary – complete with warm coats and ear muffs etc. On the slightly warmer days, I would take Ellis to Central Park, where he tobogganed and had snow fights for a couple of hours.

Across the street from our hotel was a 'Public School' – we called them Council Schools, and after two weeks we were able to get Ellis enrolled there. I think he had to stand quite a lot of leg-pulling from the other children – the kid with the funny accent, rosy cheeks and short trousers. He came home one day feeling very proud of himself because the teacher had asked him to tell his classmates about England and so, he said, 'I told them about the war and the operas, and that they hadn't had a war in America because if they had, they wouldn't have all those lights on Broadway'. Not bad thinking for a boy of five and a half years.

We settled into a routine; it was marvellous having Alice with me because she was able to cook nearly all our meals in the little kitchenette and so I was well looked after. Of course, there were lots of invitations to cocktail parties, lunches etc and we made friends in the hotel. Most

'A Wand'ring Minstrel, I'

'HMS Pinafore' on Broadway on 1947, with me as Ralph Rackstraw.

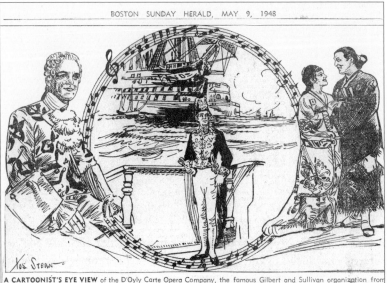

BOSTON SUNDAY HERALD, MAY 9, 1948

A CARTOONIST'S EYE VIEW of the D'Oyly Carte Opera Company, the famous Gilbert and Sullivan organization from England, which starts its final fortnight at the Shubert Theater tomorrow night. Easily recognized will be Martyn Green as Sir Joseph Porter in "H. M. S. Pinafore," which will be given for the first half of the coming week; Charles Dorning as Strephon in "Iolanthe," which will play from Thursday through Saturday; and Thomas Round and Margaret Mitchell as Nanki-Poo and Yum-Yum in "The Mikado," which will be given for the entire week, starting May 17.

Here is a selection of some reviews at the time:

There are some delightful performances ... Thomas Round, who is an ex-policeman of Britain, is tremendously engaging as that Wandr'ing Minstrel Nanki-Poo. *New York Sun*

Again Thomas Round proves himself the best singer of the pseudo-romantic leads the D'Oyly Carte group has offered within my memory. *New York Post*

Mr Round impressive ... last week I thought he was grand as Nanki-Poo in 'The Mikado' and now I know he is a first-class Gilbert and Sullivan man. His performance of Frederic, the noble and sappy hero of 'The Pirates' is a work of remarkable style, and his voice is beguiling. The *Daily News*

As the result of Gilbert's mechanical plot device, the secondary singers are busier in 'The Gondoliers' than the bigwigs. As the ranking nabobs of the company, Margaret Mitchell, Ella Halman, Thomas Round, Richard Watson and Martyn Green give capital performances in the aridly condescending style of their parts. Miss Halman's grave snobbery, Miss Mitchell's disingenuous rapture and Mr Round's gentle obsequiousness are admirable and enjoyable. The *New York Times*

Thomas Round, one of the leading tenors of the D'Oyly Carte Opera Company is to be interviewed over WFMO tomorrow morning by Marcy Hammond. He's called the Gilbert and Sullivan Sinatra. Listening in with 'One Dialler'.

Among the newcomers – meaning those who have made their first appearance on Broadway this season – I have particular fondness for Thomas Round, the handsome ex-cop who is one of the leading tenors of the D'Oyly Carte Company. Mr Round's insight into the humour of Gilbert and Sullivan is unusual and his deportment is impeccable. He should have a steady job with this find company for the next twenty years. *New York Sunday News*

I've enjoyed the antics of Martyn Green and the singing of the ex-policeman Thomas Round in the D'Oyly Carte Company. *Broadway after Dark*

Of the newcomers, I found Thomas Round, the Nanki-Poo, especially satisfying. He is tall and virile, he has a fine voice and he gives just the right tongue in cheek touch to his lines. The *Christian Science Monitor*, Boston

Thomas Round – new to the Company – flew Hurricanes and Spitfires with the Royal Air Force during the war, no doubt as skilfully as he is now singing the Nanki-Poo role in 'The Mikado'. *Boston Evening American*

of the variety acts from the next-door Madison Square Gardens stayed in the hotel and we ceased to be surprised at sharing the lift with seven-foot giants, three-foot dwarfs, fat ladies, bearded ladies and all-in wrestlers etc. The door in the apartment across the wide passage was always open and we became quite friendly with a TV wrestler who occupied it. He spent all his time in brief shorts, showing off his muscles. The apartment to our left was the residence of a very popular lady of easy virtue whom Ellis adored, and with whom we had many entertaining hours when 'business' was a bit slack. Ellis celebrated his sixth birthday in that apartment and I think all of the hotel knew!

After four and a half months, we moved to Boston for a month's season at the Schubert Theatre. Through the influence of friends we were able to book a superb apartment at the Commander Hotel in Cambridge, about twelve miles from the centre of Boston. It was there that we met Mrs Smith and her two daughters Mary and Francis. It was Mary who organised the Commander Hotel, and we have remained friends through all these years. They were great G & S fans and we seemed to spend as much time in their home at 70 Sparks Street, as at the hotel. Mrs Smith was a direct descendent of Henry Wadsworth Longfellow, the famous American poet, whose home was also in Cambridge. It is now a museum to his memory.

The end of May saw the end of our season in Boston and on our way back to New York to join the *Mauretania* for our voyage back home to England.

'A Wand'ring Minstrel, I'

LEFT: 'The Mikado' on Broadway, 1947, with Richard Watson as Pooh-Bah, Richard Walker as The Mikado, myself as Nanki-Poo, Charles Dorning as Pish-Tush, Margaret Mitchell as Yum-Yum, Denise Findlay as Peep-Bo and Joan Gillingham as Pitti-Sing.

BELOW: As Frederic in 'The Pirates of Penzance'.

CHAPTER NINE

'Does Your New Employment Please Ye?'

ONE WOULD HAVE THOUGHT that we were entitled to a break before starting out on tour again, but that wasn't Mr Rupert D'Oyly Carte's way – the sea trip was holiday enough. I had to put Alice and Ellis on the train back to Lancaster, while I made my way to digs I had booked in Hendon. We met for rehearsals next day at the Sadler's Wells Theatre, and three days later we opened for an eight-week season.

A very important event had happened before the American tour. During the week at the Coventry Hippodrome, and completely unknown to me, I had been seen playing on stage by Len Lowe of the variety duo Len and Bill Lowe. It seems he had spoken very favourably about me to his agent – Montague Lyon – and the first thing I knew about all this was when I received a letter from Montague Lyon to the effect that he was coming to see a performance and would like to see me afterwards.

I think I could call that meeting a turning point in my career. I was in a company that was not so much a career as a way of life. There were a number of principals who had been with the company more than twenty years and had never had any thoughts of leaving for another branch of the singing profession. Here I was, after only two years, daring to think of broadening my horizons. Nevertheless, 'Monty' painted a rosy picture of what my life would be in the world of the really commercial theatre.

While we were in America, I had many letters from my agent-to-be, and finally I received one with an offer from Emile Littler (a London West End impresario), to play the lead in a Johann Strauss operetta, called 'Waltzes from Vienna'.

The Sadler's Wells season was very well received and I had a very good personal press and Emile Littler was ready to confirm his offer. It was decided that I should hand in my notice to the Cartes at the end of the 1949 tour. As the time drew near, I began to feel very apprehensive and also very guilty that I should have the temerity to want to leave the D'Oyly Carte Company. I felt sure the management expected me to stay with them for years.

My contract with Emile was still being discussed, and was not finalised before we left London to go out on tour. It was arranged that my agent would write to me and send me my new contract, together with a letter of resignation in the same envelope. We were playing Derby when the letter finally arrived and I couldn't believe my eyes when I saw the salary of £75 per week that I was to be paid.

By a coincidence, I was staying in the same digs as Hugh Jones, the business manager, and as we ate breakfast together, I wondered what our relationship would be when we met for lunch and he had received my letter.

He left for the theatre and I followed about an hour later, knocked on his office door, and handed him my resignation. I felt as empty as I had when I handed in my resignation from the police force. There was a long silence before Hugh asked me to sit down while we talked, and it was all I could do to stop myself snatching back the letter and tearing it up.

Within a few hours, the news was all round the company that I was leaving at the end of the tour. For the next three months, I was treated like someone who was not quite right in the head, but also with a touch of envy.

Rupert D'Oyly Carte had died and his place was taken by his daughter Bridget, and it was from her that I received a letter wishing me the best of luck in my new venture, and an invitation to return to her company should I ever wish to do so.

Monty didn't think my name sounded right for a musical comedy star – 'Don't misunderstand me', he said, 'it is a good honest down-to-earth sort of name, but there is no romance in it.' So, believe it or not, we started to look through the London telephone books to try and find a new name. Monty made a list of likely sounding ones. I can only remember one of them – Bryan Stuart – which I disliked anyway, but my agent now guided me. He rang Emile Little and told him he was changing my name, but he was promptly told that I had been touring all over the country with the D'Oyly Cartes under the name of Thomas Round and 'that is how I want him billed in my show'.

So it was thanks to Emile that I retained my own name in show business.

I have often since wondered what effect a more romantic name would have had on my career. Anyway, down-to-earth name or not, I was soon to see it topping the bill on large theatre posters throughout the country.

I was soon to discover the difference between working in a repertory opera company, where, theoretically, there were no 'stars', and working in the truly commercial theatre. But first I had to meet the rest of

Scenes from 'Waltzes from Vienna', starring Fay Lenore as Resi, Ann Drummond Grant as Countess, George Manship as Johann Strauss and myself as Schani Strauss.

TOOK 14 CURTAIN CALLS
Barrow singer's leading role in new Emile Littler show

TOP-LINE success has been well and truly scored in the musical world by a 32-years-old Barrovian ex-fighter pilot. He is Mr. Thomas Round, son of Mr. and Mrs. Round, 177, Oxford-street, Barrow, who is now playing the leading role in the latest Emile Littler musical show, "Waltzes from Vienna."

Playing as Johann Strauss, composer of the "Blue Danube Waltz," Round's performance has been received with great enthusiasm. When the show ran at a large coastal resort, he took 14 curtain calls at the end of the show..

Mr. Round was born in Barrow and attended Holker-street School and the Barrow Technical College. He entered the Police Force at Lancaster, and while there he held the prize cup for swimming in that branch of the Force.

When the war came he entered the Royal Air Force and became a Flt.-Lieutenant.

San Antonio. Returning to England he was attached to Fighter Command.

When on leave in Barrow during the war, Mr. Round gave two Saturday night recitals in aid of local charities, one at Thwaite-street Sohcol and the other at the Town Hall.

Six months after being demobilised, he left the Lancaster City Police and joined the D'Oyly Carte Opera Company and was the Principal Tenor for 3½ years.

ON BROADWAY

Eighteen months ago, he played for six months on Broadway and in Boston. Here the "New York Post" critic said that Round "proved himself the best singer of the pseudo-romantic leads the D'Oyly Carte group has offered within my memory."

"Waltzes from Vienna" is likely to run at Manchester soon.

He spent nearly two years in Texas, U.S.A., as instructor, and while there started singing with the tenor Ivan Dneprov, principal of the Hockaday Institute of Music, and played as Canio in the "I Pagliacci" in aid of the American Red Cross.

GAINED U.S. "WINGS"

He was transferred from the R.A.F. to the American Army Air Corps and gained the U.S. Air Corps wings at Kelly Field,

Strauss Star is Ex-P.C.

PLAYING the part of Johann Strauss, junior, in Emile Littler's "Waltzes from Vienna" at Coventry Hippodrome is an ex-policeman who turned to professional singing after demobilisation from the R.A.F.

He is Thomas Round, who was born in Barrow. He went to a local school and Barrow Technical College, and then joined the Police Force at Lancaster.

When war came he joined the R.A.F. and became a Flight-Lieutenant. He spent nearly two years in Texas, U.S.A., as an instructor, and while there he started singing with the tenor Ivan Dneprov, principal of the Hockaday Institute of Music, and played Canio in a production of "I Pagliacci" in aid of the American Red Cross.

Six months after being demobilised, he left Lancaster City Police and joined the D'Oyly Carte Opera Company, staying with them for three years. On a professional return visit to the U.S.A. he played for six months on Broadway and at Boston.

"Waltzes from Vienna," which enters its second week at the Hippodrome, is enjoying a successful run.

Cartoon from *Everybody's Magazine*, July 1951.

the cast of 'Waltzes', possibly a bigger strain than when I joined the Cartes.

My leading lady 'Resi' was an experienced pantomime and summer season girl Fay Lenore, a vivacious auburn-haired girl. She was born into show business; her mother and father both performed in their own pantomimes and summer seasons. The Countess was to be played by another ex-D'Oyly Carte artist – Ann Drummond Grant, the wife of none other than Isidore Godfrey. Papa Strauss was George Manship – an actor in the Bransby Williams mould. He was to be a tremendous help and encouragement to me. A well-known baritone called Eric Starling played Leopold. There were quite a number of small part players, one or two Variety Acts, a large chorus and a fair sized orchestra. The posters proclaimed 'A Cast of Ninety' and 'Prior to London Production'. My name in the production was Schani Strauss.

The nearest we ever came to playing London was on the Mile End

I took part in two ice shows in London and in this one I am pictured with Belita (who was known only by that name) in 'London Melody' at Earl's Court. As well as the famed Belita as Catherine and myself as Paul, the great Norman Wisdom played Mike.

Road. However, the show was very successful throughout its eleven-month tour, and it is still remembered by a number of theatre managers for giving them one of their best financial weeks. The posters were still proclaiming 'Prior to London Production' when we were playing our last date at the Alhambra, Bradford. We finished to capacity business, but we were taken off the road because there wasn't a theatre available in London at the right time.

Here are a couple of amusing stories re 'Waltzes'. We were playing for a week at Hanley near Stoke-on-Trent. The final scene of the show was supposed to be a large concert hall with the orchestra on stage, and lots of dancers on the floor of the hall. This wasn't possible on tour of course, so I used to come through the curtain, step over the footlights, down a few steps into the orchestra pit, receive the baton from the regular conductor, and conduct the finale to the music of 'The Blue Danube'. One evening in Hanley, as I was bowing to receive the conductor's baton, lit by a brilliant spotlight, we heard a woman's voice from a dress circle box say to her companion, 'Isn't it wonderful that they have been able to persuade Johann Strauss to come all the way from Vienna to conduct in Hanley'.

The other show, 'Rose Marie on Ice' at Haringey Arena. This show starred world champion ice skaters Michael Kirby and Barbara Ann Scott (both pictured here with the general manager of the arena). This picture was taken at the end of a successful season.

(*Photograph courtesy of The Greyhound Racing Association*)

On another occasion, in another town, in exactly the same spot, we heard a voice say, 'There you are, I told you it was his own hair'.

The show closed, but Emile Littler wanted to sign me up on a five-year contract to play as required in pantomime, musicals, and summer shows. Monty would have none of it and he laid down quite unacceptable terms for my next show with Emile, 'Vanity Fair'. After days of bickering, I was finally left without a show, but according to Monty, 'with the world at my feet.'

A few weeks after 'Waltzes' finished, I had an unusual offer that Monty said I should accept while waiting for the right show to come along.

Tom Arnold, another West End management agent, was planning the first 'musical on ice' at Haringey Arena, London. The title was 'Rose Marie'. World-famous skaters were to be engaged to play the roles and well-known singers were to be booked to sing and speak for the skaters. Rose Marie was skated by Barbara Ann Scott, the world Olympic champion, a real live 'Sugar Plum Fairy'. Michael Kirby, the Canadian champion skated the part of Jim Kenyon and I sang and spoke for him. Heine Brock, an ice skating comedian played the part of Hard Boiled Herman. This musical was also the start of 'The George Mitchell Singers'. It was George who put the singers together for the large chorus, and also trained them. Billy Ternent conducted the orchestra.

What a wonderfully successful and spectacular show it was. To see the Mounties make their entrance marching on skates to the tune, 'On through the hail' was a real thrill, also the 'Totem Dance'. The producer Gerald Palmer, making use for the first time I think in a stage show, 'black light', was a never-to-be-forgotten sight. The skaters had to learn the dialogue and songs, and they 'goldfished' the words. I don't think it really mattered whether they knew all the lines.

Apart from playing their parts, both Barbara Ann and Michael performed solo spots. Barbara gave a marvellous display to the songs, 'I love thee' by Grieg and 'Because', which I sang for her. 'Rose Marie' was scheduled to run for eight weeks, but it was extended to twelve.

My next show, after eight or so months of 'resting' and waiting for the right one, while continuing my singing lessons with Joseph Hislop, was the following year, 'The Festival of Britain', when Claude Langdon decided to put on an enormous ice and stage show at London's Earls Court. The show was to be called 'London Melody'.

The show turned out to be a 'White Horse Inn' type of musical, with the music by Robert Farnon and conducted by Harry Rabinowitz. Again, it was an impressive line up of stars; Belita, a girl chock full of talent – singing, skating, ballet dancing, as well as being a good actress; a Spanish singing star called Elaine Streisinger; and Norman Wisdom, who it seems had been playing for years in the provinces; I had never heard of him. He was given the chance of a lifetime, which he grabbed with both hands and also his feet.

At least I was going to be able to play a part on stage – an enormous semi-circular affair, with the ice rink all around it.

For the first time I was billed as Tom Round and I didn't like it very much, but I couldn't get them to alter a fifty-foot long poster with letters a foot high in luminous paint on a giant framework on the forecourt of Earls Court.

The show opened before an audience of 5,000, with a galaxy of stage and screen stars. The show was a tremendous success and although the work on stage was secondary to the ice skating part of it, I was quite pleased with my efforts.

Belita was terrific and apart from skating, dancing and working with me on stage, she performed an aerial ballet, which had the effect of being under water. Actually I was supposed to drop a medallion over a bridge into a lake and Belita flew over a parapet, already harnessed to high wires, and performed a series of swoops and dives that had the audience gasping.

Norman Wisdom stole the show with an amazing display of knockabout comedy that had the audience rocking in their seats. His antics on skates, and he had never seriously skated in his life, were quite brilliant. In the final curtain calls, everyone was calling for

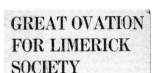

Norman, and when Gracie Fields walked across the ice onto the stage and hugged and kissed him, calling him the greatest comedy man she had ever seen, his future was assured. Belita and I were standing together in the line-up, holding hands and as Gracie Fields hugged Norman and seemingly ignored Belita, I felt her fingernails dig into my hand. From that moment on, Belita and Norman were at daggers drawn, which made my position between the two of them very awkward indeed.

'London Melody' ran for six months and before it closed, Norman Wisdom had become a household name. In both 'Rose Marie' and 'London Melody', we played nine performances a week, including two on Wednesdays and three on Saturdays at 2 p.m., 5 p.m. and 8 p.m. It was a big enough strain for me, but how Belita and Norman stood up to it, I'll never know.

At least, if I didn't have very much artistic satisfaction from 'London Melody', I had a good salary, which enabled me to continue paying Ellis's school fees, paying the flat rent and continuing my singing lessons. Joseph Hislop was good to me though; I was having three lessons a week and only paying for one.

Before 'London Melody' ended its run, I had been offered the chance to play the lead in a two-week run of 'The Student Prince' at the Opera House, Cork. It appeared that the artist who had been engaged for the show had withdrawn at the last moment and as I had nothing to follow 'London Melody', I jumped at the chance. I only had a short time in which to learn the music and dialogue and the show was due to open two weeks after we closed at Earls Court.

The operetta was very successful, and it began a long association with Ireland which spread over a number of years, singing in different parts of Ireland in such musicals and operas as 'The New Moon', 'The Desert Song', 'The Bohemian Girl', 'Viktoria and Her Hussar', and 'The Bartered Bride'. I also toured with the D'Oyly Carte in Belfast, Dublin and Cork.

After the short run of 'The Student Prince', I was once more 'resting', except for continuing my studies with Joseph Hislop. I felt I was making progress with my voice, but any improvement is very slow to show itself, although I realised that I was singing arias that would not have been possible for me two years previously. Nevertheless, I had periods of black depression, when it took all Alice's love and care to keep me from giving up. I felt I was a fool to have ever left the Cartes where I had had such a safe and comfortable job. Why should I think that I could make it in the other fields of singing? Monty was a good friend, but he couldn't produce shows out of a hat.

We trailed around to various auditions, but there was something missing. I was told several times that I had a 'good set of pipes'. For

GREAT OVATION FOR LIMERICK SOCIETY

Famous Tenor Excels In "The Bohemian Girl"

A capacity audience in St. John's Pavilion, Limerick, last night afforded the Limerick Choral Society a tumultuous ovation at the conclusion of their first performance of "The Bohemian Girl," by Balfe, which will continue for the week.

The society had as its guest artist the famous English tenor, Thomas Round, of the Sadlers Wells Operatic Society. This artist, especially in his renderings of the well-known numbers "The Fair Land of Poland" and "When Other Lips" in the concluding act, had to respond again and again to the applauding audience.

EASY SINGER.

He proved himself to be an easy singer, with a very fine presence, and played the part of Thaddeus to perfection.

Another outstanding artist was Joe Neiland, the local baritone, who was really splendid in the role of Count Arhain, which he played with great dignity and conviction, although at times there was a little uncertainty in his lower register.

The heavy soprano part was taken by Miss Noelle Fitzgerald, and she certainly distinguished herself, especially in the difficult Colotura passages. After a very nervous opening, in which there was uncertainty about her breath control, she recovered to give a really wonderful performance, especially in the later stages.

A splendid chorus, conducted by Mr. John Enright, was of tremendous help to all the vocalists, in particular the well-known number "The Gipsy Life" making a wide appeal. The gay final chorus also created a very favourable impression.

The production generally was gay and colourful, and the settings excellent.

THE CHRISTIAN BROTHERS PAST
PUPILS' UNION

—— PRESENTS ——

The Limerick Choral Society

—— IN ——

THE BOHEMIAN GIRL

(By MICHAEL WILLIAM BALFE), with

THOMAS
ROUND

TENOR, LONDON

**Star of Stage, Screen, Television
and Radio.**

—— AT ——

ST. JOHN'S PAVILION

—— FROM ——

Sunday, 23rd Feb.,

—— TO ——

Sunday, 2nd Mar.

OVERTURE · 8 P.M. NIGHTLY.

———— ★ ————

Programme   -   -   -   -   3d.

Limerick Leader, Ltd.

The programme for 'The
Bohemian Girl' in which I
starred in Ireland.

'South Pacific' I was tall enough, but not thin enough. For 'Bitter
Sweet' I was too tall and too much the romantic lead type. I was fast
becoming disenchanted with the musical comedy world and dreaming
more and more of getting into one of the opera houses.

The months dragged on with money coming in only from cabaret
appearances at various hotels and Livery dinners in the City. One
memorable day, however, Joe Hislop announced that he thought I

Myself and my beautiful co-star in 'The Student Prince', 1951. (*Photograph courtesy of The Cork Examiner*)

was ready to audition for the Sadler's Wells Opera Company (he was the advisor of singing at both Sadler's Wells and Covent Garden).

A date and time were arranged and the day arrived when I walked out onto the stage at Sadler's Wells. I had chosen to sing the aria from the beginning of the opera 'Cavallerier Rusticana'.

I had sung in so many auditions and had learnt a lot from them, but this one was the most important of them all to me, and should

TOP: 'The Student Prince'.

BOTTOM: as Pierre ('Red
Shadow') in 'The Desert Song',
Dublin, 1952.
(*Photographs courtesy of The Cork
Examiner*)

have been the most nerve racking, but I was just the opposite of
nervous. I had chosen a difficult aria, and I thoroughly enjoyed singing
it. In fact, I felt so relaxed, that at the end of the aria I wasn't satisfied
with the way I had finished it and asked Norman Tucker, the Director
of the Wells, if I could repeat the last two lines again, because I knew
I could sing it better, which I proceeded to do.

The audition was a success and almost immediately, I was offered
the chance to sing the role of Jenik in Smetana's opera 'The Bartered

Bride' for two trial shows. I was over the moon with delight and so was Alice, and I could hardly wait to get to my agent's office to break the news.

Monty Lyon had decided to retire from the agency business and had gone to live in Ireland. This had happened while I was still in 'London Melody' and when I went over there to sing in 'The Student Prince', Alice and I stayed with him and his wife Mary, in their cute little house called 'Thimble Cottage' in the seaside village of Summer Cove. His agency business had been taken over by Lew and Leslie Grade, and it was to their office that I went to tell them of the offer I'd had from Sadler's Wells. I was in the middle of my story when something happened that was to repeat itself several times in my career – the telephone rang and after a few moments Leslie Grade motioned to me to pick up the other telephone. It was Jack Hylton's office offering me the part of Camille in their forthcoming production of 'The Merry Widow' at the Stoll Theatre, London, for a run of eight weeks.

I shook my head to Leslie to turn down the offer and after several seconds of Leslie trying to mime to me to accept the part and to keep Jack Hylton interested on the other end of the line, he finally said that he would contact me right away and ring him back. He slammed down the telephone and called me all sorts of a fool, but nothing he said could change my mind. I had waited for months for a show to turn up and now, after long months of voice study, I had managed to get accepted at the Sadler's Wells, and I was not going to throw the chance away for an eight-week season at The Stoll.

So, I parted company with the Grades – I don't think they were broken-hearted and for my part, I had never felt quite at home under their banner.

I had turned down 'The Merry Widow' and a salary of £75 a week, without knowing what Sadler's Wells were going to offer me. I soon found out when I went to see Norman Tucker to discuss my contract. I must say it was something of a shock. It seemed that I was going back to the beginning again, £15 a week was the offer and even Norman Tucker thought I was more than slightly mad to give up a West End show and salary, for a junior principal's salary at the Wells.

However, I was determined to make the break and I signed a year's contract and although Alice and I were going to have to economise greatly, we both felt that I had made the right decision.

By the way, while I was in 'Rose Marie', I had auditioned for the BBC and gave my first broadcast. It was a 9 a.m. recital from Broadcasting House in August 1950. This first broadcast was quickly followed by an 11 a.m. recital, which in turn brought me a fairly regular spot in an evening programme called 'A Musical Tale of Two Cities'. I don't know how I came to forget that part of my career because it is very important and now, combined with the Sadler's Wells contract, made me feel that I was making real progress in the opera-singing world.

It felt good to be back under contract with a company again – to have a rehearsal schedule each week and to have a real purpose. My first opera was to be 'The Bartered Bride' – I had already played two performances as a guest artist – not too far removed from G & S, except that the music was more difficult. I have never had a big voice, but there have never been complaints that I couldn't be heard. However, all the singers in 'The Bartered Bride' seemed to have enormous, beautifully produced voices and for a while, I tried to emulate them. I was forgetting one of the first rules of singing, that the more one pushes at the volume, the less the sound that comes out – apart from the strain on the vocal chords. Also, I was following the footsteps of James Johnston, and Irish tenor, who had a powerful, dramatic voice. However, the reviews of my first performances were quite good and I started to settle down in my new medium.

Eisenstein in 'Die Fledermaus' was my next role. Apart from the music being more operatic than G & S, the role seemed to fit me

'Die Fledermaus' in 1954 with Victoria Elliott as Rosalinde, Marion Studholme as Adele, and myself as Eisenstein.

like a glove, and I enjoyed every performance. The cast was as follows:

Rosalinde	Victoria Elliott
Adele	Marion Studholme
Alfred	Gerald Davies
Falke	Denis Dowling
Frank	Arnold Matters
Orlofsky	Anna Pollak
Frosch	Howell Glynne

Howell was a wonderful character singer – every part he played was a gem of stagecraft and timing and his wonderful 'drunken act' as Frosch in 'Die Fledermaus' will, in my opinion, never be equalled. I always felt it was an honour to be on the same stage. He played Kecal in 'The Bartered Bride' with me and we created a record at Sadler's Wells by having to take an encore for the duet, 'This Girl I've Found You'.

Another great character in the company at that time was Owen Brannigan and I was very interested in comparing these two great singers. Off stage Howell seemed to be a rather dour man, always pleasant, but rather dull with a large pipe hardly ever out of his mouth. On stage he was completely different, far removed from the real life Howell, but deep in his role and one of the funniest and easiest artists to work with.

Owen was, in my opinion, exactly the opposite. On stage, at least to me, he was always Owen Brannigan with a costume on. His gestures and mannerisms never changed, no matter what part he was playing, but off stage, he was a very funny man indeed and to be in the same dressing room as Owen was always a continuous laughing session.

We were always in 'The Marriage of Figaro' together. Owen played Bartolo and myself Basillio. At every performance we pinned a notice on our dressing room door which read: 'Barty and Bassy Double

Two reviews at the time:

Thomas Round as Jenik provided the surprise of the evening, for since we last heard him he has developed a beautifully controlled legato, after the Tauber manner, which brings him to the forefront of English tenors. The *New Statesman*, December 1954

The current version of 'Die Fledermaus' shows little change from that presented by the same company in Bournemouth last summer. Perhaps the outstanding feature is the progress that Thomas Round has made in the role of Eisenstein. Last year his performance was promising and lively, but now he plays the role to perfection – singing well, speaking well, acting well, and all with an underlying current of good humour that is as infectious as Strauss's music. The *Bournemouth News*

'The Marriage of Figaro', with Anna Pollak (Cherabino), Patricia Howard (Sussanah), John Hargreaves (the Count), and yours truly (Basilio).

Comic Act – Thanks Norman Tucker for a very happy season. Free for Pantomimes and Summer Seasons. Can provide own Skins and Rugs.'

Other examples of Owen's wit: he never seemed to have any soap of his own and one evening he complained to me to stop buying Palmolive Green Soap because it brought him out in a rash. He also accused David Ward, the Scottish bass, of having the longest fingers in show business – they always went right down to the bottom of his Removal Cream tin.

When Sadler's Wells commissioned a new opera from John Gardner called 'The Moon and Sixpence' based on the life of the painter Gauguin, John Hargreaves was cast in the role of Strickland and Owen as Dr Coutre. It was one of the most difficult scores I had ever seen. How John Hargreaves, Anna Pollak, June Bronhill, Marion Studholme and Owen Brannigan ever learned it, I don't know. I only had a small part, but my music was bad enough. It consisted of a song, which I had to sing in a smoke-filled bar when drunk. I had to tune a guitar, out of tune, and sing the song, also out of tune.

There didn't seem to be any arias as such for any of the principals. I suppose that June and Marion came nearer to having a complete song to sing. There seemed to be page after page of speaking on notes and there was no chorus as such. When asked at a press conference if there was any chorus singing, John Gardner quite humorously replied that, if his memory served him right, there was one place in the opera where two artists actually sang together – for two bars.

I remember John Gardner rushing down the stalls during an orchestral rehearsal to tell the conductor – Alexander Gibson – that the woodwind section had played an E Natural instead of an E Flat. The whole orchestra collapsed with laughter, because the woodwind could have been playing 'God Save the Queen' for all the difference it would have made.

But back to Owen. I was sitting with him one day going through the score, when he suddenly looked up and said, 'I was told I had an aria in this opera and I can't find it anywhere and which reminds me that John Hargreaves was told he had two good arias to sing and he said he had been through the score from front to back, and he can't find them anywhere, and he can do *The Times* crossword puzzle'.

Michael Moores, one of the assistant conductors, took the music rehearsals for this opera while we were on tour and Alex Gibson took over when we returned to London only a few days before the opening night. I well remember during the interval of one performance, when the stage manager opened our dressing room door to announce that Alex had been taken ill after the first act and that Michael Moores would be conducting the rest of the opera. Owen looked across at me and said, 'Now we're in trouble – he knows the opera'. What a character.

Owen was involved in a multiple car accident on the M1 motorway and was trapped in his car for a number of hours. He was not seriously hurt but his nerves suffered and he never seemed to completely recover his old self. He died about two years after the accident, which I feel sure had a lot to do with his premature death. He was only sixty-four years old. I had the great pleasure of working with him on the concert platform on numerous occasions and also on radio and television.

Talking about difficult music, the Wells put on a production of Wolf Farari's 'The School for Fathers', a wonderfully clever and funny opera. I remember George and Alfred Black, two West End impresarios, saying that it would run for three years in a West End Theatre.

There is a very difficult and tricky octet in the second act where, apart from each trying to hold on to their own line of singing, we chased each other all around the stage throwing pillows and anything we could lay our hands on at the same time. With the orchestra playing madly and with the audience laughing loudly, I don't ever remember the octet being sung correctly. We always started together and we finished together, but the middle was just a jumble of sound. I remember one evening when I was determined to hold on to my line, come what may, and I was doing very well until I was dug in the ribs by David Ward (the Scottish bass) as he said in a broad Scottish accent, 'How you're doing Tom?' He had lost his line and of course his remark also stopped me.

At another performance Anna Pollak had lost her line and she spotted Howell Glynne at downstage right, ignoring us all and singing away quite happily and confidently. She managed to find her way down to him, amongst the chaos, hoping to be able to pick up a cue from him and so find her own line again, but on straining to catch his voice in the noise of the laughter and the orchestra, she was amazed to hear him singing, 'Why Do the Nations' from Handel's 'Messiah'.

Although I was now receiving quite a lot of concert engagements from agencies in London – mainly Ibbs and Tillett – and I was broadcasting frequently, I was beginning to think that I had made a mistake in joining the Wells and that I wasn't going to make a name in 'grand opera', when fate stepped in with a vengeance.

Alfred Nightingale, who had been the D'Oyly Carte General Manager, and had left them to become Sir Thomas Beecham's Business Manager, rang me one day to say that he had mentioned my name to Sir Thomas, who was looking for a tenor to play the lead in a Delius opera that had never been produced before; and would I go along to sing for him. Of course, I jumped at the chance to audition for Sir Thomas, and I couldn't believe my good fortune when he offered me the tenor lead in a Delius opera called 'Irmelin', that was to receive its world premiere at Oxford.

Sir Thomas thought I could do with a little more power in my top register and suggested that I have some lessons with Dino Borgoli. I was still studying with Joseph Hislop, but I didn't want to lose this chance, so I went along to see Borgoli. I don't think he was able to do much for me in the short time I had, but Sir Thomas seemed satisfied. I settled down to learn the role of Nils, a swineherd who had to find a silver stream, which would lead him to a princess, when he himself would be turned into a prince. The opera had its premiere at the New Theatre, Oxford, on 4 May 1953.

Norman Tucker and James Robertson (Sadler's Wells' Musical Director) were pleased that I was going to do this opera with Beecham. Denis Arnold was to be the producer.

It must have been a very difficult opera to produce because the score was mainly very slow in tempi, and our movements seemed to be in slow motion. I was finding it very difficult to establish a character with Nils and during the last two weeks of rehearsal, I know that Denis wasn't very satisfied with my efforts. I think I was so worried abut the actual music which was so different from anything I had tackled before, that I couldn't give much thought to my performance. It was during the last few days of rehearsal that I finally came to grips with the music and started to improve in the production and Denis told me so.

By the time the first dress rehearsal arrived, I had lost nearly ten pounds in weight. Apart from Sir Thomas not being the easiest person to work with – I think it was because everyone was in such awe of him –I was not the best musician in the land, and I did want to do everything correctly. Also Lady Beecham was telling me practically every day how much the success of the opera depended on me. I was in a pretty nervous and tense state.

Unfortunately, at the same time, I was doing some rather strenuous BBC work with Stanford Robinson, another very temperamental conductor. These broadcasts had been booked before I signed with Sir Thomas.

One incident that stands out in my mind seemed to break the tension completely; at least it did for me, because from then on I started to enjoy the opera. We were in the middle of the penultimate dress rehearsal and at one point I was off stage together with five French horn players. Brian Balkwill, the assistant conductor, was peering through a small hole in the scenery, watching Sir Thomas, ready to give a musical cue to the French horns. He gave the signal and the horns started five bars of hunting calls. On the fifth bar I had to run on stage calling 'Irmelin'. I was one bar late, so we stopped and I went off stage to repeat the entrance. Again I was one bar late. I thought I was counting correctly, but the third and fourth was still wrong. You can imagine the atmosphere in the theatre. Four times I had held up the rehearsal. A seventy-five-piece orchestra was virtually wasting its time. Sir Thomas was getting more and more irritated and the whole cast and management were reduced to an embarrassed silence.

After the fourth wrong effort, I decided to speak up and to everyone's amazement, I walked to the footlights (I must say it was difficult to be dignified dressed as a swineherd; I had on only a rough piece of sacking material and my legs were bare to the top of my thighs), and said, 'Sir Thomas, I will never get this entrance right unless you will please give me a cue.' Sir Thomas looked at me in silence for a few seconds, stroked his goatee beard and said, quite calmly, 'Very well, Mr Round, we will try again and see what we can do.'

Off I went and for the fifth time I ran on to the stage looking at Sir Thomas, who promptly let out a loud yell and shouted, 'There's your damn cue, Mr Round!' and flung his baton straight at me. For a few seconds there was silence, and then the whole theatre erupted into laughter, the orchestra were banging on their music stands and Sir Thomas was standing with a grin on his face, for all the world like a naughty little schoolboy. Needless to say, I never missed that cue again because I was always given it, but from that moment, everyone seemed to relax.

'A Wand'ring Minstrel, I'

NEW THEATRE - OXFORD

Chairman and Managing Director: Stanley C. Dorrill, M.B.E.
Proprietors: Oxford Theatre Co. Ltd.   Manager: Ben Travers

On Monday, 4th May, 1953, at 7.0

First Performance on any Stage of

I R M E L I N

An Opera in Three Acts by

FREDERICK DELIUS

Four subsequent performances will be given on
Tues., 5th May; Wed., 6th May, and Sat., 9th May, at 7 p.m.

Special Matinee of "Irmelin" will be given on
Thursday, 7th May, at 2.15

The Royal Philharmonic Orchestra

(Leader: David McCallum)

Conductor:

SIR THOMAS BEECHAM

BART.

Cast includes

EDNA GRAHAM,   CLAIRE DUCHESNEAU,   JOY PIERCE
THOMAS ROUND,   GEORGE HANCOCK,   ARTHUR COPLEY
ROBERT EDY,   NIVEN MILLER,   DAVID ODDIE

Producer: DENNIS ARUNDELL

Scenery and Properties by Mary Owen   Costumes by Beatrice Dawson
Choreography by Pauline Grant

Associated with Sir Thomas Beecham, Bart., in this enterprise are:
The Arts Council of Great Britain and The Delius Trust

OPERA PRICES OF ADMISSION (including Tax):
STALLS 21/-, 17/6, 15/-, 10/6; CIRCLE 21/-, 17/6, 12/6, 8/6; BALCONY 6/-;
UNRESERVED 3/6

Box Office open daily from 10 a.m. to 7 p.m. at the New Theatre, and at Keith Prowse,
159 New Bond Street, W.1 (REGent 6000), and usual Agents

*Special facilities will be offered to Patrons returning to London after each
performance by the provision of a train service scheduled to leave Oxford at
10.30 p.m. each evening (except Thursday) arriving London at 1.15 a.m.*

P.T.O.

The world premier of Delius'
'Irmelin' with Sir Thomas
Beecham.

'... *Your New Employment* ...'

The opera received a very good press, but the audiences were poor because of the high prices that Sir Thomas insisted on charging for the seats. His reply to one irate patron who complained through the press was, 'If you want a Rolls Royce, you must pay Rolls Royce prices'.

I was quite successful in my part and I was delighted to receive a card from Norman Tucker and James Robertson, congratulating me on an 'excellent musical performance'. This of course, pleased me more than anything else, and I felt I would now get a better chance at the Wells.

After the season at Oxford, there were no future plans for 'Irmelin' apart from an hour's television programme in which Irmelin and myself sang the long, slow love duet from the second act. For several years after, I was greeted in all sorts of strange places by members of that orchestra asking if I had found 'that bloody silver stream yet'.

Following 'Irmelin', my singing life took a definite upward turn. Sir Thomas Beecham started to use me in concerts, Sadler's Wells cast me as Tamino in their new production of 'The Magic Flute', and D'Oyly Carte invited me as a guest artist to play Hilarion in their London Season revival of 'Princess Ida' at the Savoy Theatre.

I was broadcasting practically every week in a tremendous variety of programmes, and the BBC television cast me as Alfredo in their first full-length opera 'La Traviata' with Heather Harper as Violetta.

If I had had time to think what was happening to me I think I would have panicked, but I was so busy learning new music and performing it, I didn't realise that I was becoming quite a name in the opera world. At one concert in the Festival Hall with Sir Thomas Beecham, he presented me to the Queen Mother.

It was at this concert that Sir Thomas and I again clashed, but in a friendly way. I took part in the last item of the concert – a short work by Vaughan Williams. After taking several bows, we walked off the stage. We were recalled and we took further bows and again walked off. The audience were still clapping and cheering and Sir Thomas

The *Oxford Mail* wrote:

Sir Thomas Beecham's long awaited premiere of Delius's first opera, 'Irmelin', fifty-nine years after its completion in Paris, has at last materialised with Oxford for its venue. The two principals, Edna Graham and Thomas Round, have well-matched voices of beautiful quality and their duet made a magnificent climax. Miss Graham made a moving figure of the star-rapt Princess and Mr Round was a handsome and dignified Swineherd.

And in *Music and Musicians*:

The New Zealand soprano, Edna Graham, sang satisfactorily as Irmelin and Thomas Round's tenor, free from strain and carefully phrased was ideal for Nils. Both principals acted gracefully.

In this production of 'Princess
Ida' in 1954 I played the role of
Hilarion.

started to go back on stage again, but as they opened the curtain he realised I wasn't with him. I had decided that the audience had seen enough of me and that it was Sir Thomas they wanted and I said exactly that to him. For the second time I heard that high-pitched yell, 'Get back on the stage, damn you!' Everyone in the ante-room jumped in the air and heaven knows how many in the audience heard him. Anyway, I dutifully followed him on stage for a third call.

Yes, for a couple of years or so, I was his blue-eyed tenor, and I'm sure I was all set to be his number one, but he started offering work that was beyond me and I fell behind in that area.

As Prince Hilarion again, with
Leonard Osborn as Cyril (left)
and Jeffrey Skitch as Florian.

I was still being kept busy at Sadler's Wells, playing Don Ottavio in
'Don Giovanni', Nadir in 'The Immortal Hour', Beppe in 'I Pagliacci',
Lensky in 'Eugene Onegin', the Czar in 'The Snow Maiden', and
several small parts in other operas. Of course, 'The Bartered Bride'
and 'Die Fledermaus' were both in and out of the repertoire at intervals.
There was a good team of principal tenors under contract at that time
– Rowland Jones, Robert Thomas, William McAlpine, Ronald Dowd,
Gerald Davies and Gwent Lewis. I was only really suited for certain
roles and I began to wonder how long I could last at Sadler's Wells.

I can't think why I was worried about my future, but all artists feel
insecure, not being able to see more than a few months into the
future, so I did worry.

My son Ellis, having attended the Hampden Gurney School near
our flat on Seymour Street, had been accepted at St Martins Private
School, Northwood, Middlesex, at the age of eight years and was also
accepted at Merchant Taylor's Public School. I was faced with high
fees for the foreseeable future.

My next effort with Sir Thomas was a television concert from the

As Cyril in another production of 'Princess Ida', this time at the Savoy Theatre in 1960.

studios in Maida Vale, and part of the programme was the long love duet from 'Irmelin'. The original soprano Edna Graham was not available and Joan Stuart, a principal soprano from Sadler's Wells, was engaged. Again, the concert was not without its Sir Thomas moment. The programme was to start with an introduction by Sir Thomas and he turned from acknowledging the orchestra, with all the cameras operating, and said 'Will someone kindly inform me if we are on the air, and if so, which camera am I supposed to be looking at?'

There was another big occasion which I think ended my career with Sir Thomas. I was engaged to take part in a Mozart work to be

116

'... Your New Employment ...'

broadcast from the Maida Vale studios on two separate evenings, with the Royal Philharmonic Orchestra and three international artists who had performed the work on many occasions. I felt completely out of my depth but Sir Thomas didn't seem to think so because we only had one short rehearsal around the piano at his flat. This was followed the next day by a rehearsal with the orchestra before the broadcast in the evening. I had thought there would have been several rehearsals. I was really petrified, because like the TV programme, it was a live performance. I slipped up in one of the Quartets and the next day Sir Thomas called me for a rehearsal to clear up my mistake. Everything went well that second broadcast, but I could have been a lot better with more rehearsal.

I have mentioned my difficulties with Sir Thomas Beecham during my broadcast of the Mozart work on radio as a result of my lack of music theory, which I felt was a handicap. I often wished I had been able to spend a couple of years at either the Guild Hall or the Royal College of Music – how much more confident I would have been.

I have a good ear and a good memory and I don't think I ever failed to be able to learn any work that I was asked to do, but some oratorios and musical works like 'The Canterbury Pilgrims', 'King Olaf', Rossini's 'Stabat Mater', Verdi's 'Requiem', and the Delius opera 'Irmelin' proved very taxing for me to master.

I think I managed to hide my lack of knowledge reasonably well and was even praised by some conductors for my 'musical sensitivity'. I have always felt that anyone who could conduct an orchestra or play the piano must be far cleverer than me and I rarely voiced any opinions until I had the song, oratorio or opera under my belt.

118

'... Your New Employment ...'

RIGHT: 'I Pagliacci' by Leon Cavallo, with Victoria Elliot as Nedda and me as Beppe.

I became quite friendly with several of the BBC conductors like Vilem Tausky, Stanford Robinson and Rae Jenkins who at first were quite difficult. I don't think I ever got close to Sydney Torch during my time with 'Friday Night is Music Night'.

A new production of 'The Magic Flute' followed at the Wells and the press made much of the fact that I was the only English artist in the cast, the rest coming from Scotland, Wales, Australia and New Zealand:

> The pleasing tones of Thomas Round as Tamino brought a fresh start of pleasure with each entry; his voice alone, which carried the right touch of heroic ring, was more than adequate, positively attractive. His forthright impersonation was admirable, and when he has learned to take more liberties with the music, to shape and present a phrase, he will be the Tamino for Covent Garden. *The Financial Times*, February 1955.

There was also a new production of 'Don Giovanni' in which I sang the part of Don Ottavio. I sang the aria 'Dalla Su Pace' instead of 'Il Mio Tesoro'. My personal reviews were quite good but they remarked on this and when the opera was again played, I did sing 'Il Mio Tesoro'. It was in September 1955 that I was engaged to sing the role of Alfredo in the first BBC television performance of 'La Traviata'. Heather Harper sang Violetta and Jess Walters sang Germont. George Foa was the producer.

Of course there were no recordings in those days, or colour, and

LEFT: as Nadir in 'The Immortal Hour'.

BELOW: in 'The Snow Maiden' as the Czar.

after three weeks of intensive rehearsals, followed by a technical and a dress rehearsal, we gave a live performance in the evening. I remember it was 10 October 1955. How did we do it? I also took part in a potted version of 'Die Fledermaus' and two acts of 'The Bartered Bride'.

I appeared regularly on Eric Robinson's 'Music for You' TV programmes and also on radio with his brother Stanford Robinson. Vic Oliver, too, engaged me to sing in his Viennese concerts with his British Concert Orchestra. His Christmas card to me always read 'To Tom (You are my Heart's Delight) Round'.

These were exciting times for me and I remember someone saying to me, 'What does it feel like to be a famous singer?' Famous – I hadn't thought about it; if to be famous or well-known was to be busy,

THOMAS ROUND
in Gilbert and Sullivan opera

Can this singer "go pop"?

HOVERING on the brink of mass popularity, but uncertain about taking the plunge, is that sparkling lyrical tenor, **Thomas Round.**

Don't misunderstand me. Thomas is popular enough already with audiences of the Sadler's Wells and D'Oyly Carte opera companies. His Nanki-Poo in *The Mikado*, for instance, has seldom been bettered; neither has his Count Danilo in *The Merry Widow*. For the discerning, any Thomas Round performance is welcome as the flowers that bloom in the spring.

But can that gay voice sell half a million records? Can he, as we say in show business, "go pop"?

"It's funny you should put that question, Jonah," Thomas said when we talked recently, "because **Vic Oliver** asked me exactly the same thing only the

other day. Naturally, I'd like to break into the big money class, but not if I have to sing rubbish."

I replied that **Gordon McRae** is another good singer who doesn't sing rubbish, and his records sell. So why should not some enterprising record impressario try introducing Thomas—now at the peak of his fame before a limited audience—to a larger public?

An LP all his own would prove popular, I'm sure, both here and in America; for Thomas has many friends across the Atlantic. During the war, as an R.A.F. fighter pilot, he helped to train Americans to fly at Greenville, Texas, and it was at nearby Dallas that he did a good deal of his own opera training.

I've been asked about Thomas's background several times lately. He was born at Barrow-in-Furness, Lancs. He joined the local choir as a teenager and fell in love with one of the sopranos. At nineteen, he became a policeman (they called him "the singing bobby") and married the soprano. After the war he eased himself out of the police force and into the office of the late Rupert D'Oyly Carte, who soon made him principal tenor—as nice a compliment as any singer could want.

Thomas has a devoted wife and a fine son; he's modest and bound up in his work—in fact, you couldn't meet a nicer chap. His whole career goes to prove that a policeman's lot *can* be a happy one!

FOR THE RECORD

"MANDOLINS On Capri" (Oriole CB1498), played here by the **Crawford Orchestra**, is tailor-made for moonlight picnics by the sea.

There's a message for tender-hearted teenagers in **Marty Wilde's** sad, soul-searching "Danny" (Philips PB926).

Janice Harper makes musical sunshine with the infectious "Just Whistle" (Capitol CL15026).

● **LP for fun:** It's good to hear the needle-witted **Rosalind Russell**

playing in a musical. "Wonderful Town" (Philips BBL7307), with music by the prolific **Leonard Bernstein**, provides just the right vehicle for her many-sided talents. Based on the play *My Sister Eileen*, the show is full to overflowing with good tunes, crazy situations and fun galore. Co-starring are **Sydney Chaplin**, son of a famous father, and **Jacqueline McKeever**.

● **LP for keeps:** You've probably heard the famous love-theme from Tchaikovsky's *Romeo And Juliet* very

ROSALIND RUSSELL

many times as the popular song, "Our Love." Now hear it in its rightful setting, as **Sir John Barbirolli** conducts the Hallé Orchestra in a truly thrilling performance of this glorious work (Pye CCL30128). On the same disc are Mendelssohn's "Hebrides" overture and Wagner's "Mastersingers."

★ ★ **J.B.**

23

then I must be famous, but I was much too busy learning new music and performing it to have any thoughts of being well known.

Independent television came and I was engaged to take part in a series of music programmes called 'Your King of Music' starting during the opening week of commercial television. We rehearsed and rehearsed at the new Wembley Studios, until we were ready for a first performance on closed circuit television for all the bigwigs to see and vet, before the first public transmission.

What a shock we got – the show was scrapped, the producer, the conductor and most of the cast were sacked – they hated the show.

The format was changed and a variety conductor – Billy Ternent – was engaged and it became a variety programme. Fortunately, I was retained and my contribution was a ten-minute spot in each of the six scheduled programmes.

Another aspect of my career that was starting to blossom was that of concert singing, not only taking part in oratorios such as 'The

'The Bartered Bride', broadcast
live on BBC TV in December
1955. I played Jenik and Kecal
was played by Owen Brannigan.

Messiah', 'Elijah', 'The Creation', 'The Crucifixion', 'Dream of Geron-
tius', the Verdi 'Requiem' etc, but concert performances of grand
operas such as 'The Bartered Bride', 'Carmen', 'Il Travatore', 'The
Daughter of the Regiment', 'Aida' etc. Also, what we call miscellaneous
concerts were very popular with choral societies and male voice and
mixed voice choirs. I sang three or four groups of songs and arias of
my own choosing and perhaps sang an item with the choir or the
soprano or baritone, if one had been engaged.

I enjoyed this part of my work as much as any, because your success
depended on just your voice and your presentation. I also liked to see
the audience, and still do, and the concert hall lights were usually left
on and there was no stage lighting as such. Of course, it meant an
awful lot of travelling up and down the country, from the north of
Scotland to the South Coast and from east to west. I hadn't a car then
and so there were many complicated travel plans to work out, especially
if I had several consecutive dates in different towns.

To perform in one of these concerts and to feel that I had given a
vocally good performance gave me tremendous satisfaction and the
feeling that I was a real professional, and also that I was being engaged
because I gave value for money as a professional should.

My son Ellis was now attending Northwood Primary School as a
boarder and he came home every third weekend. We hoped that he
would be accepted into the Merchant Taylor's School at Sandy Lodge,

'... *Your New*
Employment ...'

Patricia Bartlett as Marjenka with
me as Jenik in 'The Bartered
Bride'.
(*Photograph courtesy of*
BBC Television)

where we had had his name down for quite a while. I had already
decided that if he were accepted, we would move out of London to the
Northwood area, then Ellis would be able to attend there as a day boy.

Of course, there was a written test and an interview and I remember
taking Ellis to the meeting with the Principal – Hugh Elder – in his
office. We were greeted with great enthusiasm. Hugh Elder was a
great G & S follower and he had seen me perform many times and
I also learned that John Steane, the Head of Music at the school, had
seen some of my performances.

Mr Elder produced a G & S opera every year at the school, and lots
of photographs were brought out for me to see. Poor Ellis just sat

quietly, wondering what was going on, and it wasn't until we had exhausted our talk about music that the question of Ellis getting a place at the school came up. He was accepted!

The next thing was to find a house, and so started a long and weary round of house hunting. After several weeks of virtually daily train journeys out to the Pinner, Harrow and Northwood areas, Alice finally gave in. The houses we could afford didn't suit us and the ones we liked were too expensive. I continued hunting on my own. We had bought our first house in Lancaster for £550 and we later sold it for £2,000, but we couldn't find anything as good as the one we had in Lancaster, even for £4–5,000.

We were really depressed and in desperation, I had all but settled on a house in Pinner, and was on the point of signing a cheque for the deposit in the house agent's office, when I stood up and said that I must have another look round to find something more to our liking. The agent wasn't very pleased because I had taken up quite a lot of his time, but to me £4,500 was an awful lot of money that required earning and I wasn't about to give up so easily. I went into the nearest telephone booth and telephoned our friend Irmgard Warren at Moor Park, to ask if she would meet me in Pinner, to have a look at the house. Thirty minutes later we were sitting outside the house in the car. It looked quite nice and was situated at the end of a cul-de-sac. Inside, though, it was very ordinary.

Mrs Warren then suggested that we had a look in Northwood itself, and although I thought the area would be too expensive, agreed to have a look. We were standing outside an agent's office looking at photographs of houses for sale, when I spotted one that looked exactly what Alice and I would like – with the added advantage of being virtually on the edge of the Merchant Taylor's School grounds.

When Irmgard stopped her MG sports car opposite 203 Hampermill Lane, I knew the house was just what we were looking for, and when we were shown over it, I was more convinced than ever. I immediately telephoned Alice to meet me at Moor Park Station right away. From leaving the flat on Seymour Street, to get to Baker Street Station and then the Metropolitan Line to Moor Park, took at least an hour and a half, so I was hoping she would also like the house. From Moor Park Station we had about a ten-minute walk down Sandy Lodge Lane, past the gates of the school on the left and Sandy Lodge Golf Course on the right.

Alice was quite convinced that we were in the middle of the country and after living near Marble Arch for nearly five years, she couldn't contemplate living in this country area. We arrived at the house and she liked the first view of it, and although the inside was all brown and

Me in my work outfit.

203, Hampermill Lane, Oxhey, in Hertfordshire, as it looked when we purchased it in August 1952. It was to be our home for thirty-seven years.

green, she very much liked the rooms and the unusual layout. We bought it in May 1951, and we were to stay there for thirty-seven years.

Another bonus in buying '203' was that, by an amazing coincidence, it was only five houses away from Maude 'Brownie' Evans' house, where I had studied the G & S operas.

Through many years, I spent some part of every day at Brownie's working on my various Sadler's Wells roles and also the BBC programmes concerts and oratorios with which I was kept busy.

Brownie, who was well into her eighties, took on a new lease of life, so much so that she was invited to give an interview about her life on BBC Radio.

Brownie had a cat that definitely did not like tenors. Each time I arrived at the house, I opened the door to her small sitting room, where her baby grand was placed, and the cat, who was always on the armchair, looked up at me and immediately dashed through the door that I was holding open, never to return until I was leaving the house again.

Ellis started his studies at Merchant Taylor's as a day boy, and he immediately started to look and behave better. Over the next few years, I was invited to give several lunchtime recitals at the school with John Steane at the piano and Ellis never once mentioned to his school friends that I was his father!

Life now settled down into a reasonable routine of music – travelling to Sadler's Wells, concerts, the BBC in London, Manchester, and Glasgow etc., and of course, rearing Ellis.

Before the end of the 1957 season at Sadler's Wells, Norman Tucker

and his Committee had decided that the company should present an operetta and that their first venture should be 'The Merry Widow'. I was offered the part of Danillo which I gladly accepted, June Bronhill was to play Hannah Glavari – the Widow, Howell Glynne as Zeta, William McAlpine as Camille and Marion Lowe as Valencien. The libretto was by Christopher Hassell and the producer, Charles Hickman.

Rehearsals started and scenery and costumes were being planned. Everything seemed to be moving along smoothly when one morning, Norman Tucker came into one of our rehearsals and dropped the bombshell that, owing to a legal dispute between the descendants of Franz Lehar and the Metro Goldwyn Mayer Film Company over the question of royalties, all rehearsals must cease and the production indefinitely postponed until it was decided who should receive the royalties from the production.

They had turned down Norman's offer that Sadler's Wells would pay the royalties to whoever was entitled to them when the dispute was settled. We were all very disappointed with the news because we were all enjoying the rehearsals so much, and it was a change from working on the more serious operas.

'The Merry Widow', performed on the BBC by the Sadler's Wells Company, with me in the role of Count Danilo Danilovitch and June Bronhill as the Widow.

My Count Danilo played opposite June Bronhill as Anna Glavari; Zeta was Howell Glynn and Camille, William Mc Apline.

A few weeks later my contract came up for discussion and it was decided not to renew my regular contract, but for me to continue working with the company as a guest artist. Although I wasn't keen on the idea, it proved to be financially better for me, because I was paid for each performance and also relieved me of the pressure of always having to apply for permission to accept engagements outside the company. In other words, I was a complete 'freelance artist'.

I think all this happened at the beginning of August 1957, and when the new season started at the Wells, I found myself performing two and even three times a week with the company, and together with my broadcasting, television and concert work, I was being kept very busy.

I had also been invited by the D'Oyly Carte Company to record 'The Mikado' and 'The Pirates of Penzance' with the Decca Record

Company, to commence in October. I was thrilled to be making my first professional recordings.

My guest artist status with Sadler's Wells didn't last very long because later in October, a very excited Norman Tucker rang me to say he had just received the news that the 'The Merry Widow' dispute had been resolved and they could now go ahead with the production. Would I please come down to the theatre to discuss my contract? My reaction to this news took Norman by surprise. I said that now I'd had time to think about the role of Danilo, I wasn't at all sure that I was the right artist to take it on. I felt sure I would be up against unfavourable comparison with such famous musical comedy stars like Joseph Coyne, Jack Buchannan and Peter Graves. Norman pooh-poohed these thoughts and I finally agreed to go to the theatre to discuss the project.

Alice told me that, virtually on the same day, Frederic Lloyd – Bridget D'Oyly Carte's general manager – also telephoned with an offer to return to the company, and offering me a five-year contract, which was the first offer of this kind in their history

I still wanted to stay with Sadler's Wells and when I met with Norman Tucker and Stephen Arlen to discuss my new contract with them, I told them of the offer I'd had from the D'Oyly Carte Company to re-join their company. I didn't tell them of the long contract the Cartes had offered me because they had requested that we keep it between ourselves for the time being. I did, however, infer that the contract was a very good one but if they – the Sadler's Wells – could offer me at least a two-year contract, I would consider turning down the offer from the D'Oyly Carte Company.

Their reply was that staging 'The Merry Widow' was an entirely new venture for them and that the production could just become another opera in their repertoire, so Stephen Arlen's reply to my request received a very definite no; they could not take the chance of having me under a two-year contract if 'The Widow' failed. If I wished to leave when my contract ran out at the end of August 1958 to join the Cartes, that would be OK.

I agreed to their terms, but if this discussion had taken place after the great success of 'The Widow', then I think the result would have been very different.

My diary shows that rehearsals re-started on Monday, 23 December and the show opened on Monday 20 January 1958.

Life at home had become difficult during 'The Widow' rehearsals, and the discussions between Norman Tucker and the D'Oyly Carte. Alice's mother had become quite ill and she was making frequent visits to Barrow to look after her. Ellis and I were managing on our own. It was finally decided that we should have both her mother and

'A Wand'ring Minstrel, I'

The window of the HMV store in London, when our record topped the LP charts.

128

'... Your New Employment ...'

father come to stay with us. Matilda was so ill that special arrangements had to be made both by train and ambulance, but it was finally accomplished. We knew that 'Tilly' had not got long to live and Alice's sister, Jenny, who lived in New Zealand, decided to come back home. Our house became rather full and sad. Fortunately we had plenty of room at '203'.

Matilda died in the early hours of 16 January 1958, only a few days before my opening night. I wasn't even able to attend her funeral on Saturday 18, because of the final dress rehearsal of 'The Widow', which was scheduled for that day. Imagine trying to portray a role like Danilo when our house was so full of grief. 'The Merry Widow' opened on Monday 20 January 1958 and Alice, Jenny and Ellis attended that performance in full mourning, sitting in the front row of the dress circle.

'The Widow' was a tremendous success and we played it three times a week to capacity houses. It became the show of the season in London and June Bronhill and I were invited everywhere, interviewed and photographed, and the final accolade was to be invited to transfer 'The Widow' to the London Coliseum for a month's season. Even this had to be extended.

If only the Sadler's Wells management had been able to foresee the great success of 'The Widow'; I wonder what would have happened. Would I have signed up with the Cartes? Would the Wells have offered me a more permanent contract?

Negotiations were under way to televise 'The Widow' and I remember being paged at Heathrow Airport as I was waiting to fly to Ireland to take part in a week's performance of 'The Bohemian Girl', virtually ordering me to agree to accept the BBC's fee offer before I left.

'The Merry Widow' was performed on BBC television on Easter Monday, 7 April 1958, watched by an audience of twelve million people.

The Wells went on tour in April and I remember in Dundee that my voice suddenly left me during the first act of 'The Widow', and my understudy had to take over. The following day, having made an appointment with Ivor Griffiths, a throat specialist in Harley Street, I took the train to London and went straight from Euston Station to see Ivor, who within minutes had diagnosed blocked Antrim's. He proceeded to clear them in no uncertain manner, and I immediately felt much better, but when I suggested that I should take the next train back to Scotland, he told me that I should rest my voice for a few days. I rang Sadler's Wells and told them the news, and they suggested that I join the company a week later in Aberdeen – which I did. I think it was the only time I ever missed a performance of 'The Widow'.

A very proud moment for me on that tour was in Leeds when my

COLISEUM

CHARING CROSS · TEM 3161

Managing Director: PRINCE LITTLER   General Manager: SAM HARBOUR

For a Limited Season commencing THURSDAY, JULY 31st

EVENINGS MON. to SAT. 7.30   MATINEE: SAT. 2.30 (NO MATINEE on AUGUST 2nd)

Sadler's Wells Trust Ltd. in association with the Arts Council of Great Britain
present

SADLER'S WELLS OPERA

THE

MERRY WIDOW

FRANZ LEHAR

English version CHRISTOPHER HASSALL   From the German of VICTOR LEON and LEO STEIN

JUNE BRONHILL   THOMAS ROUND

HOWELL GLYNNE

CHARLES CRAIG   ROWLAND JONES

MARION LOWE

DENIS DOWLING   JOHN KENTISH

GWILYM JONES

JOYCE BLACKHAM   JOHN LARSEN

SHEILA REX   LILY GRIBBIN

RAIMUND HERINCX

WILLIAM BOOTH   DEIDREE THURLOW

Conductors:

ALEXANDER GIBSON   WILLIAM REID

Directed by CHARLES HICKMAN

Choreography by PAULINE GRANT   Designs by THEA NEU

SADLER'S WELLS ORCHESTRA, CHORUS AND OPERA BALLET

Subject to Alteration

parents travelled over from their home in Barrow-in-Furness to see me in 'The Widow' at the Grand Theatre on Whit Monday, 26 May.

Final arrangements had been completed to transfer 'The Widow' to the London Coliseum for a month's season and a few days after our tour ended we went into rehearsals to adapt the production for the much larger stage at the Coliseum.

MERRY!

AMAZING but true! "The Merry Widow" selection by the Sadler's Wells company looks as though it will get into the L.P. Hit Parade.

It has been on sale for only ten days. But popular demand is so great that the H.M.V. factory is postponing rush orders for Tin Pan Alley tunes.

They're having to work overtime on making music that was old in grandma's day

But it's only fair to point out that this long-player is a very fine disc indeed—even by the most modern standards.

OPERA

Quite ageless and quite irresistible

By PERCY CATER

*T*HE MERRY WIDOW—quite, quite ageless—was back at Sadler's Wells last night, practically with the cast that staged the operetta's Wells debut nearly two years ago.

It is more than ever irresistible. Experts are at work. From start to finish it goes with a click.

I doubt if, since it began its conquering course, the piece has been presented with more polish and speed, swish, and assurance. How freshly it comes up under this effortlessly high-spirited treatment.

The Widow herself, June Bronhill, is more than ever irresistible (I 'requote). I do not know if there has been a Widow so petite. But the simply enormous vitality, the feminine acuteness in repartee and the abundance of style carry all before them.

Thomas Round must be one of the handsomest and most dashing Danilos in the operetta's history. How he, one of the busiest of singing stars, contrives to appear so casual and debonair, as though being the slim Count of the crinkly hair and flashing teeth were his life's work, is completely baffling.

Rubbed their eyes, looked again

BRISSON'S DOUBLE—EVEN THE SUIT FITS

By PHILIP McDONNELL
Our Film and Theatre Correspondent

*T*HE older members of the audience rubbed their eyes and looked again. For the tall, elegant figure playing Count Danilo in the Sadler's Wells production of "The Merry Widow" looked the double of old matinee idol Carl Brisson.

Without the photographs, which show the remarkable resemblance, I wouldn't know. I was being pushed about in a pram at the time Mr. Brisson had the women at his feet with his debonair Danilo.

So I asked Wells Danilo, Thomas Round about it.

"I don't know myself, because I never actually saw Brisson," he said.

"But friends who have, say I am tremendously like him, and my work is often compared with his.

"Perhaps the most remarkable thing is that when I played the Student Prince, the evening suit I wore had been made for Carl Brisson. It fitted me perfectly, so we must have even measured the same.

"I can't say much about the comparisons between us but I can tell you I take them as a compliment."

Who said nothing was the same any more?

LOOK at the picture on the left, then at the one on the right. See the resemblance? On the left we have Thomas Round as he appears in "The Merry Widow." On the right is old matinee idol Carl Brisson, pictured with Tilly Brisson. The picture was taken in 1933.

CARL BRISSON

We opened on Thursday 30 July and we were all thrilled with the reception. This started the negotiations to transfer the Sadler's Wells Company from Rosebery Avenue to the Coliseum on a permanent basis. It was during this season that we recorded 'The Widow' with EMI in three mornings and part afternoon sessions, which gave us a few hours' break before the performances in the evening.

The LP records sold really well and compared well with the sales of Frank Sinatra's new record.

The season was extended by a week ending on Saturday 6 September and on Sunday the 7th I travelled to Coventry and opened with the D'Oyly Carte Company on Monday 8 September in 'The Mikado'. 'The Pirates of Penzance' followed on the Tuesday, a matinée and evening of 'The Mikado' on the Thursday, followed by a matinée and evening of 'The Gondoliers' on the Saturday – quite a hectic first week.

So started a six-year contract (the five years had been extended to six) with the D'Oyly Carte Opera Company. The agreement allowed me to continue performing in 'The Merry Widow' when required and also to continue with my broadcasting and concert work.

I quote from the April 1958 issue of *Music and Musicians*:

Thomas Round, who has had a resounding success as Count Danillo in 'The Merry Widow' at Sadler's Wells, is leaving the company this summer. He goes back to the D'Oyly Carte Opera Company, which he left to join The Wells, a few years ago.

But I understand that, considering his success in 'The Merry Widow', the Wells and D'Oyly Carte Companies have come to a friendly arrangement, and Round will continue to sing as Danilo. Probably, they will arrange things so that performances of 'The Merry Widow' will go on when Round is not singing Gilbert & Sullivan heroes.

All the same, it will be something of a Cox and Box existence for him, with a great deal of dashing about the country, considering all the touring of The D'Oyly Carte Company – and in addition, the tours of The Sadler's Wells Company.

To crown the enormous success of 'The Widow', the Sadler's Wells Company were invited to present a selection of items from the operetta at the London Coliseum before Her Majesty Queen Elizabeth II in the Royal Variety Performance of November 1958. I was very proud and thrilled to receive a letter and certificate.

Life became even more hectic as I was flying, driving or taking the train from various parts of the country to play Danilo (now back in rep at the Wells), or for broadcasts or concerts, and travelling back the following day to sing in one of the G & S operas.

When the Cartes arrived in London for a season at the Savoy Theatre,

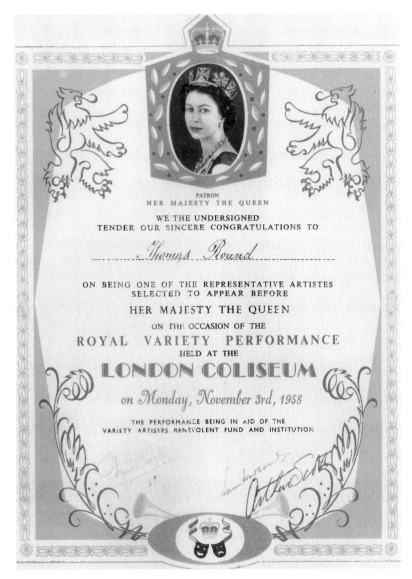

PATRON
HER MAJESTY THE QUEEN

WE THE UNDERSIGNED
TENDER OUR SINCERE CONGRATULATIONS TO

Thomas Round

ON BEING ONE OF THE REPRESENTATIVE ARTISTES
SELECTED TO APPEAR BEFORE

HER MAJESTY THE QUEEN

ON THE OCCASION OF THE

ROYAL VARIETY PERFORMANCE

HELD AT THE

LONDON COLISEUM

on *Monday, November 3rd, 1958*

THE PERFORMANCE BEING IN AID OF THE
VARIETY ARTISTES BENEVOLENT FUND AND INSTITUTION

life became much easier because, as the London *Evening Standard* wrote, 'It's a good thing for Thomas Round that the No. 38 bus runs from the Savoy Theatre on the Strand to the Sadler's Wells Theatre on Rosebery Avenue'. During this season I was also appearing in the film of 'The Story of Gilbert & Sullivan' which was showing at the Empire Cinema in Leicester Square.

EMI Records also engaged me to record Schubert's operetta 'Lilac Time' with June Bronhill and John Cameron, followed by Grieg's 'The Song of Norway' with Victoria Elliott and John Lawrenson.

At the end of 1961 the copyright on Gilbert's words in the G & S operas ran out and with the copyright on Sullivan's music having

'... *Your New Employment* ...'

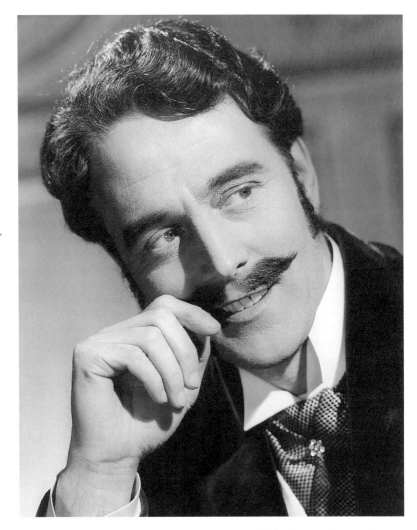

The Defendant.

expired in 1950, the operas were now available for professional companies to perform them.

The BBC was the first organisation to take advantage of this and on 6 January 1962, I took part in the first-ever broadcast – together with other D'Oyly Carte principals – of 'The Gondoliers' out of copyright. Another broadcast on 20 January followed this, and then a BBC series of G & S operas. At least I didn't have to spend hours learning new music for these broadcasts and so I welcomed the offers to sing G & S on the air.

In the spring of 1962, the year of the Festival of London, the D'Oyly Carte were approached to present a production of 'The Yeomen of the Guard' at the Tower of London. I don't know the full facts of the ensuing discussions but, incredibly, the management turned down the offer on the grounds that it would be too difficult technically to

135

produce it successfully on Tower Green. The whole company heard about the offer and we were all very disappointed that it was turned down.

A few weeks later, both Kenneth Sandford, a principal baritone in the company, and myself were approached to play the roles of Shadbolt and Colonel Fairfax respectively. So, in spite of the Cartes turning down the offer, the Festival of London Committee intended going ahead with the idea and had contacted Anthony Besch to produce it.

The production was to take place during the Carte's summer break, so I was delighted to be able to accept.

It had been decided to present the opera, not from inside the Tower, but on an enormous stage built in the moat, against the Tower walls, facing Tower Hill, with the audience seated on football stadium-like stands.

What a thrill it was to start the rehearsals in the historic Tower and

OPPOSITE: The 1962 production of 'The Yeomen of the Guard' at the Tower of London was quite a spectacle. I was Colonel Fairfax, with Elizabeth Robson as Elsie Maynard.

'Strange Adventure' with, left to right: Anne Pashley, Joanna Peters, myself and Bryan Drake.

'The Grim Old Tower' and 'Is Life a Boon?' with, left to right: Anne Pashley as Phoebe, Bryan Drake as Sergeant Merryl, me as Fairfax, and John Carol Case as Lieutenant of the Tower.

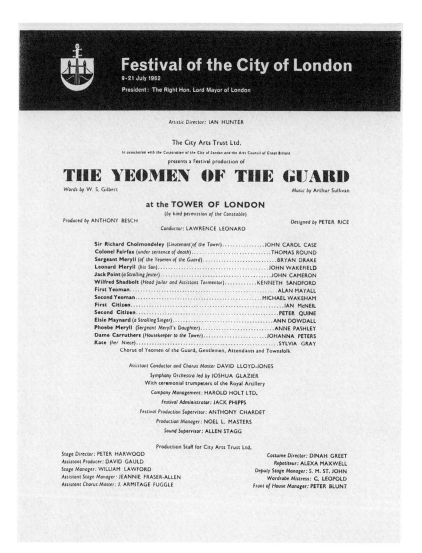

Festival of the City of London
9-21 July 1962
President: The Right Hon. Lord Mayor of London

Artistic Director: IAN HUNTER

The City Arts Trust Ltd.

In association with the Corporation of the City of London and the Arts Council of Great Britain

presents a Festival production of

THE YEOMEN OF THE GUARD

Words by W. S. Gilbert   Music by Arthur Sullivan

at the TOWER OF LONDON
(by kind permission of the Constable)

Produced by ANTHONY BESCH   *Designed by* PETER RICE

Conductor: LAWRENCE LEONARD

Sir Richard Cholmondeley (*Lieutenant of the Tower*)	JOHN CAROL CASE
Colonel Fairfax (*under sentence of death*)	THOMAS ROUND
Sergeant Meryll (*of the Yeomen of the Guard*)	BRYAN DRAKE
Leonard Meryll (*his Son*)	JOHN WAKEFIELD
Jack Point (*a Strolling Jester*)	JOHN CAMERON
Wilfred Shadbolt (*Head Jailor and Assistant Tormentor*)	KENNETH SANDFORD
First Yeoman	ALAN MAYALL
Second Yeoman	MICHAEL WAKEHAM
First Citizen	IAN McNEIL
Second Citizen	PETER QUINE
Elsie Maynard (*a Strolling Singer*)	ANN DOWDALL
Phoebe Meryll (*Sergeant Meryll's Daughter*)	ANNE PASHLEY
Dame Carruthers (*Housekeeper to the Tower*)	JOHANNA PETERS
Kate (*her Niece*)	SYLVIA GRAY

Chorus of Yeomen of the Guard, Gentlemen, Attendants and Townsfolk

Assistant Conductor and Chorus Master DAVID LLOYD-JONES

Symphony Orchestra led by JOSHUA GLAZIER
With ceremonial trumpeters of the Royal Artillery
Company Management: HAROLD HOLT LTD.
Festival Administrator: JACK PHIPPS
Festival Production Supervisor: ANTHONY CHARDET
Production Manager: NOEL L. MASTERS
Sound Supervisor: ALLEN STAGG

Production Staff for City Arts Trust Ltd.

Stage Director: PETER HARWOOD	*Costume Director:* DINAH GREET
Assistant Producer: DAVID GAULD	*Repetiteur:* ALEXA MAXWELL
Stage Manager: WILLIAM LAWFORD	*Deputy Stage Manager:* S. M. ST. JOHN
Assistant Stage Manager: JEANNIE FRASER-ALLEN	*Wardrobe Mistress:* C. LEOPOLD
Assistant Chorus Master: J. ARMITAGE FUGGLE	*Front of House Manager:* PETER BLUNT

'A Wand'ring Minstrel, I'

The cast list for 1962 'The Yeoman of the Guard' at the Tower.

with artists such as John Cameron as Jack Point, Ann Dowdall as Elsie Maynard, and Kenneth Sandford as Shadbolt.

By the time the opening night arrived, I felt I was living in those far-off days as I was led up the steep steps over the battlements of the Tower; and more especially when the tenor bell was sounded and lit by a pinpoint white spot light as the time of my supposed execution was announced. There was one incident that caused some amusement in the audience. The weather forecast for that evening was that thundery showers would develop. It stayed dry until just after I started my solo in the first act, 'Is Life a Boon?', when heavy drops of thundery rain started to beat a tattoo on the hollow wooden stage. I finished the song with the rain falling faster and faster. I started my dialogue and had just reached the line, 'And now Sir Richard, I have a boon

'... *Your New Employment* ...'

'The Yeomen of the Guard'
1969, with Don Adams, 'In an
Comtemplative Fashion'.
(*Photograph courtesy of the Newark
Advertiser*)

to beg' when, as though on a signal, hundreds of umbrellas opened and Sir Richard and I (Colonel Fairfax) abandoned the stage and the audience to the elements. Fifteen minutes later the rain had stopped and we both walked onto the stage, took up our positions and I started my dialogue, 'And now Sir Richard' – and I added, with my eyes raised to the heavens, 'As I was saying before I was so very rudely interrupted – I have a boon to beg'. Everyone burst out laughing.

Incidentally there were to be other times when the locations of our productions meant that our scenery designer had to excel in unusual ways. In 1971 we were invited to mount an open-air production of 'The Yeomen of the Guard' in the grounds of Newark Castle, Nottingham-shire. Our scenery designer, John Griffin, did a wonderful job in building extra pieces of castle against the existing walls, hardly distinguishable from the original castle masonry. The venture was highly successful and the following year we produced 'The Mikado' with the castle walls turned into the Japanese town of 'Titipu' – very spectacular.

It was to be twenty years before we were again invited to present 'The Yeomen' at Newark Castle. Norman Meadmore had long since broken away from Gilbert & Sullivan for All, and I took on the task of producing the opera as well as playing the role of Colonel Fairfax. The following year, I produced 'Iolanthe' at Newark Castle, turning it into the Houses of Parliament. We also produced 'The Yeomen of the Guard' at Nottingham Castle.

My career continued between the Cartes and the Wells, and other singing activities through 1960 and 1961, when the Cartes announced they were planning a long tour of the USA in 1962.

My son Ellis – now nineteen – had ended his education at Merchant Taylor's and was now at the London University studying Aeronautics, and was living in a bedsit in Bayswater Road. We didn't like the idea of leaving Ellis, even though he was not living at home, and neither did I like the idea of going to America for months and leaving Alice alone at '203'. We chose the lesser of the two evils and decided that Alice should accompany me. We then decided that we didn't want to fly together, in case of accidents, so we decided that Alice should sail over to New York and then take the train down to Pasadena, where we were opening the tour.

Donald Adams, who suffered from claustrophobia and couldn't fly, had also decided to sail over and then take the train down south. This was a great relief to me that Alice would have company on the long journey with someone she knew so well.

So, a week or more before we were due to fly, Alice and Don left for Southampton to board the *Queen Mary*. They had a wonderful voyage and an even more wonderful train journey to Pasadena, but first they had to stop in Chicago, where they had a few hours to wait for the train to Pasadena, which gave Alice the opportunity to renew her friendship with Barbara Ann Scott (of 'Rose Marie' on ice fame).

They finally boarded the 'Super Chief' train for the two-day and one night journey to Pasadena. They arrived in Pasadena the day after the company and I was able to meet her and Don from the train. The whole company was booked into the Greens Hotel – a large old fashioned style building and yes, painted a dark green.

Widows and widowers mainly occupied the hotel and, I suppose, elderly retired people. It was not air conditioned so it was very interesting to walk along the wide corridors, past the doors of the apartments – left open to allow a small movement of the hot air to circulate – to catch a glimpse of the elderly occupants. I'm sure the large swimming pool had never been used for a long time before the D'Oyly Carte Company descended on the hotel. We spent most of our days in and around the pool.

I don't think the hotel had its own restaurant because I well remember having to walk to a nearby coffee shop each morning for bacon, waffles and coffee.

At 9 a.m. the temperature signs in the streets were already showing 75 degrees and by the time we had finished breakfast and started back to the hotel, the signs were registering between 83 and 85 degrees. Also, by this time, the smog was getting thicker and my eyes smarted unbearably, and I couldn't wait to get back to my room to bathe and close my eyes to ease the stinging. Of course, we did leave our rooms to make various sightseeing trips. Jeffrey Skitch and I hired a car to visit Disneyland, the Observatory and Marine Land, always hidden by the smog. I have cine film of these trips but no stills.

After Pasadena we moved to San Francisco, where we had to get used to temperatures around the 50s with thick fog each morning and brilliant hot sunshine in the 80s by noontime. I think we only saw the Golden Gate Bridge once completely free of fog.

We had a surprise telephone call one morning from a chap from our hometown of Barrow-in-Furness, called Bill Mulhearn. He was an engineer employed by the Coca-Cola Company, and he serviced the vending machines in the San Francisco area. Our first outing with him was on a Sunday morning when he had arranged to take us to a Highland Games in San Jose. We woke up on that Sunday morning to the usual thick fog, so I rang Bill to ask if the trip was still on and if so what should we wear. He replied that he would be with us in an hour and that he would be wearing shorts and a tee shirt. Sure enough, he duly arrived in his shorts and tee shirt – Alice and I were in warmer clothes. We set off and very soon we were crossing the Golden Gate Bridge with headlights blazing in the fog, feeling very smug that we were wearing sensible clothes. We were amazed when, two thirds of the way over the bridge, we burst out of the fog into brilliant sunshine and by the time we had driven the fifty or so miles to the Games, we were getting very hot indeed in the car. We had a marvellous day and I'm sure we saw more variety of kilts than they had in Scotland. In the evening, we again ran into fog on the bridge.

Another great trip we had with Bill was to see the San Quentin Prison, and to an area of the California redwoods. To top it all, Bill arrived one day with a suit of Coca-Cola overalls and said that he was going out to Alcatraz to service the vending machines in the prison and that I was to accompany him as his assistant. We boarded a motor launch at Fisherman's Wharf, and duly arrived at Alcatraz. Bill warned me not to speak too much to any of the guards, which would give away the fact that I was English and arouse their suspicions. We passed through X-ray machines and then into the prison itself, where Bill inspected the various machines that were scattered about. I tried not to appear too curious, but it was very difficult as we passed along the passages with the barred gates sliding open and crashing closed behind us. I wonder how many English people have had that experience. Twelve months later, Alcatraz was no longer a prison.

From San Francisco we moved to Portland, Oregon, and then on to Vancouver, where Alice's brother, Bernard, was a schoolteacher. Of course we stayed with him and his wife Ethel and their two boys for the week that we were in Vancouver.

Our next venue was back in the USA, to Seattle, and as we were due to return through Vancouver on our way from Seattle to Edmonton, Alberta, Alice decided to stay on with her brother, and I picked her up on the return journey.

What a wonderful night trip we had through the Rockies to Edmonton – very romantic – we couldn't sleep, the moonlit views were marvellous.

My last performance in Edmonton was on the Friday, which meant that I was free until the Monday performance in Calgary, our next town, so we decided to go on ahead. We booked into our hotel and then hired a car to visit Lake Louise, a real blue water lake – very lovely. We saw our first brown bears on that trip.

From Calgary we started back across Canada towards Winnipeg, stopping at a town called Saskatoon for one performance only of 'The Pirates of Penzance'. We arrived in the town at about 11 a.m., moved into a hotel room for the day and later gave our performance. We then had a meal and made our way to the train coaches that were waiting for us in a siding to take us to Winnipeg.

Alice and I overheard a conversation between two ladies in the next booth to us where we were having our late meal. They had obviously been to see 'The Pirates' and one remarked to the other, 'Did you really enjoy the show tonight?' The reply was, 'Yes, I did enjoy it but I had difficulty following the words – I think the English accent interfered with the dialogue'.

From Winnipeg we moved to Ottawa and then finally by ship, *The Aquitannia* I think, back to England.

You might have thought that we would have had a few days' break before starting again, but this was the D'Oyly Carte and time out was money lost; and after all, we'd had a holiday on board ship, hadn't we?

We arrived home in bitter weather, with ice and snow covering the country. Icicles hung around '203' and deep snow covered our steep driveway.

'... Your New Employment ...'

Our son Ellis, who was now at London University and in digs in Bayswater Road, had paid occasional visits to the house, but could not prevent the water pipes becoming frozen. We had a very difficult couple of days getting organised with plumbers etc. before I had to leave to start another tour with the Cartes.

CHAPTER TEN

G & S For All

THE NEXT EVENT that was, eventually, to have a major effect on my career was when we were playing Brighton in the early summer of 1963. Norman Meadmore, the stage manager of the D'Oyly Carte company at that time, approached Donald Adams and myself with an idea to form a concert group of four principals of the company, together with the present chorus master and rehearsal pianist, William Cox-Ife, to present a programme of Gilbert & Sullivan at various seaside venues on Sunday evenings during the summer.

Don and I agreed to have a meeting with Norman to discuss the details of the idea, and we met one morning in Don's caravan. By lunchtime, 'Gilbert & Sullivan for All' was born.

We worked out a programme of solos, duets, trios, quartets, and scenes with dialogue, with Don and myself introducing each item, together with anecdotes from each of us.

We then approached Jean Hindmarsh (principal soprano), Gillian Knight (principal contralto) and William Cox-Ife (chorus master), who all readily agreed to join us. The D'Oyly Carte Management, amazingly, gave their permission to go ahead with the concerts, thinking quite rightly that concerts with their own principals would give added publicity to the stage performances.

I personally thought that the idea would run out of steam in a couple of years, but it would be fun while it lasted and would give us something to do on Sunday evenings when we couldn't get home. How wrong I was.

What we hadn't thought about was where the money was to come from to pay the artists after each concert, while waiting to receive the cheque for our fee from each venue. It was decided that both Don and I would take turns in paying them, plus any other expenses until we had some capital behind us. Norman was to be our road manager/ general administrator.

Our first date was in Aberystwyth, Wales, but I don't remember very much about that first concert. For me the first date that put us on the track was in the Leas Cliff Hall, Folkestone, in August 1963. With the backing of three local amateur societies, the Leas Cliff Hall manager and a good publicity system, we had a full house, with a recipe for a unique and potentially successful format. For a number

Gilbert and Sullivan For All

SOUVENIR PROGRAMME

of years we were to give performances twice a year at the Leas Cliff Hall, interspersed with full weekends of opera workshops.

Using the excellent reviews from that first effort, Meadmore circulated venues around the country, theatre managers and entertainment managers, especially in areas reasonably close to where the D'Oyly Carte were due to play. The reasons for this were twofold; to avoid us having long car journeys after a concert to the next town on the Carte's tour (we didn't want the management to say that we were tiring ourselves to the detriment of their performances), and to give added publicity to the company and boost their bookings.

Of course, we were limited to Sunday concerts only, for whereas

Jean and I had a couple of nights off each week, Gillian Knight performed every night and Don was only off when we performed 'The Gondoliers'.

Sunday Celebrity Concerts were very popular around the seaside resorts during the summer and I was already involved in these before we had started Gilbert & Sullivan for All, but we soon found that our own group was proving more and more in demand and that G & S for All was fast becoming a musical power around the country.

We finally decided that we should form some sort of legal operation. I think we all had our own personal accountants at that time and a meeting was arranged at my solicitor's office in Old Bond Street, London, to discuss the formation of a company.

I think it was first decided to form a partnership, and we later became a limited company. When my solicitor, Graham Hunt, suggested that there should be provision in our agreement to guard against any disagreement that may arise between us, we three were horrified. How could three chaps, who were good friends and colleagues, ever have disagreements? But it was agreed that there should be clauses in our contracts to cover any eventuality. How right he was – if only we could have looked into the future.

Myself and Kenneth Sandford are presented to Her Majesty Queen Elizabeth and Prince Philip in 1962.

G & S For All'

The little company went from strength to strength; nearly every venue we played re-booked us for the same date the following year, some twice a year. It soon became apparent that Sunday concerts were not sufficient. Theatre managements and particularly local authorities wanted dates during the week, which in our circumstances we could not fulfil.

However, in 1964 and after my five-year contract with the Cartes had been extended to six years, I received an offer from a London impresario, Tom Arnold, to tour South Africa with the operetta 'Lilac Time' based on work by the composer Schubert.

I had already been approached to repeat my role of Colonel Fairfax in another production of 'The Yeomen of the Guard' at the Tower of London, with some changes in the original cast. Again the opera was very successful and was highlighted when the Queen and Prince Philip went to see a performance. The cast and the producer were presented to them both and I had a very interesting short conversation with the Queen.

The Queen discussed my difficulties in walking up and down the steep staircase that was built from the moat up the side of the Tower walls to the battlements. Prince Philip asked me what my future plans were and when I told him that I was leaving for South Africa immediately after the 'Yeomen' ended, he remarked that he hoped that the weather had improved, because it was very damp when he had left there only a day or so before.

My long contract with the Cartes had ended in August 1964, and after two or three weeks' rehearsals of 'Lilac Time' at the Victoria Palace Theatre, the company of twenty-seven left for Johannesburg, taking Alice with them. I followed a few days later because I had to perform at several G & S for All concerts in Wales.

With Donald Adams still in the Cartes and myself in South Africa, our company had to take a back seat once again.

I arrived home in the early hours after my last concert in Wales and, after a few hours' sleep, I left home for the long flight to South Africa. I think it was about lunchtime when the aeroplane landed at Johannesburg and I took a taxi direct to His Majesty's Theatre and joined the 'Lilac Time' company for rehearsal that afternoon – suffering badly from jet-lag.

The cast were delighted to see me safely with them, especially Marion Studholme the leading lady and Alfred Hallett playing Schubert. I was cast as Baron Schober. Of course, Alice was more than delighted to see me and to escort me to our suite at the Library Hotel, where she had been made very welcome.

The opening night was very successful and the reviews next day were terrific. It had been many years since a British company had performed in South Africa because of apartheid, and we were welcomed warmly.

There had been great difficulties with the artists' union Equity before we were allowed to perform in South Africa, because they had placed a ban on all British artists performing there. Permission was finally granted when the Consolidated Theatres of South Africa finally agreed to Equity's demand that we give one performance every week before a wholly black audience. At that time, no white South African would have attended a show with black people in the audience.

It was an experience to play to a wholly black audience, the majority of whom had never seen a musical show before. Schubert's 'Lilac Time', telling the story of Schubert's ability to write beautiful love songs, but because of his shyness, his inability to express his love for Lilli, was perhaps a little beyond them.

When Schubert asks his friend, Baron Schober, to plead his love for Lilli on his behalf and finally loses her to the Baron in a very emotional scene, the ladies in the white audience were in floods of tears for poor Schubert. However, the black audience was convulsed with laughter that a man should be so silly as to ask another man to speak for him, and so he deserved to lose her. Which audience was right, I wonder? *The Black World*, Johannesburg's black newspaper, reported it thus in September 1964:

HISTORY IS MADE AT POSH HIS MAJESTY'S: SOCIALITES FLOCK TO STAGE MUSICAL TREAT. History was made last night when hundreds of socialites packed the posh Joburg Theatre for a grand gala performance of 'Lilac Time'.

This was the first time our people had been allowed into this all-white cinema and theatre in the heart of Joburg's theatreland in Commissioner Street.

Hundreds of cars from all over the Reef, Vareeniging and Pretoria jammed Commissioner Street as theatre lovers arrived for this Joburg Festival Performance.

There were grand gowns on the ladies, smart evening wear on the gentlemen, who had come to enjoy this enchanting musical.

Marion Studholme was also staying in the Library Hotel with us, and as the theatre company had provided us with a car – covered I may say, with posters advertising 'Lilac Time' – we were able to get around quite easily.

Alice had relatives in Johannesburg who made us very welcome and took us on several trips around the city, including a long trip to the Kruger National Park.

Alice's cousin met Alice, Marion and myself outside the stage door after our two performances one Saturday evening. We jumped into his car and drove all through the night arriving at the Kruger Park at about 8.30 a.m. on the Sunday morning. We booked into a 'rondo',

A performance of 'Lilac Time' in South Africa.

The company with the South African president.

a circular thatched-roof type of bungalow, had breakfast and then spent the whole day driving around looking for wild animals. Our biggest thrill was to witness a lion kill. Two lionesses pulled down a 'kudu' (a kind of buffalo), and we joined three other cars watching the gory feasting. I had my cine camera with me and I filmed the scene through the windscreen, but when I opened the window and held my camera outside to get a clearer view, the lion's head shot up in warning and I quickly withdrew into the car.

I filmed many exciting animal and bird scenes that day and after a very tiring day – remember we hadn't slept the night before and I had developed a bad headache – we virtually collapsed in our rondo and I awoke in the morning feeling marvellous. We had a sumptuous breakfast and set off on the long drive to Johannesburg. I do hope that Marion and I gave a good performance that evening – I can't remember! – but I do remember being very glad to get back to our hotel for a refreshing shower and a good night's sleep.

On another Sunday we were taken to the Durban Deep Diamond Mines to see the Tribal Dances, another wonderful experience. Again I took lots of footage of cine film. In all, I took 2,400 feet of cine film during our stay in South Africa. We visited Pretoria and were entertained by Government officials. Alice's cousin took us to the N'dbele Native Village and we were also entertained at the Johannesburg Country Club and played golf there.

After eight weeks we moved on to Durban. The company travelled by train but another of Alice's relatives took us by car through the Drackenburg Mountains, a wonderful drive. Alice, Marion and I were booked into a very handsome hotel and we were immediately pounced upon for publicity photographs and interviews, including feeding the dolphins. Again we were supplied with a car, which was a boon, and Alice also had relatives in Durban who entertained us.

After a very successful three weeks in Durban, we moved to Port Elizabeth for two weeks, followed by a three-week stay in Cape Town. The company travelled to Cape Town by the famous Blue Train on a really spectacular route. I wish Marion, Alice and I had been able to do that, but we had to fly down in order to fulfil publicity engagements before the opening night.

We were booked into a hotel called Sea Point and we had marvellous views of Table Mountain and Lion's Head from our balcony. Again we had a car, covered with posters advertising 'Lilac Time', and one day we drove down to the southernmost point of South Africa, where the Pacific and Atlantic Oceans meet in a line of foam. On this trip, we were invaded by a troop of baboons, who swarmed all over our car and proceeded to peel off all our 'Lilac Time' posters. They had obviously seen our show! I have film of the baboons staring in through the windscreen and side windows. Of course, we kept all the windows tightly closed and we nearly died in the awful heat, but we were too scared to drive away for fear of antagonising the animals. We also found the loveliest of all the South African flowers, the 'protea'.

Another memorable trip was in the cable car to the top of Table Mountain, where we spent several hours walking along its flat top,

'A Wand'ring Minstrel, I'

'Lilac Time' with, pictured above, Alfred Hallet as Schubert, Marion Studholme as Lili and myself as Schober.

with the most staggering views of Cape Town, Table Bay and the mountains to the north.

One of our favourite drives was along the coastal road with the Twelve Apostles Mountains on one side. Our last day in Cape Town was spent on this drive and on a last dash in the cable car to the top of Table Mountain.

I forgot to mention that in Johannesburg we met Webster Booth and Anne Zeigler, the famous tenor and soprano duo, who entertained a number of us at their home, including Sunday evening. I mention this because a peculiarity of South African hospitality was that while we were often invited to a Sunday 'Bri Fleis' – barbecue – the party always broke up at about 3 p.m. and we found ourselves on our own through the rest of the day. It was an extra treat, therefore, to be entertained during the evening. There were no cinemas open or any entertainment at all and we would spend the rest of the day walking on the beaches or in our hotel – very nice of course. I remember the theatre manager opening one of their cinemas especially for our company and he showed us the films for the following week.

Alice, Marion and myself were usually looked after, but the rest of the company was at a loose end in a strange country and a strange town. We three had a wonderful Sunday at a vine-growing farm in the Stellenbosch area.

The company were booked to fly back to the UK, but a friend suggested to Alice and I that he could exchange our air tickets to enable us to sail back home, taking about two weeks. I had no immediate engagements back home and so we duly booked on a ship of the Union Castle Line. Again, a friend suggested that we change our tickets and sail back on the Ellerman Line, which would be on a smaller ship – about 19,000 tonnes – carrying cargo and only about sixty passengers. He said that the difference would be like changing from a Butlin's Holiday Camp holiday to a luxury hotel. We agreed to do this and our tickets were once again changed to sail back on *The City of Port Elizabeth*, taking fifteen days for the voyage.

After a gala night performance, during which Alice took cine film, we said goodbye to the rest of the company, including Marion, and spent our last night in South Africa. We were not due to sail until 10.30 p.m. on the Sunday so we spent our last day re-visiting some of our favourite places once again and taking a last ride to the top of Table Mountain. We finally loaded the car with our luggage and drove to the docks where we left the car to be collected by the hire firm, and went on board.

The Purser must have had news of our sailing with the Ellerman Line, because we were greeted with the music of 'The Merry Widow', playing over the sound system. It was a very nice welcome.

A Gilbert and Sullivan For All production of 'Cox and Box', with Donald Adams as Cox and myself as Box.

Table Bay is noted for its 'rollers' (waves), and for the first few hours of the trip Alice was very ill with seasickness, as were many of the sixty passengers on board. Once clear of the Bay, we sailed into calm waters in tropical heat. I took cine film of the receding Table Mountain.

We had done the right thing in changing our flight tickets – our stateroom was great, the food marvellous and the people on board were very nice. Of course, I was put in charge of entertainment and we had some wonderful evenings. Virtually every afternoon I was invited to play deck tennis with the Captain and the Chief Engineer. Crossing the Equator, it was Alice who was initiated and finally thrown into the swimming pool. A really wonderful voyage until we reached the Bay of Biscay, when Alice and many others were again laid low with seasickness. We arrived at Tilbury Docks where our son Ellis was waiting to greet us with a beautiful new Humber Hawk car. So ended a really wonderful trip.

Three days later I was driving my new car, loaded with artists and luggage, through the snow to a G & S for All concert tour in Scotland – we were in the month of December.

Norman Meadmore had been busy while I was abroad and G & S for All started to take off in earnest with two, three or four concerts a week. Don went on tour with the D'Oyly Carte Company to the USA, but the concerts went on with a baritone called John Cartier. John had been the principal understudy to the comic character parts in the Cartes, a real trouper of the old school with an excellent singing voice, who proved to be a great asset to our company.

We had now added three more sopranos and three contraltos to our list of singers and also another musical director. We had also now devised twenty-six different programmes, with either four or five artists taking part. Don and I were the 'common denominators' and managements would not accept a booking unless we were both taking part, unless prevented by unavoidable circumstances.

Norman had, several times, broached the subject of us mounting full productions of the G & S operas, but Don and I always resisted the suggestions. We were busy enough with the concerts and both Don and I were in demand for other engagements, and so we did not want the added stress of full productions.

However, several theatres were asking if we would put on a stage show saying that they could not afford the fees that the Cartes were demanding. We finally gave in and gradually we built up our repertoire presenting 'The Mikado', 'The Pirates', 'The Gondoliers', 'The Yeomen', 'Pinafore', 'Ruddigore' and 'Patience'. We used professional principals and chorus, augmented by amateur societies. We gradually acquired our own scenery and costumes as we produced each opera. We were able to hand-pick the principals and to assemble the best possible cast for each opera, and we soon became rivals of the D'Oyly Carte company.

As Don and I had predicted, it gave us a lot more work. Norman Meadmore was the producer in the early years and he would rehearse and produce the amateur chorus for three weeks in whichever town we were booked. This of course left the running of our office, which was in London, to Don and myself, together with arranging the transport of scenery and costumes and the collection of various properties from places in London.

It was while we were occupying the office in Liverpool Street that John Seabourne asked if we would be interested in making films of the highlights of the G & S operas for television and educational purposes. Naturally, we were thrilled by the idea.

It seemed that John Seabourne had first contacted the D'Oyly Carte office with his idea, but that had been turned down. A member of the office staff told him of our company, and within three weeks of his telephone call, we were starting to film. We hand-picked the chorus from ex-D'Oyly Carte members and were able to cast the principals from our own pool of artists.

The soundtracks were made of eight operas at the Denham Film studios, and the operas themselves were filmed on the stage of the Odeon Cinema in Slough. The orchestra was fixed and conducted by Peter Murray, an ex-assistant conductor with D'Oyly Carte. Each opera took five days to shoot, working from 8 a.m. to 6 p.m. Two Royal Shakespeare Company artists were engaged to share the linking narration. They were shown twice on ITV television and the sound-tracks were issued on LP records by BASF.

It was during the filming sessions that we had to move from our office in Liverpool Street and look for new premises. John Seabourne solved our problem by offering us two rooms above his film office in Vauxhall Bridge Road. The films were made in 1972.

I think it was about 1971 when we were approached by the London County Council with a view to presenting an open-air concert in Holland Park, Kensington.

A stage had been erected in front of Holland Park House, with dressing rooms in the house itself, and the audience were accommo-dated on football stadium-type stands. Following the success of our concert, we were invited to stage a full-scale production of a Gilbert & Sullivan opera for one week, which also proved very successful.

For the next eight years, in either July or August, we presented a short season of a Gilbert & Sullivan opera and, when the weather was kind, we generally played to good houses.

Of course, performing *al fresco* brought its own special problems; for instance, at about 8 o'clock each evening, we were treated to the sight and sound of Concorde flying over us, which virtually drowned out our performance for a few seconds. Also, some of our dialogue scenes were accompanied by the screeching of the park's famous peacocks.

A very amusing incident occurred during a Saturday matinée of 'The Gondoliers'; we had just started the gavotte in the second act, when we noticed that the majority of the audience were looking off to their right and starting to smile and then to laugh.

Naturally, all of us on stage looked to our left to see what the distraction was and were amazed to see a procession of small ducklings, led by their mother duck, slowly walking along the pathway in front of our stage, seemingly oblivious of everyone. Of course we couldn't continue with the scene, the orchestra stopped playing, and we stopped singing until the parade had disappeared – stage right.

The most amusing (and also a little frightening) incident occurred on several evenings during the production of 'The Pirates of Penzance'.

G & S
For All'

'Iolanthe' at Holland Park. Donald Adams is shown in the role of Earl Mountarrat and I played Lord Tolloller.

When Donald Adams as the Pirate King made his entrance at the beginning of the first act of our opening performance, he strode down the stage towards the footlights with the black feather plumes of his Pirate King hat blowing in the breeze. Suddenly, there was a startled gasp from the audience as a large black crow swooped down from the right-hand side lighting gantry; it would have collided with Don's hat, had he not ducked just in time. Of course we all laughed about it, but the following evening, we all spotted the crow perched on top of the gantry and at exactly at the same point down it swooped again, missing Don's head by inches. It obviously thought Don's plumes were a rival crow. Don had already christened the bird 'Bridget'.

The Park authorities decided that the situation was becoming dangerous and the bird would have to shot, but we all strongly objected to this idea, and the following evening when the crow had again taken up its position, it was scared away by firing shots in the air. The crow took the hint and we were never bothered with it again.

Those seasons in Holland Park were happy ones for Gilbert & Sullivan for All and Harry Brammer, who was the official in charge of the Park productions, became a real friend and I still hear from him each Christmas.

Don and I used to say that they sold the best ice-cream in London at the little café in Holland Park and we always bought a large cone of vanilla on our way to our dressing rooms before the performance.

It was during one of our seasons in the Park that I was contacted with the offer to play the part of Arthur Sullivan in a musical play called 'Tarantara Tarantara'. Stratford Johns was to play the role of William Gilbert. It was to be presented at the Connaught Theatre in Worthing for a three-week season, and I was delighted to accept.

I had never worked with a real acting company before and it was a great experience to be on stage with Stratford (Alan) Johns and other well-known actors. I had to make a sacrifice, though. Alice and I had booked a holiday in Rome, together with her brother and his wife, which clashed with this engagement. As far as I was concerned, there wasn't any competition; they went on the holiday without me.

I had already seen the play at the Westminster Theatre in London, presented by the Young Vic Company from Bristol, and thought what a clever idea it was to present Gilbert & Sullivan's collaboration in such a way. I never thought that I would be invited to take part in a production.

The production received a good press in the local papers and also in the actors' newspaper, *The Stage*.

During the season Basil Soper, the business manager, suggested that we put on a variety Midnight Matinée with each member of the cast doing their own thing. I, of course, sang a couple of arias and also several ballads. One item that set the theatre alight was the trio, 'Three little Girls from School' from 'The Black Mikado' with Stratford, Basil and myself in which we virtually did a striptease act.

Stratford and I became quite good friends during our six weeks in Worthing. We were in great demand for publicity projects and I had a taste of what it was like to be in the company of a well-known TV star.

Whereas perhaps one person in a hundred might recognise me on the street, every other person recognised Stratford and we were continually stopped for his autograph or just to greet him with some catchphrase from the 'Softly, Softly' or 'Z Cars' series.

To get away from this pressure we would take walks along the sands, at the edge of the water, as far out as possible. In the hotel dining room we had a corner table and Stratford would sit with his back to the other guests and I would sit opposite, facing them. I didn't

'A Wand'ring Minstrel, I'

OPPOSITE TOP: 'Tarantara Tarantara' at Worthing, with Stratford Johns as Gilbert, Paul Bacon as Richard D'Oyly Carte and me as Sullivan.

OPPOSITE BOTTOM: 'The Story of Gilbert and Sullivan' on tour. Donald Adams and I played Gilbert and Sullivan again.

157

envy him his fame one little bit. Even in the shops he was invariably recognised, which made it awkward to purchase even the bare necessities. You can imagine a star-struck shop assistant relating to her friends how she sold a tube of toothpaste to Stratford Johns.

We always remembered each other at Christmas time and now he has died – ah me.

'Oft in the still night, when slumber's chain has bound me,
Fond memory brings the light, of other days around me.'

A few weeks after the success of 'Tarantara' in Worthing, a three-month tour of the play was suggested. However, Stratford Johns was not available and I suggested that Donald Adams would be ideal as Gilbert. He certainly proved so. We enjoyed the tour and we had very good reviews, but the business was poor. I think the title put people off – some thought it was something to do with spiders!

Not too long after this episode, both Don and I were invited to the Connaught Theatre to take part in a three week season of 'My Fair Lady,' with Don as Doolittle (perfect) and myself as Professor Higgins (not perfect, but in the event quite successful). To quote from *The Stage* review, I 'stepped out from Rex Harrison's shadow'. It was a real *tour de force* for me and at one point in rehearsal I felt I would never master the part; in fact it made me ill for a couple of days, so much so that Alice had to join me in Worthing to nurse and coddle me.

We played to capacity houses for the whole three-week season, including the matinées.

On 23 June 1962, I took part in my first BBC International Festival of Light Music from the Festival Hall, with Stanford Robinson conducting the BBC Concert Orchestra. My fellow artists were Jacqueline Delman (soprano) and John Cameron (baritone). Max Schonherr from Vienna was the guest conductor.

In June 1971 the BBC engaged Gilbert & Sullivan for All to present one of our programmes on the International Festival of Light Music with our own conductor, Michael Moores. We did the same in June 1972.

Gilbert & Sullivan for All was now acknowledged to be a musical force in the UK and was soon to become an international company.

In 1968 an American agent approached us, asking us to present a two-week tour of the USA. Unfortunately, Don wasn't available, but we decided to go ahead with the tour. The artists were Jean Hindmarsh, Jean Allister, John Cartier, Anthony Raffael and myself. William Cox-Ife, the D'Oyly Carte chorus master, was our accompanist. This was our first taste of G & S for All's international career.

During Don's last tour of the USA with the D'Oyly Carte Company in New York he met Nancy Tuttle, an associate of the Columbia Artists

'A Wand'ring Minstrel, I'

In 'My Fair Lady' at Worthing, I played Professor Higgins …

… and my great friend Donald Adams played Alfred Doolittle!

Max Schonherr, the great
conductor (above), and (below)
the kind message he wrote to me.

To Mr. Thomas Round,
the charming artist,
who might nearly be a
Viennese!

With kindest regards

1962

Management, and when he told her of our popular concerts, she immediately showed a keen interest. Shortly afterwards we received a call from Nancy asking if we would like to consider a tour of the USA. Of course we were delighted to accept and soon found ourselves with a three-month tour of the USA on our books. So began a long and happy association with Columbia Artists, resulting in twelve three-month tours of the USA and Canada, presenting between fifty and fifty-five concerts on each tour.

Don and I always looked back on these tours as the highlight of our company's career. We agreed with Columbia Artists that we should change our company's name for the USA to 'The World of Gilbert & Sullivan' and for the following ten or twelve years we flew and drove all over the USA and Canada, sometimes with two tours in the one year. We often flew to New York in early September and toured until approximately the middle of December, covering approximately 15,000 miles on each tour. The artists usually consisted of Valerie Masterson, Helen Landis, John Cartier, Donald Adams and myself. The accompanist was Clive Timms. The three male singers were always the same, but we alternated the ladies between Angela Jenkins, Marilyn Hill Smith, Anna Burnadin, Anna Cooper and Jean Temperley. The pianists alternated between Clive Timms, Ian Kennedy and Michael Moores.

On arriving in New York, Don and I spent the first two days in the offices of Columbia Artists completing the tour arrangements and collecting the two cars – usually station wagons – making sure that they were fitted out for driving in the heat of the southern states and the freezing cold of the northern states in November and December.

The Exxon Petrol Company supplied us with a complete set of road maps for each of our tours, all clearly marked with our day-to-day journeys. Don and I were the licensed drivers, alternatively leading and following each day. The distances between concerts varied from two hundred to six hundred miles. On the long journeys we would stop off at a motel for the night and continue the journey next day. We would arrive in a town at approximately 4 p.m., check into our pre-booked Holiday Inn, Ricky Hyart or Western Motel, telephone the concert organiser to confirm that we had

Gilbert and Sullivan For All's first
venture abroad, with John Cartier,
Jean Hindmarsh and Anthony
Raffael.

arrived in the town, relax for an hour and then meet in the hotel
coffee shop for a meal before driving to the concert hall to prepare
the stage for our performance. The performances usually started at
8.15 p.m. or 8.30 p.m.

Let me explain what the Community Concerts really are. Columbia
Artists Management had area agents throughout the USA and Canada
who contacted the music clubs in both large and small towns. The
members of the clubs contributed so many dollars each year, and
depending how much money they had collected, the agent could tell
them what attractions they could afford. There were usually four
concerts in the autumn and winter season, and they discussed with
the agent the type of concert they would like – such as a small
orchestra, a solo singer, a pianist, an instrumental trio etc. I don't
know how Nancy Tuttle 'sold' our group to the various clubs; perhaps
the attraction was because we were from the UK and also that we

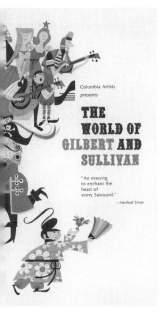

A new logo and a new name (below) for the USA – we became The World of Gilbert and Sullivan. This Columbia Artists playbill included several rave reviews (right).

THE WORLD OF GILBERT AND SULLIVAN

"Blow the trumpets . . . bang the brasses . . . tan-tan-ta-ra, tan-tara!!"

Once again from England comes THE WORLD OF GILBERT & SULLIVAN, that unique band of Savoyards which has so enchanted audiences in the U.S. and abroad with its sparkling anthology of G & S favorites. Cheering crowds of G & S buffs and just plain concert goers have thunderously echoed the joyous critical acclaim accorded these six stylish and witty artists for their delightful potpourri of songs and scenes. With consummate musicality and an unerring sense of theatre they recreate, without the need of costumes, scenery or props, the elegance, the zest, the satire and the sublime nonsense of the world of Gilbert & Sullivan.

"With gusto and abundant high spirits, The World of Gilbert and Sullivan came to Alice Tully Hall. The various solo and ensemble numbers were assembled in sequences that kept the pacing brisk, the balance good between familiar and comparatively rarefied material."—The New York Times

". . . they sang and danced—how they danced!—a healthy selection of arias and ensembles from nine of the operas. The pieces were tied together neatly with snippets of dialogue; some amiably inane and unrelated anecdotes; and a pair of overtures."
—Los Angeles Times

"The very model of a modern G&S celebration . . . It must have been a difficult chore to choose from the wealth of material offered by G&S for a single program. But the expertness with which this was done, together with the ease with which it was performed combined to double my admiration for this band of artists . . . Thank you all."
—Dallas Morning News

"Without the aid of scenery and props, and while wearing formal modern dress, the group sang, acted and charmed their way into the hearts of the audience members from the moment they appeared on stage. The ladies and the gentlemen demonstrated their musical skills in recreating the humorous and dramatic scenes from G&S favorites . . ."
—Rocky Mountain News, Denver, Colorado

"OVERFLOW CROWD GIVES STANDING OVATION (headline)
Gilbert and Sullivan Performance Simply Magnificent."
—The Phoenix Gazette, Phoenix, Arizona

COLUMBIA ARTISTS MANAGEMENT INC.   Personal Direction: MICHAEL RIES   Associate: Nancy P. Tuttle
165 West 57th Street, New York, N.Y. 10019 • (212) 247-6900

were singing Gilbert & Sullivan. However, she did it, and we proved to be very successful, receiving standing ovations in many towns.

We were nearly always invited to a reception after the concert and so it was usually around 1 a.m. when we got back to the motel. We were up again by 8 a.m. and back on the road by 9.30 a.m., heading for the next town on our tour. Sometimes the distance was too great between the towns to reach in one day and so we were booked into a motel on our route.

Publicity photographs taken for
the USA in an English country
garden. From left to right: Ian
Kennedy, Anna Cooper, me,
Marilyn Hill Smith, Donald
Adams, John Cartier.

We looked forward very much to this arrangement because it gave us a night off to relax, which usually meant meeting in the motel bar for a drink before going into the restaurant for a meal. We were generally back in our respective rooms by about 10 p.m. Don and I usually had rooms next to each other and so we would watch some TV and also discuss any business matter – there were nearly always some points to discuss. Don knocking on the wall always awakened me next morning.

On each of our tours there would be three or four orchestral concerts (these were not community concerts), which was a wonderful experience for our pianists, but gave Don and I much extra work that we could have done without. This included the transport of parts for a fifty-piece orchestra, as well as arranging for them to be sent on to the next orchestral venue so that the conductor could rehearse the orchestra before our arrival.

Our programme consisted of about twenty-six items from the various G & S operas with very important pick-up cues between each item. These concerts meant us arriving at the town at least two days before the concert date, when we would go through a piano rehearsal with the local conductor, followed the next day with an orchestral rehearsal, and then the performance the following day.

We performed in some wonderful venues, including three concerts at the famous Hollywood Bowl with the Los Angeles Philharmonic Orchestra, conducted on our first concert by Neville Marriner. We were voted the Highlight of the Season that year with an audience of approximately 18,000. Other orchestral concerts were at Tempe,

Myself and Don dancing a merry jig to 'You Understand' from 'Ruddigore'.

Arizona; El Paso, East Texas; Detroit, San Diego, San Antonio, Santa Barbara and the Mormon Tabernacle at Salt Lake City, Utah.

It was much easier for us when our own pianist was able to conduct these concerts because of the tempi's and the dialogue cues, and both Clive Timms and Ian Kennedy gained valuable experience on these tours.

On some occasions we had to hire drivers to take our cars to the next town because we could not make the trip in one day, driving across mountain ranges usually covered in snow. We would fly to the town and our cars would arrive two days later.

We drove seemingly endless miles across the plains and hills of Arizona, the Salt Lake flats of Utah and the plains of Nevada, from Los Angeles across Arizona into Louisiana to New Orleans, up into Missouri and the Carolinas to Pennsylvania and to Washington DC; and by the middle of November we were by passing New York on our way to Massachusetts and Maine, Vermont and New England, where we usually ran into the snow, which started in earnest about the beginning of December.

Our drives became more and more hazardous and I think one of our most frightening journeys was crossing the border from Canada into Michigan, when we ran into a horrendous blizzard. We were on our way to Ann Arbor in Michigan. We were not fitted with snow tyres and we were slipping and sliding on the freeway, passing cars that had skidded off the road into the wide ditch that separated the east and west carriageways. My passengers managed to film some of these accidents with my cine camera.

We finally reached the slip road into Ann Arbor and also ran into trouble. Cars were coming to a halt and then starting to slide backwards into the ditch. I did exactly the same. Local tractor drivers were making quite a lot of money, charging ten dollars to tow vehicles out of the ditch and up to the main road.

Eventually we arrived at our hotel and watching TV while checking in, we learned that the slip road we had used only thirty minutes earlier was now closed and the freeway had become impassable. We were very lucky because hundreds of people were stranded and had to abandon their cars, to be housed in schools, farm buildings etc. Our tour would have really been disrupted by this but luckily we were able to carry on. Next day our cars were completely buried in snow and it took a long time to clear them before we could drive to the concert.

We sang in towns in Wyoming and Colorado as high as 11,000 feet where we were supplied with oxygen tanks on both sides of the stage, and where we had to move about slowly because of the thin air. How we sang I don't know.

I remember waking up one morning in a small town in Connecticut at 6.30 a.m. and being hardly able open my room door because of the force of the snow blizzard outside. We were due to drive to Kennedy Airport. We managed to get some breakfast, load our cars and set off on a slipping, sliding drive to the outskirts of New York, where we handed over our cars to the Hertz people and boarded our aeroplane to fly to St Thomas in the Virgin Islands. We left in temperatures of twenty-five degrees and three hours later landed in temperatures of eighty-three degrees. We nearly died!

Nancy Tuttle in New York had thoughtfully given us a three-day break in St Thomas, where we gave one concert, to enable to us recover from a very exhausting tour. We had a marvellous time in St Thomas and it ended that particular tour in the USA.

I've just discovered a daily diary that I kept on the 1970 USA and Canada concert tour; here it is, just as I wrote it in 1970, at Alice's request.

'A Wand'ring Minstrel, I'

CHAPTER ELEVEN

USA Tour Diary, 1970

WONDERFUL FLIGHT ON BOARD TWA 747 Jumbo Jet – choice of two films – we chose 'Kelly's Heroes'. Free to walk up one side of the plane and down the other. We were not flying first class so we were not allowed in the upper deck bar.

Arrived dead on time at Kennedy Airport and met by CAMI (Columbia Artists Management Incorporated) Rep, with two cars to deliver us to the Wellington Hotel on West 57th Street, New York.

After resting for three hours, we all met and went for our first meal in the US, at 'Mama Leone's', after which we staggered back to the hotel and straight to bed.

Friday was an adjusting day, time- and food-wise etc. Don and I had conferences at the Columbia offices re the imminent tour. CAMI had thought of everything – comprehensive lists of concert dates, concert halls, representatives to contact on arrival at each town, time of performance and hotels booked. List No. 2 gave mileage between each town and approximate time of travel.

After an inspection of the Dodge station wagon hired for the tour, we decided it was not capacious enough for the comfort of six of us with our luggage, for a tour of 9–10,000 miles. Another car, a Plymouth Satellite was hired, Don and myself to be the drivers.

Saturday we left for our first concert at the Bushnell Auditorium, Hartford, Connecticut. A capacity house of 2,800 thrilled us with their reception of our performance, which we hoped was setting the seal for our tour ahead.

We stayed at the lovely Hilton Hotel and in the hour or so available to us, revisited Mark Twain's house and had quick look at Hartford's lovely buildings, new of course to Helen and Michael, who with his camera hoped to provide us with a pictorial record of the tour. We left Hartford at about lunchtime, not before I'd had a five-minute chat with film star Barbara Stanwyck whom I spotted in the hotel lobby, to go back to the Wellington, New York.

Monday: our second concert – Bridgeport, Connecticut – another successful concert with 1,500 audience, back to New York the same night. Tuesday free, with seats booked at a theatre by CAMI to see 'Applause, Applause' with Lauren Bacall – good show. Wednesday morning 8 a.m. we left for a difficult journey to Newark, New Jersey, for a 10 a.m. concert for schools – the kids loved it. We all sang marvellously well at that hour. Back to New York for our last night there before leaving on Thursday morning for Cinnaminson, New Jersey and the real start of our travels. Stayed in the Ivy Stone Motor Inn. Again concert well received in a beautiful auditorium. Left the next morning for the 635-mile drive to Clinton, South Carolina, stopping on the way in Washington where we had lunch and I renewed acquaintance with the city's beautiful buildings. A very helpful and knowledgeable taxi driver took John, Helen and myself on a lightning tour of the capital. Michael was off on his own with his camera and Don and Valerie chose to stay in the restaurant to wait for us. We arrived at our first Holiday Inn, at Henderson and drove on the next day to Clinton, South Carolina, arriving at the Gala Motor Inn after driving most of the trip on Interstate highways through continuous forestland. The Clinton Concert held on Sunday afternoon was well received. The temperature so far never fell below eighty degrees – phew! We were entertained in the organisers' home afterwards and after an early night, we left for Greenville next day, a journey of only forty-four miles. We settled in at the Pointsett Hotel and Don and I contacted the concert hosts – our first job at each new town – and arranged to view the concert hall. We drove out to the Firman University and we both thrilled with the lovely settings and buildings. We met our hosts and were entertained to lunch at the school's cafeteria and then went into the hall – another lovely building, the McAllister Auditorium. Our two concerts there were rapturously received and we were honoured with a standing ovation – a great thrill.

Our second day in Greenville we again spent on the campus – had lunch and were then taken to the organiser's home – halfway up a wooded mountain, where we were able to look down on the University campus and the surrounding country. By 3 p.m. we were back at the hotel to rest before our second concert.

We left next morning for Charleston, SC. We had been told that this was a lovely city, but our first glimpse disappointed us all. We arrived at about 2.30 p.m. and promptly got lost trying to find the Francis Marin Hotel. We checked in, had lunch, contacted the organisers and went to our rooms to rest.

We drove out to the Citadel, which proved to be a Military Academy, and were escorted by smart young lieutenants in sparkling white uniforms. We were apprehensive to learn that our audience would be comprised of officers and their wives and large contingents of men, who I felt sure had been ordered to attend the concert. (I was to be proved wrong in this assumption.) This was our smallest hall so far, 800 or so and within minutes of the start of the concert, we had those cadets right with us – a great concert and a standing ovation, led by General Duckett. Later, on stage the cadets and officers mingled with us to hear more of our English accents and of course, escorting our girls in strength to our cars and very reluctant to leave us.

We were escorted to General Duckett's home on the campus, and there entertained – everyone thrilled with the performance.

Next morning we were picked up by General Duckett's wife for a quick tour of Charleston – how wrong were our first impressions – the streets and the homes are among the most beautiful I have ever seen – Georgian style. We saw the location of the musical 'Porgy and Bess' and Catfish Row, and the Sumter Fort, where the first shots of the Civil War were fired. We were very grateful to Mrs Duckett for this lightning tour and we left Charleston converted to its beauty and quaintness.

On to Aiken, South Carolina, a small town, but again with an enormous auditorium. Heavy rain and sticky heat but a great concert.

Next day we moved on to Greenville, South Carolina where a very happy surprise was waiting for me in the form of a cablegram from Alice, informing me that my son's wife Margaret had given birth to a baby girl who was to be christened Susannah Louise. This news called for a celebration and we arranged with the manager of our hotel to put a bottle of champagne on ice for when we returned from our concert.

After an excellent concert we returned to the hotel, after the inevitable reception, and enjoyed wetting the new baby's head with champagne and everyone singing – 'O Susannah, don't you cry for me, for I'm off to Louisiana, with a banjo on my knee'. We left next morning for Atlanta, Georgia; what a city, beautiful shops and lovely buildings. We booked into our hotel, the Georgian Terrace Hotel, and after a rest and clean up, we met for our only real entertainment – eating. We were recommended to 'Mammy's Restaurant' and after a good dinner, we took a taxi back to the hotel and bed, having driven through the 'hippy' section of the town – quite weird.

Next morning, Don, Michael and myself took a bus tour of the city and its suburbs, which included the wonderful 'Cyclorama' display of the Battle of Atlanta. We also saw Martin Luther King's grave and church.

It was on this tour that the driver told us about 'Charity Hospital' and a rather sick saying about the number of killings that took place in a week – 'You stab 'em, we slab 'em'. Ouch!

The Memorial Arts Centre was the most wonderful building, but when we saw everyone arriving in full evening dress, we worried about the reaction to our concert – completely unfounded – we had a great night – the audience loved every minute of it and the whole audience rose to its feet applauding at the end of it. We were entertained to a cocktail party afterwards, where we met the British Consul.

Driving back to the hotel, the police diverted us – riots in Hippy Town were the reason and all night long police sirens and fire engines constantly roared past our rooms.

We left at 9 o'clock next morning and arrived in Mont, Alabama, for a concert at 2.30 p.m. Another packed house on a hot Sunday afternoon.

Next morning we left for the long drive to Dallas, Texas – we drove out of Alabama across the Mississippi and across the mighty Mississippi River, across Louisiana to Shreveport, where we stopped for the night, after 500 miles of driving. On the next day for the final 187 miles drive to Dallas – not the Dallas I remember from the war years but a fabulous skyscraper city with complicated flyovers and underpasses. You really had to know where you were headed – we didn't, and found ourselves in downtown Dallas, instead of on the North Express Freeway. We soon righted ourselves and arrived in the most sumptuous Holiday Inn – it could only be in Dallas.

What a small world; I found myself checking in at the desk at the side of Faye Griffis, a lady who had travelled in from Waco, and who was one of my best friends in America. She did not know we were staying at the Holiday Inn – what a delightful surprise.

I rang as many of my friends as I could and some came out to the Inn to see me, knowing it would be difficult after the concert. Before the concert, a large bouquet of Texas yellow roses was delivered to my dressing room, sent by my good friends the Brewer sisters from Terrell, where I had trained as a pilot. The concert was splendid; 2,800 in the Southern Methodist University Concert Hall, and afterwards it seemed that nearly that number came round to see me – what a reunion, it was difficult to talk with them all, but I managed it. I drove away to Terrell – about thirty miles – to spend the night with friends and the following morning I started a round of visits – all very nice. All had enjoyed the concert and all were delighted to see me on stage, and all were amazed that I could dance as well as sing!

At 2 p.m. I was at Love Field Airport ready to take off at 3 p.m. for San Antonio, more friends to see me off. I was very sad to leave after so short a visit. A long article in the *Dallas Morning News* welcomed me back and, fortunately, gave the concert a good review.

A short flight to San Antonio; met by the organisers and driven to the Crockett Motor Inn, across the road from the famous Alamo Mission.

We rehearsed that evening and all felt a bit worried about the sound. Met again the next morning and felt much better about everything. Our first concert that evening was a big success – again a standing ovation – even the orchestra stood for us. A great thrill and a job well done, confirmed by the press next day, one critic finishing his article with – 'Heck, I might even go back again on Saturday'.

Friday was spent sightseeing, and Don and I took a boat ride through the city on the San Antonio River, which winds through the town. We went up the Hemisfair Needle for lunch – 675 feet above the city, revolving slowly the while.

At 2.30 p.m. we were all picked up and driven to the San Jose Mission – beautiful. That evening there was an official cocktail party and dinner given by the Symphony Orchestral Society. Everyone was delighted with the concert and extra seats were to be arranged in the orchestra pit for overflow audience.

Saturday, I was taken to Austin to see more friends who had moved from Terrell. I had a lovely day with them at their home and all drove back to hear the concert that evening. A really great night – no doubt we shall be returning here.

Sunday morning we left the airport at 10.50 a.m. to fly back to Dallas, pick up the cars from Avis and set off for Texarkana – we thought. I first rang my friends in Dallas to say a fond farewell and then we set off – first to visit friends of Don and Valerie, who had a ranch near Tyler, Texas (G & S fans who had seen Don and Val in New York with the D'Oyly Cartes). They have a wonderful ranch with a glorious Southern style home. I was introduced to Suzette and Overton Shelmire and their children, Day and Clare – what a marvellous family.

We were all so relaxed that we accepted the invitation to stay the night and not go on to Texarkana. We all had a good night's rest and set off for Little Rock, Arkansas at 10 a.m. next morning.

The ranch is called 'Holly Tree Farm' and the day we were there was my birthday and I couldn't have had a nicer one without my family.

Arrived safely at Little Rock and after the usual telephone calls we had a splendid concert and were entertained afterwards at the home of the organisers.

We left Little Rock at 10 a.m. and drove back to Mississippi and across that splendid river once more, to Oxford, Mississippi, through mile after mile of cotton fields – looking as though they were covered in snow. I have a cine film of the gangs picking cotton.

We settled in once again at a Holiday Inn – we have unpacking and packing down to a fine art, and also we know where everything is to be found in these Inns.

Here is a description of a typical Holiday Inn room:

At least 25 feet by 15 feet
Three reading lamps

Two easy chairs
A 13-foot long desk and drawers with chair
Queen-size double bed
Coffee table
Bedside table with telephone and TV remote
Magic vibrator for sleep inducing
A 19-inch TV
Bathroom with always at least eleven towels
Large wardrobe
Air-conditioned
Beautifully carpeted and decorated

Oxford is a very small town grouped around a central town hall. The concert was in the University Campus and the audience was comprised mostly of students who received it tremendously. Isn't this the university where several students were shot and killed by the National Guard?

No reception afterwards and we were all pleased to be able to have a quick snack at 'Bemzo's Hamburger Shop' and back in our rooms by 11.30 p.m.

We left next morning at ten o'clock on the dot, and drove 250 miles in three and three quarter hours on the straightest Interstate highway we have struck – mile after mile of nothing except, of course, cotton fields. Once more over the Mississippi River skirting Memphis, Tennessee, where years before, I had landed my aircraft, had lunch and flew out again – this also happened at Little Rock!

The last thirty miles of this journey took us into lovely wooded country – the leaves are turning and the colours are wonderful. The sun is bright now, but we drove the first 150 miles in thick mist – so, they do have fog over here!

Another Holiday Inn – if we had swimsuits we'd be in the pool this afternoon it is so warm – seventy-five degrees.

Contact made with the hall and all arrangements made for tonight's concert. Another University campus – a splendid audience with a large percentage of young people and an amazing number of children from nine to twelve years, and they were all still there at the end of the concert!

We stopped off at a Pizza House on the way back to the Inn and inside six students who had heard our concert greeted us, and all enthused and thanked us for a wonderful evening. The pizzas were great, but Don and I settled for a couple of doughnuts. We all retired to our rooms and our own personal colour TV.

The next day, Thursday, Don and I went through our weekly routine of going to the bank and collecting the dollars that were always waiting for us – then we paid the artists and we were once more on the road by 11 a.m.

This business system never failed; CAMI had arranged that every Thursday in whatever town we were on that day, we attended the designated bank and introduced ourselves to the manager, who was expecting us, and collected our dollars. Don and I knew exactly what denominations we wanted and there were never any problems.

At 11 a.m., we were on our way through beautiful wooded country, trees now turning, brilliant sunshine for the first hundred miles and then into rain – pouring slashing rain, and on into St Louis, where we stopped on the outskirts at one of our favourite eating places – the Howard Johnson Road House. On Wednesdays, they served 'All the fried chicken you can eat for three dollars fifty', and on Monday 'All the fish you can eat for three dollars' – we loved it!

After many hours driving and 421 miles later, we stopped at our Holiday Inn in Iowa City, at 8.00 p.m. A clean-up, a meal and at 10.30 p.m. bed and an hour's TV.

At 9.30 a.m., we drove away from Iowa City, not having seen it, still raining and misty. No Interstate highway, just a narrow two-way road, driving with great care because of the width of our own cars and approaching cars and trucks. Why the two-way roads should be so narrow, I do not know.

The State of Iowa is purely agricultural – corn, cattle, hogs (pigs) and turkeys. Rich black soil and dozens of farmhouses, all beautifully painted red or white. We drove through lots of small towns – I suppose we would call them villages – very attractive streets with the autumn leaves lying thick on the ground in lovely colours. What a difference from four days ago when we were 1,000 miles further south – everything was still so green.

The atmosphere makes us all feel very homesick; dusk falling, lights coming on in the houses – I feel like stopping and knocking on any door and asking to be taken in to a family, or jumping on a plane and flying home.

We arrived in Minneapolis at 4.15 p.m., and settled into our hotel – we were met by two of the Symphony Orchestra officials. It is still raining hard so we must hope for a fine day tomorrow. This evening we are to have a meal at John Troy's home. Michael has gone off to hear a concert by the Symphony Orchestra – we are all too weary for that.

Saturday morning we all had a late breakfast and took a taxi to the Hilton Hotel, St Paul's (twin city of Minneapolis) where we were met by the press and taken up to the top of the Hilton to be photographed and interviewed. Back to our hotel where we split up to our own devices. Don and I made a sentimental journey to the Dykeman Hotel where he and Alice and I stayed on our tour with the D'Oyly Carte. We couldn't even get lunch there – the coffee shop was closed.

Sunday morning at ten we met in the lobby to be transported to the Northrop Auditorium for a rehearsal with the orchestra – all very satisfactory, except that the orchestra had to be cut down from seventy-five to fifty-five – too many fiddles etc.

Rehearsal finished at 12.30 p.m. and we returned to the hotel for lunch and a rest before returning to the auditorium for the 4 p.m. concert – a big success, with an audience of 3,200. This format with orchestra is very successful. Afterwards, we were entertained to dinner by the Minneapolis G & S Society, together with Symphony officials.

At 10.30 next morning, we left for Stevens Point, Wisconsin – at least we tried to, because forty-five minutes later we were still trying to find our way to Highway 94 East – finally we made it and after a drive of 195 miles we arrived at a super, super Holiday Inn – with their big sign lit up with the words, 'Welcome to the World of Gilbert & Sullivan' (this happened quite a few times at various Holiday Inns). I am looking out on to a beautiful indoor swimming pool.

Weather reports are becoming a little grim.

After the magnificent auditorium in Minneapolis, the High School hall and changing accommodation was a bit of a shock. We men were three floors under the hall in a teacher's room and the girls, one floor below the hall in a classroom. A great concert though and highly appreciated.

We left Stevens Point at eleven o'clock the following morning and drove through some of the most beautiful countryside yet – rolling hills covered with pine and fir trees – mile after mile of Christmas trees for sale – and beautiful lakes. Finally into La Crosse, Wisconsin itself, which sits astride the Mississippi River. Very autumnal weather and snow can be expected any time, according to the locals – we'll keep our fingers crossed.

A funny experience before leaving the Holiday Inn; I put a call through to the CAMI office in New York, and after a short wait a voice said, 'This is the White House, could I have your name please?' I replied, 'I am ringing New York, and you can't mean the White House, Washington.' The voice replied, 'Yes, this is the White House, Washington, there must be a mistake.' I replied, 'There certainly is a mistake, but please give my regards to President Kennedy,' and hung up.

We had a really enjoyable concert – a nice atmosphere – we had everyone swinging along with us in no time. A Mr Gilbert Schiliter came round at the interval, wanting to hug us all. He had already issued an invitation to the group to 'partake of a little libation and food at his house' after the concert. This we did and it was very

USA Tour Diary

enjoyable – the other guests were members of the Community Concert Association, and all were loud in their praise.

We left next day at noon after a look around the shops – we had only fifty-eight miles to drive to our next venue. A bright, sunny morning and really lovely wooded countryside for the drive out of Wisconsin into a corner of Minnesota and then in Decorah, Iowa. We telephoned the organiser as usual, a Mr Lunnewold. He came round to the motel and drove us to a large gymnasium, where the concert was to be held – all very reminiscent of the Sports Centre at Bracknell, Essex. The concert should be fun, in unusual surroundings. It was fun – when we arrived that evening, they had erected football-type stands all down one side of the arena and chairs down the centre – 1,500 in all. A stage of rostra had been set up and steps to get onto it. We would be in full view making our entrances and exits. I should say that half of the audience were students and by the interval a number of them decided they would be better off sitting on the floor in front of us. Lots of children there and they all seemed to enjoy it. According to the organisers who entertained us afterwards, it was the best evening they'd had for years and a splendid opening to their concert season. We seem to be giving the opening concert to quite a few Community Concert seasons.

I must say we are seeing the inside of a number of American houses, which is very good.

We left at 9 o'clock this morning for Fairfield, Iowa – two hundred miles to go and no Interstate highway – of course we see the country-side better on the ordinary roads and we can still keep up a good average speed.

We are all keeping remarkably fit and well in spite of the tight schedule and exhausting drives. The cars are behaving well but drinking gallons and gallons of gas (petrol).

A beautiful crisp, sunny morning – nearly all the leaves off the trees, but there are some that have turned a glorious yellow gold and are still clinging on and looking lovely. Arrived in Fairfield at 1.45 p.m. – dropped everyone off at the Dream Motel! Don and I left immediately to go to the local bank. By 4 p.m. we had completed the 'business of the day'. We had a late lunch and checked with the organisers and departed to our rooms to rest.

We arrived at the hall – again in a high school, to find our smallest audience yet (Fairfield is only a small town), about 250 and all so quiet about it all as if they did not know whether they were supposed to enjoy the concert or not. We were highly amused at this and the invitation we'd had for afterwards seemed as though it would be a dull affair. How wrong I was – they had loved every second of the concert and they admitted that the people around them knew little or nothing about G & S and although they enjoyed it, they were not sure whether we were being purposely funny or not. We were taken to the country club and within minutes, we were left in no doubt at all as to whether we had been successful or not. For many of the committee, it was the first time they had seen or heard G & S performed professionally and they were stunned by it.

We stayed until midnight and then we got up to leave after a very nice meal. We are making it a rule, at least Don and I are, that we make our excuses at midnight – we must think of the next day.

We had another invitation – we learned that no breakfast was served at our Dream Motel (our Dream Motel was turning out to be a 'Nightmare Hotel', because Don and I had missed out on lunch because they were closed – most unusual for America). The concert committee knew this and we were all invited back to the country club at 9.30 a.m. for breakfast. We will be all packed and ready to leave for Oskaloosa, Iowa, immediately after our pancakes and bacon – only fifty-three miles away!

We duly arrived in the town, which was built around a central square and checked into our motel. It was a very raw, cold day, so after a meal we got back to the motel at about 8 p.m. and I wasn't feeling too good – I had developed, of all things, boils under both arms. Next day a local doctor told me that they were caused by pores being blocked by talcum powder so, no more of that – in the meantime, it is very sore.

We drove to the concert hall at the appointed time of 6.45 p.m. on a very cold evening, to find every door locked and not a soul in sight. At seven, audience started to arrive and still no doors were open. After much dashing about – not by us – we finally got into the building at 7.20 p.m. You can imagine the panic for the girls to get ready – not helped by the worst dressing rooms we had seen.

After all this, we played to our smallest audience of the tour, about 250 people plus a very slippery stage – but we sailed through in our usual way and all enjoyed the concert. Not that we were told by anyone, because not one of the committee came to see us. We arrived, we sang, we left – that was Oskaloosa.

Sunday morning turned out beautiful and we left town on the dot of 9.30 a.m. and had a wonderful drive to Chicago – all on the Interstate – arriving at the hotel at 3.30 p.m., after stopping for lunch at our first 'Ramada Inn'.

We contacted the organisers and left the hotel at 5.45 p.m. to drive the twenty-three miles to Glen Ellyn, Illinois. A large auditorium this time and everything fine except for the so-called dressing rooms – dusty and dirty. How the girls will keep their dresses clean if we have much more of this, I don't know.

A large audience – the second largest audience in five years they

'A Wand'ring Minstrel, I'

said – the biggest being for the St Louis Symphony Orchestra. A great place to sing in and it holds 2,500 people. The concert went with a swing and we earned our sixth standing ovation. I've never seen so many children at a concert and they all came backstage together with dozens of adults after the performance, for autographs and to talk. We were entertained at a home afterwards – I don't know the name of our hosts – and given a wonderful meal, buffet style. We hadn't eaten since our lunch on the highway so you can imagine we did full justice to it. I also had my first cup of tea since arriving in America – because it was made in a teapot with boiling water.

A very enjoyable evening – we left at 11.45 p.m. and drove back the twenty-three miles to our hotel in Chicago, and so to bed.

I feel much better now and the boils are fast disappearing under my arms.

Monday morning and it's pouring down, so sightseeing will be difficult. It rained all day and the temperature was at forty-eight degrees. I walked out for an hour, determined to recall some of the sights I had seen on my last visit in 1962 with the D'Oyly Carte. I think the others have spent their time in the hotel or in some of the many fine shops. We left for the concert, still in pouring rain and we played to a full house – people having to be turned away who had seen our show the night before at Glen Ellyn, and wanted to again. Another lovely hall, the type we have learned to like and in which we seem to give of our best. We really don't like to be held up after a concert, but there is something quite depressing about being backstage, when we come out of our dressing rooms and find only the janitor waiting impatiently for us to get out of his building so that he can get home. Not a soul to be seen outside the hall – it's too cold. Back to the hotel and bed, ready for a 10 a.m. start in the morning.

We left Chicago at 10 a.m. as planned and left this great and beautiful city via the Eisenhower Expressway and within the hour we were speeding along the Ohio Turnpike at a constant speed of fifty-seven miles per hour, through flat wooded country where the trees have now turned into brilliant autumn colours – we were on our way to Wooster, Ohio. We arrived at the Wooster Inn at 6.15 p.m. – a really lovely Colonial-style building. All the rooms are furnished in this style, even the TV set and stand. We have had a splendid meal and at 9.15 p.m. we are all in our rooms. The US Senate elections are in full swing and every TV station is on to it so there is nothing for us to watch – so, it's a book and sleep.

We went into the town of Wooster for a couple of hours this morning and then at lunchtime Don and I went to a diner we had spotted, advertising 'All the fried chicken you can eat – one dollar fifty'. John and Michael also joined us.

Back to the Inn, rest, ready to leave at 6.45 p.m. to drive the fifteen miles to Oriville. Another High School Hall and changing in class-rooms. About four hundred people received our concert with enthusiasm. Before we had started, the school band had played to the audience for forty-five minutes. Lots of students stayed on for the concert and afterwards, the organisers were very thrilled and said that it was the biggest audience they had ever had and that it was the best reception any audience had given a concert in their eight years of Community Concerts.

One eighty-year-old man was heard to remark, 'I'm glad I'm not an animal and I'm very grateful and proud that I'm a human being, after seeing and hearing that concert'. That has got to be original.

Next day, an excellent drive to Flint, Michigan – Interstate all the way – all flat country – arrived about 6 p.m. Dinner and bed by nine o'clock – we all wanted to watch the nine o'clock movie, 'The Shuttered Room'.

A quiet day in Flint – everyone wanting to catch up with his or her bits of shopping, laundry, letter writing etc. Helen went to visit friends in Detroit.

Nancy Tuttle surprised us by arriving at 6.50 p.m. – no time to talk – straight to concert. A lovely 700-seat theatre in the middle of an art exhibition. A full house and a splendid concert with our seventh standing ovation. Glad Nancy was there to witness it. She told us that not a day passed without a letter or a telephone call from sponsors to tell us how successful our concerts were.

We left Flint at 9.30 a.m. next day and drove 300 miles on Interstate highways to reach the wonderful 'Mackinac Bridge', spanning the Lakes Michigan and Huron.

Real logging country – thousands of logs floating and rafted together in the water.

We arrived in Sault St Marie, Ontario. The concert was held in the most modern of theatres holding 850 people and it was full (why do these places not have dressing rooms?). We changed in the shower room!

A great concert and our eighth standing ovation. At the reception afterwards we learned that the audience was very knowledgeable re G & S and they loved every minute of it.

We left St Marie at 10.00 a.m. next day and drove 300 miles to Orillia, Ontario, through seemingly endless miles of winding road between endless lakes to left and right – quite beautiful and in lovely sunshine.

Our hotel, the Birchmere, is on the edge of Lake Couchiching and Lake Simcoe – really beautiful in the sunshine. There are black squirrels running about the lawns.

Another great concert – a full house and very responsive. There were twelve Toronto G & S people in the audience, including Doris Dingle, who entertained Alice and I on our tour with the Cartes.

We have now reached eight and a half standing ovations – only the circle stood last night. I wanted to call out to the people in the stalls, look round to the circle and see what is happening, but I didn't, so we'll have to settle for a half.

We are leaving at 11 a.m. this morning – only seventy-five miles to go and it's raining. We arrived in Peterborough, Ontario, at 1 p.m. and checked into our old friend, the Holiday Inn.

The concert was really great – the hall held 950 and it was full. A very friendly crowd and we all really slammed into it and the show sparkled. You'll never believe it – right in the middle of my John o'Groats story, we heard the wail of the bagpipes – there was quite a laugh – it was coming from the Armoury across the road.

There was a pleasant reception afterwards; it didn't match up to Nancy Tuttle's directive on the concert contracts that at any reception, before the artists socialised they had to be supplied with 'hot food and strong drink'. Back to the Inn and bed.

We left at 11.00 this morning for the short drive to Trenton, Ontario – pouring rain and very misty, arriving at the Dutch Mill Inn at 1 p.m. An excellent concert with lots of Scots and Lancashire people in the audience. Rain, rain and more rain – better than snow.

We left at 10.30 next morning and drove Interstate all the way to Montreal, where we booked into the Queens Hotel at about 4.30 p.m. Next day, still raining, we left at 12.30 p.m. and drove alongside the St Lawrence River to Riviera-de-Loup where we are settled in for the night at La Berge-du-Pont, overlooking the river. We'll see it in the morning – we hope!

Over 7,000 miles on the clock.

Yes, it's a clear morning, but snow falling in flurries. We left at 10 a.m. a lovely drive through hilly country covered with the short, I think, birch or larch trees, and on the outskirts of each small town, a mill for cutting logs – mountains of sawdust and mountains of logs, all about six feet in diameter. I believe they are cut into boards for packing cases.

The amazing thing about these small towns is that a magnificent church or cathedral – seemingly far too grand for what are obviously only poor towns – dominates each.

Out of the Province of Quebec now and into New Brunswick and we immediately alter our watches by one hour forward. It's strange, one side of the river is 3 p.m. and on the other it's 4 p.m. Snow still falling, but not very much.

An excellent concert with the full membership of 500 present. One of the best receptions yet – plenty of 'hot food and strong drink' – in my case coffee. Late to bed – the concert didn't start until 9 p.m. Rang Alice at 2.15 a.m.

Left at 10.00 next morning for Moncton, New Brunswick, through small snowstorms but after a hundred miles we ran out of them and we arrived in Moncton in pouring rain. This is the first town that I was stationed in during the war, and my first-ever radio broadcast was done from here.

I rang my good friends Jessie and her son Jack Armstrong, and visited with them during the evening – after twenty-eight years, we meet again.

A great concert – aren't they all – followed by a little get-together at the home of Elsie Bovier, the pianist who played for me all those years ago and who, with her mother, were in Scarborough, England last year and came to our concert there.

We left Moncton at 11 a.m. and arrived in Truro at lunchtime. Already, Jack Armstrong had been to see me and will be at the concert tonight. Another standing ovation and we thought the audience was a bit on the quiet side – I think we would rather have more enthusiasm during the concert – perhaps they are afraid of missing some of the words.

A small reception afterwards and it was held in the motel restaurant, so we are home.

The following morning at breakfast came a telephone call from Michael – he'd had a bad night and was feeling ill, could we please call a doctor. Fortunately, it was nothing serious – a stomach upset.

Jack Armstrong called round and I did a radio talk with him, how we first met etc, and what I had been doing since then.

We left Truro at 11 a.m. – a beautiful day – and drove the forty miles to New Glasgow, Nova Scotia. We could see for miles over the rolling hills, covered with the small fir trees and birch.

It was bitterly cold when we arrived and our rooms were the best places to be. An excellent concert and a nice reception afterwards in a very lovely home.

A drive of 165 miles through the most spectacular country – rolling hills and miles of lakes and waterways – across two causeways from one piece of land to another, until we reached Sydney, Nova Scotia, an industrial area, quite out of keeping with the surrounding beautiful countryside.

A great concert and yet another standing ovation – making nine and a half all together. A very nice reception afterwards I'm told – I did not attend because of a headache.

We left Sydney at 11 a.m. and drove back down the same stretch of the Trans-Canada Highway in glorious sunshine. We stopped several times to allow our photographers to take pictures.

U S A Tour Diary

We are now in Antigonish (accent on 'ti'), Nova Scotia, a Catholic university town. A really great concert – how do we keep it up? – the audience was with us right from the start. We were worried about the long low-ceilinged hall, but it turned out to be very easy to sing in.

At the reception afterwards, I met a Catholic priest who had seen me in 'The Student Prince' in Cork and also in opera at Sadler's Wells and in 'The Merry Widow' at the London Coliseum. Another Englishman there had seen me in 'The Merry Widow' and also in 'The Magic Flute' and 'The Marriage of Figaro'. A small world!

Helen Landis not at all well and we took her straight back to the hotel after the concert. Both Helen Landis and Valerie Masterson have borne up well on the tour and have sung beautifully at every concert.

We left Antigonish at 11 a.m. next day and drove through really frightening rainstorms and high winds – the cars behaving really well, no problems.

Helen still not well, upset stomach and a cold I think.

The weather is so bad that I shan't see much of Dartmouth or Halifax – except from my Holiday Inn room window. At least I can see the enormous suspension bridge between the two towns.

An excellent hall and a splendid concert, in spite of Helen being under the weather. It appears that the announcement of our concerts in the Community Series has led to an increase in the membership – not only here, but also in many other towns. The CAMI representative of this area was present and she couldn't wait to ring the New York office to say how much she had enjoyed the concert.

The inevitable reception followed – we all know the questions that we shall be asked and we all know the answers we shall give – it has to be done I suppose.

We are due to take off from the airport in Halifax to fly to St John's, Newfoundland at 5.30 p.m. so won't be leaving the hotel until 2 p.m.

It dawned a beautiful Sunday morning, so Don and I decided to walk across one of the suspension bridges – what a walk, frosty, clean air. Warships lying in mothballs and a general view of the docks.

At the airport, we abandoned our cars and took off at 5.30 p.m. – we can't believe it – a normal one-hour flight is going to take us four hours, with stops at Sydney, Nova Scotia, Deer Lake, Newfoundland, Gander, Newfoundland, and finally St John's. We arrived over Deer Lake in a snowstorm and what a shaky, bouncy landing we made, to the cheers of the local football team who were on the plane with us. The same thing at Gander, the pilots are used to it – but clear at St John's.

By 10.30 p.m. we were settled in our hotel. We rang the organisers who insisted on coming round to see us.

Monday morning at 11.30 a.m. a Mr Herbert Wyatt picked us up and took us on a sightseeing trip for a couple of hours, including Signal Hill, where Marconi received the first wireless signals from across the Atlantic.

A lovely auditorium and a splendid concert before the Lieutenant Governor, to whom we were presented at the reception after the concert. He was a really charming man and he had thoroughly enjoyed the concert – they want us back next year. We were invited to sign our names in the Government House Visitors Book.

The theatre manager wanted to put on a second concert on the Tuesday evening as we were free, but we couldn't consider it. We had to be up very early on Tuesday morning to catch the 7.35 a.m. flight to Halifax. We landed at 9 a.m. – collected our cars and drove the 260 miles to Saint John, New Brunswick through rain, fog and finally snow. Thank goodness we are free tonight and can rest.

Heavy snow is reported in the west of Ontario but we may yet escape it this far east. How long a day can be, just waiting (supposed to be relaxing) for the concert time. Finally it arrived and it was a splendid concert, wonderfully received. Helen is fit again – not that her performances have been affected by her illness.

This is a town where twice in every twenty-four hours, the river flows backwards. The tide comes in against the flow of the river – the tide wins and amid a great tumbling and tossing, the river is forced backwards.

On to Fredericton, New Brunswick, the next day. Another great concert and another standing ovation, making ten and a half in all. A nice reception afterwards and we were delighted to meet the CAMI rep who was speechless – or practically – with delight at our performance and couldn't wait to telephone Columbia in New York this morning.

By the way, this is where Lord Beaverbrook of our *Daily Express* newspaper was born. There is a statue of him in the main street.

We left the town at 11 a.m. A superb journey along the St John River, now starting to get frozen over, in brilliant sunshine – a light covering of snow and the fir forests – beautiful. We've never seen so much water in the three weeks we have been in Canada. Through the customs, and once more in the USA – we are lodged in the Trade Winds Motel, facing the sea – very nice. We are in Rockland, Maine.

Saturday was spent looking at the few shops here and then we drove to Camden, a lovely little village by the sea.

After a meal at the motel, we are all in our separate rooms by 9 p.m. in time for the movie. Sunday morning Don and I went for a walk in the keen frosty air, and at noon we went to see the concert hall, and everything OK. We were back there again at 2.15 p.m. in time for the concert at 3.00 p.m. It's strange to arrive at the school campus with not a soul or car in sight.

USA Tour Diary

We get ready for the concert and suddenly, the hall is packed with 800 people and about 400 cars parked outside. Within minutes of the end of the show, we are once more alone, getting changed – the hall is empty and when we walk out to our car there is not a soul in sight and the car park completely empty. We wonder if anything has happened and had there really been a concert. We were told some time later that evening and I don't know by whom, that it was the best concert they had ever had!

Well – we've had dinner and are back in our rooms once more and ready for TV – we have an early start tomorrow for the 220-mile drive to St Johnsbury, Vermont. We left early in pouring rain and for the first hundred miles we didn't see any of the beautiful, wooded hills with the clouds slowly clearing from the valleys.

We arrived in the lovely town of St Johnsbury and checked in.

The concert was a real success and the reception afterwards was very nice – everyone was thrilled with the concert and once again it seems to have been the best they have ever had.

One of the patrons, Senator Douglas Kitchell, owns amongst other things, a mountain called Mt Burke, and we were invited to go up to the ski area the next morning. We were duly collected and driven to the mountain, which had a light covering of snow. All our ambitions were realised – we got to ride a 'skidoo', virtually a two-seater tractor with skis fitted, plus a 500cc engine, which can drive it at 35 mph through the snow. I reached, as we all did, about 10 mph before I fell off. A delightful two hours was spent on the mountain, with breathtaking views in clear sunshine. The locals are amazed at the long autumn – normally at this time of the year in Vermont there is two feet of snow – the luck of G & S for All! We left the town at 2 p.m. and after a drive of only sixty miles, we are in Hanover, New Hampshire, a beautiful town and the theatre is out of this world. What lovely states are Maine, New Hampshire and Vermont!

An excellent concert before 850 people – no reception – so I was in my room by 11 p.m. and in bed by 11.45 p.m.

We left at eleven o'clock in the morning, with not a cloud in the sky and we drove the thirty miles to Springfield, Vermont, in about forty minutes and as we approached the Howard Johnson Motor Inn we could see, in large flashing letters – 'Welcome to the World of Gilbert & Sullivan'. What a wonderful surprise; naturally, we had photographs taken standing below it. A lovely Inn in beautiful surroundings – and what a picture postcard town – one can easily imagine Christmas here, the spires of the churches set against the wooded hills.

An audience of about 350 – but one of the most responsive yet – gave us another standing ovation, making ten and a half in all. Michael says that all the other audiences that didn't stand were 'sitting ovations'.

We had a reception at the home of the President of the Society with lots of lovely food. He was completely over the moon about our concert – he couldn't believe he had managed to get such talented artists (his words, not mine) to the small town of Springfield. The CAMI rep, Jack Trevithick, was also at our concert for the third time and was equally delighted. Someone remarked that Jack had booked another 'Trevithick Concert' – that's a new word for us.

Late to bed I'm, afraid, 1.30 a.m., and now it's 8.30 a.m. and we leave at 10 a.m. for Boston Massachusetts; it's another beautiful morning.

Arrived in Boston at about 1 p.m. and checked in at the Madison Motor Hotel. We collected again at 6.30 p.m. and drove the sixteen miles to Lynn, Massachusetts. Quite a large audience – a good concert and one of Michael's 'sitting ovations'. No reception afterwards, thank goodness.

Next day we were picked up the Smiths, good friends with whom Alice and I had stayed on our D'Oyly Carte Tour of 1962, at their home in Cambridge Massachusetts. It was Thursday, 19 November; America's Thanksgiving Day, and we were invited to their traditional turkey lunch. Very enjoyable and wonderful to see Mrs Smith and her two daughters Mary and Francis again.

Back at the hotel for 4 p.m. to rest before leaving again at 5.30 p.m. for the thirty-mile drive to North Andover, Massachusetts. The snow started in real earnest and we thought we were going to be caught after all – it didn't last, but it froze which was tricky.

Well. We have sung in all sorts of places both here and in the UK, but never have we performed in a Roman Catholic church. We couldn't believe it – we actually gave our concert from the high altar at the back of the communion rail, with the altar lights as stage lighting. The dancing that we do was very difficult on the highly polished tiles, especially for John Cartier, our comedy patter man. The church held 800 and it was packed to the doors. It turned out to be a very unusual, enjoyable concert. Two lovely bouquets were presented to the girls. A clear, frosty, slippy night for the drive back to Boston.

We leave at 10 a.m. for the last drive between concerts on this tour, to Milford, Connecticut. We are booked in at the Howard Johnson Motor Inn and the weather is bitter.

Some of the CAMI staff have arrived and we are off to give our last concert on the mainland. Excellent concert and about twenty-four people stood, so we consider we have achieved ten point five standing ovations.

After the concert we had a drink with Nancy and Co., and a snack – we were in bed at 1 a.m. and up again at 6.30 a.m. which came all too soon.

USA Tour Diary

I soon found out why I had difficulty in opening my motel room door on to the balcony – there was a howling blizzard, which had piled the snow against the door.

What a thing to happen for our last drive, which was to Kennedy Airport, on the outskirts of New York.

We took it very carefully indeed and we passed six pile-ups, including a car straddling the crash barrier. We said goodbye to our cars, which had served us so well and boarded the aircraft, which was to take us to the Virgin Islands. Three hours later we landed at St Thomas, the Virgin Islands, in tropical sunshine and the temperature at eighty degrees – unbelievable after the biting cold of New York. We were met at the airport, and immediately piled into two small cars for a sightseeing trip around St Thomas, before checking in at our motel. Poor John Cartier had developed a very bad headache on the flight, and now with our heavy clothes and the heat, it was made much worse. In his typical way, he didn't complain. What a fabulous place it is – as I write this, it is noisy with crickets outside.

Within fifteen minutes of checking in, Don and I were in the hotel pool – wonderful. We lay about on deck chairs and could feel the strains of the last ten weeks draining away from us.

It is dark now and the lights are on all over town and the harbour, which I can see from my room window. We are all going into town to find a place to eat – except for Johnny – this hotel hasn't a restaurant.

At 10 a.m. Monday morning, we took a taxi to a beach called Morning Star and there we swam in the Caribbean – absolutely out of this world. We lay in deck chairs, trying not to get too much sun, yet not wanting to leave it. I think we left just in time.

Today Tuesday, believe it or not, we have only had tiny glimpses of the sun and there have been heavy storms on the nearby Island of St Crois, but it is still very warm and I'm wearing only a tee shirt and slacks.

Don and I went for an hour's trip on a glass-bottomed boat that sailed slowly over the wonderful coral reefs. Afterwards, we went up a mountain in a cable car for a meal in Trader Vic's restaurant on top.

I have spent the whole afternoon waiting for the time to leave for our last concert of the tour – we are being picked up at 7 p.m. and now it is 6.20 p.m. I'll finish this later.

This is the noisiest hotel we have stayed in on the whole tour and last night I couldn't sleep much because of it – what a din! Two reasons: the noise of the crickets and millions of other insects chirping and squeaking all night long – even now at 6 p.m., I can hardly think for the noise. Tropical trees surround us and they are full of little things that you never see, but who make an absolute orchestra of sound.

The second reason for my lack of sleep was the human one of shouting and cheering in the early hours and which I thought was a riot but was actually an open air sports arena where Mohammed Ali was fighting Joe Frazier – I wish I had known.

Certainly not one of the best halls to finish our tour in – the usual high school auditorium and we changed in the usual classrooms.

A great concert though, and all of us on top form – an excellent reception afterwards at the Brittany Hotel – a real sit-down dinner to end our eleven-week marathon tour.

Wednesday morning and still dull and raining so, no beach again, instead last minute shopping before we are collected at 12.30 p.m. to be taken to the airport for our flight to New York, where Nancy met us to see us safely off on our flight home, with promises of future tours ringing in our ears.

'A Wand'ring Minstrel, I'

CHAPTER TWELVE

Tour Highlights

I THINK IT WILL BE VERY DIFFICULT to separate the many tours of the USA and Canada from the one described in my diary, which gives a good idea of the day-to-day happenings, so I will write about our tours in general and their various highlights.

In August 1971 we gave our first concert at the Hollywood Bowl, with Neville Marriner conducting the Los Angeles Philharmonic Orchestra. The day before the Bowl concert, we gave a concert in San Diego with the same orchestra and conductor.

I don't think I shall ever forget the overwhelming feelings I had when I walked out on the stage of that enormous shell-shaped structure in front of an audience of nearly 18,000, which seemed to disappear skywards up the mountainside.

In front of the stage was an ornamental lake with underwater coloured lighting, followed by fifty or so rows of picnic tables and chairs, each with a table lamp. Families and friends brought their own picnic or purchased one on the premises, which they could enjoy before or during the performance. My friend Michael Kirby, the skater, and his wife Mary and their children had booked one of these tables and I was able to chat with them before the concert. These tables were followed by row upon row of bench-like seats for thousands of people, with escalators running up the side of the arena.

I remember that during the interval of that first concert, Danny Kaye came into the ante-room just off stage and shouted to the stage staff, 'For God's sake get more light on the singers – if you can't see them, you can't hear them!' His language was a bit fruitier than that, but he was quite right. The sound system was very good because Don and I not only introduced each item, we also told anecdotes and from the audience reaction, they could definitely hear our spoken word.

This was the concert that was voted in the press to be the highlight of that Hollywood Bowl season.

It was in Hollywood that I first met Milt Larson, the owner of the Magic Castle on Sunset Boulevard, the Mecca of all magicians worldwide; and Dr Thomas Heric, who was also involved in the Magic Castle, and the Mayfair Music Hall in Santa Monica. Tom Heric was, and still is, a great admirer of G & S and possesses one of the finest G & S memorabilia collections in the world. They were great friends and admirers of Donald Adams and I was honoured to be accepted into their circle of friends.

Tom Heric had written a script on the lives of Gilbert and Sullivan and Milt Larson and Tom invited Don and I to record it in his private studio, with a view to marketing it on LP records. It told their story from their first meeting until their deaths. Don and I were to speak as ourselves and then as Gilbert and Sullivan – Don as Gilbert and myself as Sullivan. We were given that afternoon to practise it and then after our concert at the Bowl on the Saturday evening, we went back to the studio on Sunday morning and recorded it.

It sold reasonably well in the US and I'm sure it would have sold even better in the UK, but it was difficult and expensive to market. The copyright has since been transferred to me and it is now issued on cassette.

Our first concert in Dallas, Texas was especially good for me, as I had spent nearly two years of my war service in and around Dallas learning to fly and afterwards as a flying instructor in the American Air Force. After having studied singing at the city's Hockaday School of Music, and sung in Dallas as an amateur many times, it was marvellous to be back there as a professional. I was presented with a bouquet of yellow Texas roses to celebrate my return to the city.

We were able to divert off the Expressway on our way to San Antonio for our next date to visit Terrell and its air field, where 2,000 other RAF pilots and I were trained. We also visited the Memorial Park where a number of my comrades were buried, as a result of fatal flying accidents.

We also gave three or four concerts at the Stanford University, Palo Alto, California, about thirty miles out of San Francisco, and from there we flew up to Alaska to give concerts in both Anchorage and Fairbanks, taking professional G & S to Alaska for the first time.

I remember an amusing incident on the flight up to Alaska. Don and I were sitting on the port side of the aeroplane where there was a row of three seats. Don sat on the aisle seat with myself in the middle seat – there was already a man sitting in the window seat. About thirty minutes into the flight, I got into conversation with this rather tough-looking chap, who turned out to be an American. He told me he was a truck driver and that he was employed on the oil pipeline that was being laid from Prudo Bay down to Anchorage. He was returning there after a two-week break at home. He then asked me if Don and I were also going up there to work on the pipeline. I told him that we were part of a British opera group and we were going to give concerts in Fairbanks and Anchorage, and that we were known as The World of Gilbert & Sullivan. He leaned forward to look at Don, who was fast asleep, and said, 'I bet he's Gilbert'.

Tour Highlights

That story reminds me of others that we used to include in our concert programme. Here is a sample of them; unfortunately, I cannot remember all of Don's stories. Some of Don's stories and mine were a little truer than others and I can't vouch for this one.

A small village in the north of England, which shall be nameless, decided to form a choral society and they advertised in *The Times* and *The Telegraph* for a musical director. They had only one reply, from a young man living in London. He duly arrived in the village at the appointed time to meet the committee at the local pub. He was shown into a room where they were sitting and after introducing himself, he made the request that the interview be as brief as possible because he had to catch the 5.05 p.m. train back to London.

'Right,' said the Chairman, 'we would like to ask you a few questions – what do you know about this fellow, Beethoven?' 'Well,' said the young man, 'I happen to know him quite well, we were at the same school together.' 'Very good,' said the Chairman. 'What about Mozart, do you know anything about him?' 'I certainly do, we are members of the same club in London.'

'That's good; now then, what about Arthur Sullivan?' 'I'm afraid I don't know him myself, but my father often plays a round of golf with him.'

'Well,' said the Chairman, 'I don't think we need to know any more about you; will you please wait outside for a minute while we have a little discussion?'

'Yes, I will, but please could I remind you that I really must catch the 5.05 train back to London.'

'We'll only keep you a couple of minutes.' The Chairman then turned to one of the committee and said, 'What do you think of that young man George?' 'Well, for my money,' said George, 'I don't think he is a very truthful young man.' 'Not very truthful?' said the Chairman. 'Whatever makes you think that?'

'Well,' said George, 'there's no 5.05 train back to London.'

A baritone on tour with an opera company developed a bad throat and he went to see a local doctor, who diagnosed laryngitis. He gave him a prescription and also recommended that he had lots of ice-cream. He left the prescription with a chemist and then found an ice-cream shop. He spoke to the man behind the counter and asked him, in a very gruff voice, what flavour ice-cream he had. The man replied, also in a very gruff voice, that he had strawberry and vanilla. The singer replied, 'Have you got laryngitis too?'

'No,' replied the man, 'only strawberry and vanilla.'

Here are few more of Don's stories:

Sir Thomas Beecham was rehearsing his orchestra at the West Hampstead Studios. It was a very foggy morning and after waiting for half an hour for latecomers to arrive, he finally announced that he must get on with the rehearsal. Halfway through the first piece, he stopped the players and said that the principal horn player was playing too loudly.

The orchestra leader said, 'Sir Thomas, the French horn player hasn't arrived yet.'

After a few moments' pause, Sir Thomas then said: 'Well, when he does arrive, tell him he still plays too loud.'

One Boxing Day, Don, who lived in Cambridge, caught a train into London for a matinée performance of 'The Mikado' at the Princes Theatre. All went well until the train reached Bishop's Stortford, where it stopped for half an hour.

As Don didn't appear until well into the second act of 'The Mikado', he wasn't unduly worried. When it stopped again outside Liverpool Street Station, and an hour later it was still there, he began to get really bothered and he went through to the bar to get a strong cup of coffee or a whisky to calm his nerves.

A passenger standing at the bar said, 'This is very annoying, I have brought my wife and family all the way from Bishop's Stortford to see a performance of 'The Mikado' and here we are stuck on this train.'

Don replied, 'I don't know what you are worried about – I *am* the Mikado!'

He always added a tailpiece to the story that he did arrive in time, much to his understudy's frustration.

The D'Oyly Carte Company was playing at the Opera House in Cork. At the beginning of the second act of 'Ruddigore', Dick Dauntless and his new bride, Rose Maybud, run onto the stage followed by all the bridesmaids. Suddenly the bad Baronet, Sir Ruthven Murgatroyd, threatens Rose Maybud. Dick Dauntless steps forward with these words: 'Hold!' he says, 'We are prepared for this,' and takes out from his uniform, of all things in Southern Ireland, a Union Jack, and proceeds to wave it over Rose Maybud's head with these words: 'Here is a flag that none dare defy, and while this glorious rag floats over Rose Maybud's head, the man does not live who would dare to lay unlicensed hands upon her.'

An Irish voice called down from the gallery: 'Sez you.'

Our first concert on one of the Scottish tours was in the border town of Hawick. It was a cold and wet night and not many people were turning up for the concert; in fact, we couldn't hear any movement in the hall at all. We were all on stage waiting for the curtain to go up, when Norman Meadmore ran on, pretending to be all breathless, to announce to us that we would have to hold the curtain because there were another 'three people pouring in'.

'A Wand'ring Minstrel, I'

Again we were in Scotland and we were due to give an afternoon concert in the open air at Craigtoun Park, St Andrews. Unfortunately, it was raining so hard that the concert had to be cancelled, so we artists went to the pictures instead. The next day, a newspaper carried an excellent review of the performance that never took place, which amused us but, I understand, cost the critic his job.

We once arrived in a small town called Prescott, Arizona and I was talking to one of the committee members who told me that she had telephoned an elderly lady of the concert group, who lived a little way out of town, to inquire if she intended to come to our concert. The lady had replied that she didn't want to make the journey unless she could be assured that the 'British group' had arrived safely and that they were all well and that no understudies would be appearing, and that Mr Gilbert and Mr Sullivan would definitely be performing.

Even in our own country there are people who have not heard of Gilbert & Sullivan. We were on tour in Scotland and had been singing in the town of Wick, only a few miles from John o'Groats. The next morning, we drove up there, and like all tourists we decided to have our photographs taken around the signpost they have there, with all the arms pointing to various points north, south, east and west, giving the mileage, including one pointing south to London – 600 miles.

We all gathered round the sign ready to be photographed, when the man looked up from his camera and said, 'It would be nice if two of the three men could stand on either side of the signpost – which is Gilbert and which is Sullivan?'

Again, in Scotland: Don and I always took our golf clubs on the Scottish tours and we were walking off the eighteenth green back to

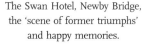

The Swan Hotel, Newby Bridge, the 'scene of former triumphs' and happy memories.

the club house of a course in Aberdour, when we were passed by a couple of players going out to the first tee. As we passed, one of the men said, 'Aren't you Thomas Round?' After the pleasant shock of being recognised on a golf course, I replied, 'Yes I am, but I don't seem to recognise you.' He replied, 'We were in the same squadron in the Air Force, and I always remember you saying that when you were demobbed you were going to make a career in singing.' I replied, 'Yes, I do remember saying that.' He replied, 'Well, what happened?'

In 1981 Gilbert & Sullivan for All were approached by James Birtlin, the manager of the Swan Hotel at Newby Bridge in the Lake District. He and his wife Jill were, and still are, great admirers of the Gilbert & Sullivan operas and he wanted to ask if we would be interested in presenting a Gilbert & Sullivan weekend at his hotel.

Don and I were always open to new ideas so of course we agreed to discuss the project. The result was that in November 1981, we successfully presented the first of eleven three-day weekends at the Swan, nine while James and Jill were managers and two under the new management. The weekends proved very successful so much so that we artists agreed to be placed in nearby hotels, to provide more rooms for the guests. I also celebrated my forty – and later my fifty – years as a professional with James and Jill.

One incident that will never be forgotten occurred in November 1991. The usual format was for me to present a solo entertainment on the Friday evening, followed by a film show on the Saturday morning.

The other artists usually arrived in time for lunch on the Saturday, followed by a rehearsal for the evening concert that started about 9.30 p.m. after the banquet. How-

Thomas celebrates a Round 50 in style

OPERATIC tenor Thomas Round will celebrate half a century as a professional singer in style at the weekend.

During a long and celebrated career since leaving Barrow to join the famous D'Oyly Carte Opera Company, Mr Round has performed with many of the world's leading conductors and orchestras.

Last week, at the age of 79, Mr Round gave one of his renowned Gilbert and Sullivan performances before 2,000 people in Birmingham Symphony Hall.

This weekend he will be performing before a more modest but, nevertheless, just as enthusiastic audience of 100 when he stars in an Gilbert and Sullivan festival at the Swan Hotel, Newby Bridge, to mark his 50th anniversary.

On Friday Mr Round, former principal tenor with the Sadlers Wells Opera Company, will be giving a concert and recount his time with the D'Oyly Carte.

On Saturday morning Mr Round, whose wife Alice is also from Barrow, will show films about Gilbert and Sullivan before joining an all-star cast for a concert spectacular later that evening.

ever, on the Saturday morning of 15 November, James and I went to Barrow-in-Furness – about fifteen miles away – to give an interview on Radio Cumbria. We returned to the hotel at lunchtime and as I walked over the cobbled entrance to the hotel door, I tripped and fell with my right foot trapped under the doorstep. I felt a tearing sensation in my lower right leg, but did not mention my fall to the group, who had just arrived, and it wasn't until during the afternoon rehearsal that I felt increasing pain and realised that I was finding it very difficult to move. We decided to have a look at my leg and we were all horrified to see that it was very badly swollen. James immediately stated that we should see a doctor he knew in nearby Backbarrow. Of course I had to agree and promising Don and the other artists that I would be back in time for the concert, I was helped into James's car and driven to the surgery. The doctor took one look at my leg and said that I should proceed without delay to the Abbey Park Hospital in Barrow for an immediate operation because I was bleeding heavily inside my leg. When I told him that I had to perform in a concert that evening, he flatly stated that I could do the concert and risk losing my foot, or go to the hospital. It seems that because there was no external cut in my leg, there was no escape for the blood, which had started to compress the arteries leading to my foot and so was starving my foot of its supply.

We sped off to the hospital and after an examination by the resident doctor – it was now early evening – the registrar was called in, who in turn contacted the consultant surgeon. By the time he arrived my lower leg resembled a rugby football and he said that we had approximately two hours in which to save my foot and that I was to be prepared for an immediate operation. It took place at about 10 p.m. I won't go into the gory details, but it was to be twelve days later before I was allowed to leave the hospital, with my leg still in plaster and wearing a surgical boot. I performed in numerous concerts up and down the country until the plaster was finally removed.

A year and a half later, again at the Swan, I quoted Katisha's lines in Act II of 'The Mikado', when she states that 'I have a left shoulder blade that is a miracle of loveliness, people come miles to see it – it is on view Tuesdays and Fridays, on presentation of Visiting Card.' I changed the lines to, 'I have a six–inch scar on my right leg that people come miles to see – it is on view throughout this weekend on presentation of a Mastercard'.

Even though I shall shortly be presenting my fourth Gilbert & Sullivan Weekend in the lovely town of Richmond, North Yorkshire, organised by my good friend, Les Jobson, I shall never forget our weekends in the Lake District.

Our weekends always finish with a Sunday morning Forum, when we have a question and answer session from the audience, which is quite fun. After a superb buffet lunch the artists and guests depart to cries of, 'Here's to the next time.'

CHAPTER THIRTEEN

'Oh Don't The Days Seem Lank and Long, When All Goes Right and Nothing Goes Wrong?'

*I*MENTIONED EARLIER that after a couple of days in New York, arranging the business side of the US tour, we would finally wave goodbye to Nancy Tuttle and set off for our first concert. Nancy had always done a good job of arranging our travel routes and hotels and so on, and everything always worked smoothly. The artists were generally happy, apart from the little irritating upsets as a result of us living in such an unusual way, or one of us not feeling too good. But on a long tour there were bound to be a few problems and minor disasters.

Possibly the worst moments were trying to get away from the motels on the time that Don and I had previously arranged – say 8 to 9 a.m., depending on how far we had to travel that day. I'm sure it was more difficult for the two girls to be ready on time and Don, John and myself would be standing around the cars with our cases ready to be loaded in a certain way, or else we couldn't get it all in the two boots. One of the girls would remember that she had left something in their room or that they hadn't paid their hotel bill. Don used to get really uptight and I remember one morning my car was loaded up and my group settled in the car. Don was still waiting impatiently for Jean Temperley, who was running late and had left her big case out of the boot while she dashed off to pay her bill. Don was furious, and had got into the car, leaving Jean to load her own final case herself. He had completely forgotten this and decided to reverse out of the parking space while he was waiting for her. We frantically tried to signal for him to stop, but it was too late and he reversed right over Jean's case. The next few minutes were very fraught – Jean was very angry to see her squashed case and Don was torn between being angry and also sorry for what he had done. I never knew what the atmosphere was like in his car, until we stopped for lunch when I was told that there had been 'no-speakies'.

There was another incident involving Don's car. After each concert

The Days Seem Lank and Long

there was nearly always a reception, either in the motel or at one of the organisers' homes. This was all very nice, of course, but when the concert didn't start until 8.15 p.m. and didn't end until turned 10.30, it was nearly 11.30 p.m. before we arrived at the reception, then around 1 a.m. before we got back to our motel. We had to be up again before 8 a.m. – so the reception issue became a bone of contention among the artists. Don and I felt obliged to accept the invitations, but the others attended sometimes under protest.

One evening Valerie stated quite flatly that she didn't want to attend any more receptions and wanted to be taken straight back to the motel after each concert. We drove back to the motel in stony silence, dropped Valerie off and then went on to the reception.

The atmosphere was still not very good the next morning, and there was a decidedly frosty feeling in Don's car as we set off. Don was leading that day and after about fifty miles, we were driving through a small town when Don signalled that he was stopping. I pulled up behind him thinking that someone wanted a toilet or to buy something. Don walked back to my car, and I could see that something was badly wrong. I rolled down my window and he announced that he would have to drive back to the motel because Valerie had left her evening dress hanging behind her bathroom door. It was nearly two hours later before we could continue on our way.

Another incident, this time involving my car, happened when we were loading the cars outside the hotel in Hertford, Connecticut. I had opened the boot of my car and the entire luggage was loaded. I took off my jacket, put it on top of the cases, and slammed the lid down – completely forgetting that I had put the ignition keys in my jacket pocket and they were now securely locked inside the boot. There was no way in, except to force the lock or break in through the back seats in some way. The hotel desk telephoned a garage and a mechanic finally came out. After trying countless keys, he decided that the only way was to get through to the boot by the back seats. By the way, the car doors were still locked, but he managed to get one of the windows down and get a door opened. After an age, he managed to prise the back of the seat forward a few inches, which allowed him to put his arm through, grab my jacket and pull it through into the car. That incident lost us one and a half hours and cost me thirty dollars.

On one tour, Don and I were very unhappy with our cars. Avis in New York had been particularly unhelpful. After all, we were hiring the cars for approximately three months and virtually living in them, driving thousands of miles from tropical heat into freezing conditions and we wanted all the comfort we could get – like air conditioning, a good heating system and cloth seats (plastic seats were awful in hot weather).

We had been on the road for about two weeks and were driving along a road way out in the wilds, when there was a loud bang and my car swerved badly. A rear tyre had burst. We unloaded the boot to get at the spare tyre, only to find that the wheel didn't even belong to the car. Our two cars, fortunately, were the same make and when we unloaded Don's car we found his spare wheel was the correct one. When we reached the next town, we bought two new wheels and tyres.

Incredibly, a few days later when it was my day for leading, I glanced in my rear mirror just in time to see pieces of tyre flying off from one of Don's front wheels and his car swerving all over the road. He managed to pull up safely and went through the procedure of changing the wheel while thanking our lucky stars that we hadn't had a serious accident. Poor John Cartier, who was helping with the change, had taken his expensive wristwatch off and put it on the roof of the car for safety. He completely forgot it and we were many miles on our way when he remembered about it. It was hopeless to think that we could ever find it, even if we'd had the time to retrace our steps.

You can imagine the reports that went to Nancy in New York, and then to Avis. Nancy, of course, claimed the cost of the new tyres from them.

But, as I said earlier, generally all went well, so much so that Nancy used to ring us at our motel, many hundreds of miles from New York, to enquire if everything was OK with us. When we replied that all was well and was there a problem, she replied that she had never had a group on a tour that didn't contact her virtually every week with some complaint or other, and she was worrying because we hadn't been telephoning her!

Nancy and her co-directors would always try to catch the last concert of a tour, which was usually within a few miles of New York, and they were always genuinely amazed that we seemed as fresh as though it was the start of the tour – a great compliment.

Spreading Our Wings

The summer of 1972 proved to be very hectic in the life of Gilbert & Sullivan for All and involved Alice in a very important way.

CAMI had booked us for a short tour of the USA, which would last just less than one month, starting with a second concert at the Hollywood Bowl. We would then return to the UK have a three-week break, during which we would fulfil a few concert dates and then return to the USA for an eleven-week tour, taking us to the middle of December.

The Days Seem Lank and Long

Alice and I discussed this busy summer and autumn and decided that she should pay a long visit to her sister Jenny, in Auckland, New Zealand.

Our first concert was to be at the Hollywood Bowl on Saturday, 15 July and Alice was to accompany us. Again, the concert was very successful before an audience of 14,000 and with our own musical director, Ian Kennedy, conducting the orchestra. Alice was thrilled to see me at the Bowl.

We then flew to Palo Alto, California, where we gave six concerts at the Stanford University's Dinklespiel Auditorium. Palo Alto is a lovely town and we very much enjoyed our stay there. The daughter of the former conductor of the BBC Variety Orchestra, Charlie Shadwell, ran an 'English Shop' selling everything English: jams, tea, cakes, scones, and a café serving Lancashire hotpot, sausage and mash, roast beef and Yorkshire pudding, and the like – we visited her shop quite often.

I remember one concert when there was no reception afterwards, and we drove back to our Ricky Hyatt Motel to find that Alice had prepared a surprise Kentucky Fried Chicken party – better than any reception.

From Palo Alto we flew to Tempe, Arizona, where the temperature rose to 105 degrees. We stayed in a Howard Johnson Motel and we were welcomed by their large outside screen saying: 'Welcome to The World of Gilbert & Sullivan.' I have cine film of this, with Alice and me standing in front of the screen. I also have film of the beautiful, circular Pink Stone Music Theatre, where we sang on July 25.

On 26 July, Alice flew on to Auckland. We flew up to New York to fulfil several more concert dates and then flew back to the UK, where we had more concerts, before I was able to fly out to Auckland to join Alice and her sister and husband for a three-week holiday. After my holiday, during which we hired a car and toured all around the North Island, I flew back to New York to join Don for another eleven-week tour, which would finish on 10 December.

Alice had taken some information about G & S for All with her to Auckland, including programmes and reviews, and had done some excellent spadework on our behalf. She had contacted a concert agency called Impact Talent Associates who expressed an interest in our concerts and arranged for them to meet me when I arrived in Auckland.

Shortly after arriving in New Zealand, I had my first meeting with Impact Talent. Before I left to fly to New York, we had virtually finalised our first tour of Australia, New Zealand and the Far East, with the added attraction of possibly taking part in the Inaugural Ceremonies of the new Sydney Opera House.

We arrived in Auckland on 1 August 1974 but our flight was fraught with difficulties. I think we first landed at Brisbane where we were supposed to change planes to fly on to Sydney, but owing to an industrial dispute, all commercial flights had been cancelled and all passengers were to be accommodated in a hotel for the night and to be taken back to the airport the next morning.

However, the strike was still on, but our tour manager, Robert Raymond, had been busy. He had contacted a small commercial airline owned by Jack Brabham – a former racing driver – who ran a fleet of small seven-seater aircraft. When we arrived at the airport there was a call over the sound system requesting that the Gilbert & Sullivan for All Company should report immediately to the departure lounge.

We made our way as requested and in full view of the hundreds of frustrated passengers, we were led out to a small aircraft and a few minutes later, we were on our way to Sydney.

We landed at a private airfield and were transported into Sydney only twenty-four hours before we were due to perform at the Opera House. The concert was very successful, before 2,500 in the beautiful new concert hall.

However, there was a new problem awaiting Don and me in the form of a letter from Frederic Lloyd, the general manager of the D'Oyly Carte Company, enclosing a ticket for our concert in the Opera House.

Unbeknown to Don and I, our manager had authorised the printing of the posters and theatre tickets to read that the concert was being presented by 'Stars of the D'Oyly Carte Opera Company', instead of by 'Former Stars'. We'd had this kind of problem before and we were always very careful with the form of billing we sent out and also, we always asked to see proofs of the billing before printing.

We had followed this procedure for this tour, but had not seen any proofs for the Sydney Concert, and our manager had purposely used the above wording.

Mr Lloyd's letter stated that the D'Oyly Carte Company would take legal action to cancel our tour unless they received definite assurance that the billing would be corrected immediately. Of course it was too late to do anything about the Opera House concert and after a very fierce discussion with our manager, he very reluctantly agreed to alter the billing for our future concerts.

We wrote to Mr Lloyd apologising for the mistake and enclosing the form of billing that Don and I had submitted, explaining that we had been powerless to do anything about it. We never heard anything further from London and assumed that they were satisfied with our explanation.

After the trauma of our journey to Sydney, the long hours of flying, the strain of the billing problem and the tension of performing on

The Days Seem Lank and Long

On tour in Australia, we made a stop off to refuel our private jet at Wagga Wagga. From left to right: Clive Timms, John Cartier, Robert Raymond (manager), Anna Beradin, Donald Adams, me and Helen Landis.

such a prestigious occasion, we were still able to present a successful concert; but the next day, I had practically lost my voice.

The airport strike was still on and our journeys to the other towns in Australia continued in Jack Brabham's aircraft. Our manager did us proud because there were always champagne and exotic fruits on board to cheer us up. I had been promoted to the co-pilot's seat to make more room in the small saloon and I was able to take the controls on several occasions, which was a great thrill for me and took my mind off my voice problems.

I took lots of cine film of our flights along the various coastlines and our very friendly pilot dropped down to 500 feet on several occasions to give me close-up shots of the Australian countryside.

I can't remember what caused the delay, but we arrived at one major town very much behind time and we arrived at the concert hall only thirty minutes before the start. The organisers were relieved to receive a call from our manager that we had landed and were on our way to the hall.

I remember when we landed at Perth, we climbed out of our little aircraft and started to walk towards a small reception group of people. We were all puzzled that they seemed to be performing some kind of ritual hand movements about their heads. We soon found out why, and joined in the same ritual – it was the season of the flies, hundreds of them continually flying around us; it was a relief to get to the hotel.

Our manager made an appointment for me to see a doctor about my throat and when he had examined me he said that he had never seen a singer's vocal chords before, but he couldn't see anything wrong and that a couple of weeks' rest would put me right. I told him that

I still had a number of concerts still to do in Australia and at least twenty in New Zealand, and that in one way or another I had to keep going. I did keep going, by keeping my talking to a minimum and with a few alterations to the programme.

The strike had not affected the New Zealand Airlines and so we were able to fly out to start our tour in New Zealand, starting in Christchurch. From then on, we toured both South and North Islands by car, except for a short flight from Nelson in the South Island, to Wellington in the North Island.

One incident that stands out – I think it was at Invarcargill – was when in the middle of a scene from 'Iolanthe', the police came on stage and ordered everyone to leave the theatre because of a bomb scare. We all trouped outside and for over an hour, we mingled with the audience, before being given the all-clear to continue. Obviously, word had got about that the English were in town.

My voice was slowly improving as the tour progressed and by the time we had reached Auckland, I was nearly, but not quite, back to normal. Alice's sister, Jenny, lived in Auckland and I wanted to be at my best for the concert there. I don't think she, or anyone else, noticed that there was anything wrong with me.

The bomb scare story reminds me that the same thing happened to us in a town in Long Island, New York. We had gone into a local restaurant for a meal before our concert and we were sitting at the bar. Apart from a group of men at the other end of the bar, there was no one else in the place. The barman came down and told us he had received a telephone call saying that a bomb had been planted in the restaurant and that if the British did not leave it would be exploded. We had the feeling that it was a set-up and we told the barman that they could leave if they wanted to, but we were going to stay – which we did – and our meal was served to us.

It happened to us twice in England. We had just started an orchestral rehearsal in Bath when the police ordered everyone out because they had received a call that a bomb had been planted under the stage; a hoax of course.

We had to announce from the stage in the City Hall, Sheffield, that a call had been received that a bomb was planted somewhere in the hall. The police thought it was a hoax call, but though members of the audience were invited to leave, no one did.

I had a very pleasant experience after our concert in Wellington. Graham Clifford, who was playing the principal comedy parts when I first joined the D'Oyly Carte Company in 1946, had retired to New Zealand and now lived in Wellington. He came round to see me and invited me back to their house for a meal. I was delighted to accept and was further delighted to find the dining room table covered with a cloth that had been signed by all the members of the company – including myself – when he left.

We flew out of Auckland about the end of August 1974, and headed for Hong Kong where we were booked to give two concerts in the ballroom of the Mandarin Hotel. A stage of rostra was set up on the highly polished dance floor and the first row of seats was only about three feet from the edge of the stage. We had a wonderful audience, including Chinese ladies in very colourful kimonos, reminding us of 'The Mikado'.

In the second half of the concert we presented a scene from Act II of 'Iolanthe', which ends with the trio 'If you go in', in which Don, John and myself perform quite a lively dance. At one point we all three push backwards on one foot and immediately the front row of rostra slid forward into the front row of the audience – who instinctively threw up their legs to protect themselves. No one was hurt and everyone had a good laugh.

From Hong Kong we flew to Singapore where a very good concert again took place in a very up-market hotel – I think the Singapore Hilton. The following morning we had a last swim in the rooftop pool followed by breakfast and then a taxi ride to the airport for the flight home with Britannia Airlines.

'The Sons of the Tillage who Dwell in this Village'

In 1965 we had acquired a bungalow in the little village of Bolton-le-Sands – just five miles north of the seaside resort of Morecambe and six miles north of the city of Lancaster where I had been a policeman.

We used it for holidays and long weekend, or if I had a few engagements in the north of the country, Alice would drive up in her little red Austin Mini and I would join her when I could. Our son Ellis and his wife Margaret spent their honeymoon there and relatives and friends used it for their annual holidays.

We had a lovely room built on the top of it, which had a twelve-foot long picture window facing to the west, giving us wonderful views across Morecambe Bay to the Cumbrian hills and, of course, of Morecambe Bay's renowned sunsets.

We enjoyed it for nearly twenty years before we decided to sell it, because we seemed to be using it less and less. Our neighbours, Lydia and Jim Mayall, were wonderful in keeping a careful watch on the house and keeping the place warm in the cold weather. We never had to worry about the little garden and they always kept in constant touch with us.

Alice and I often talked about selling our house at 203 Hampermill Lane, Oxhey, Hertfordshire with a view to retiring to a smaller one – but where? Even though we had lived in Oxhey for thirty-seven years, I had never felt that I belonged down there and I always missed seeing the sea and the mountains.

As I mentioned earlier, for ten years Gilbert & Sullivan for All had presented a series of three-day Gilbert & Sullivan Weekends at the Swan Hotel, Newby Bridge, managed by James and Jill Bertlin, great followers of G & S. After one such weekend, Alice and I stayed on with friends for a few days and we both agreed that we should look for a house in the Bolton-le-Sands area. It was the middle of November and we saw a few properties, but nothing that we really liked.

When we left for home, our good friends Ian and Phyll Robertson said that they would keep looking for a house that they thought would suit us.

A week later, Ian rang us to say that he had seen a house that he thought we would like – because *he* certainly did. I drove up the next day and agreed that it was indeed a lovely house, so I rang Alice and she travelled up, saw the house and also liked it.

It was now nearly the end of November. We put our house in the hands of an estate agent and in less than a week an offer was agreed. We quickly agreed a price for the new house and on 19 December 1988, we moved.

After thirty-seven years at 203 Hampermill Lane, it was a big decision to make and of course, all our friends and business colleagues tried to dissuade us because '203' had become a focal point for all our artists.

'A Wand'ring Minstrel, I'

'In Sailing O'er Life's Ocean Wide'

Don Adams also had a second home in Sheringham on the Norfolk Coast, which he was preparing for his retirement, and we were trying to slow down our company's activities.

So we moved, and we have never regretted it, although I missed my friends in the various clubs I belonged to in London, including the two sailing clubs. Yes – in the summer of 1980, Ellis surprised me with the news that he would like to buy a yacht!

He had obviously already done some research and had seen a number of yachts at the London Boat Show, and had decided that the

The Days Seem Lank and Long

boat he would like was a Southerly 28-foot built at the Northshore Boatyard, Itchenor, near Chichester.

When he first spoke to me about the idea, I wasn't particularly interested until he said that he had already investigated various finance schemes, which involved borrowing about £23,000 and paying interest rates of between 12 and 14 per cent. I discussed the scheme with Alice and we decided that we would supply the capital to Ellis at a much lower interest rate.

Ellis had already contacted Northshore, the builders of the Southerly range of yachts, and they had informed him that they had a Southerly 28 'in build' and which would be completed in time for the Southampton Boat Show. If we would agree to buy it and allow them to display it at the Boat Show in September that year, 1980, they would grant us various concessions. We agreed, and Ellis and I had great pleasure in watching the Northshore salesmen showing prospective buyers of a Southerly yacht, over our brand new boat, making sure they took off their shoes before walking on our gleaming decks and spruce carpets.

Ellis and his wife decided they would like to call the yacht *Born Free*. That was the easy bit – I didn't realise just what I had let myself in for. It was all very well to dream of sailing in sun-dappled waters with drinks and coffee being served at regular intervals by our 'galley slaves' (meaning our wives) but when *Born Free* was transported back to Itchenor and duly launched into the waters of Chichester Harbour, the moment of truth arrived. Accompanied by two expert sailors from Northshore we set sail on our Commissioning Voyage – or Shake-Down Cruise.

We sailed the eight miles of the harbour towards the open sea of the Solent and the English Channel. Ellis took to sailing and all the jargon like a duck to water, but I was completely baffled by the shouts of 'ready about' – 'lee ho' – 'close hauled' – 'broad reach' – 'starboard tack' – 'port tack' – 'let go this, let go that'. Every order shouted at double *forte* over the noise of the wind and the slapping and banging of the sails, while at the same time I was feeling more and more queasy as the boat pitched and heeled. Before we had cleared the Chichester Bar Beacon I shouted to Ellis that the sooner we got back to Northshore the better, and that I was too old a dog to learn these new tricks.

After a couple of hours, we sailed back into the comparatively quiet waters of the harbour and dropped our anchor off Easthead, where our crew opened the hamper supplied by Northshore and we enjoyed a good lunch with good wine thrown in. I began to feel better, but was still determined that I'd had my first and last sail and that Ellis would have to find another crew.

The following weekend I reluctantly agreed to give it another try, but again I was seasick. The following week I took seasickness pills and wore pressure bands on my wrists and lo and behold, I started to enjoy sailing.

We sailed regularly all through that autumn and even on New Year's Day, when we had to break the ice from around the hull. Ellis was becoming a real expert sailor and the Bukh 20 engine and the electrics were an open book to him, and any problems were quickly solved. I was acquiring some sailing skills, but I had a lot to learn.

I decided to attend a Yacht Masters Course and I also did a week's intensive sailing course with the Cowes Sailing Centre and obtained my Competent Crew and Day Skipper Certificates. At the end of twenty-five weeks, I obtained my Yacht Masters Certificate – just! I also obtained my VHF Ship's Radio Licence and took a course on diesel engines.

After about three years sailing *Born Free* I decided we needed a larger yacht and longed to own a 32-foot Southerly 95 with six feet headroom throughout. I had grown tired of continually banging my head.

One day in the Northshore boatyard, Ellis and I were looking at the new version of the Southerly 28 when we were joined by another man who told us that he already owned a 95, but now that his wife wanted to give up sailing he felt that the 95 was just too big to single-hand and that he was thinking of dropping down to a 28.

When I said that we owned a 28 and that I wanted to move up to a 95, we were in business.

Three weeks later, we tied up together in Bosham Reach; personal items were handed over into each boat and when we were both satisfied, I handed over a cheque plus *Born Free* in exchange for, can you believe it, the aptly named *Minuet*. We celebrated together with food and wine and parted company, leaving us with our 32-foot Southerly 95.

How's this for a coincidence – both yachts were on display next to each other at that same Southampton Boat Show, September 1980.

Ellis and I soon found ourselves becoming more and more involved with sailing. Northshore staged an open day at their boatyard and we met other Southerly owners. It was suggested that we form a Southerly Owners Association, so ten owners held a meeting that weekend and I became a founder

The aptly named *Minuet*, on a rough day in the Solent. Although Alice didn't enjoy sailing she did consent to a few trips and made an excellent galley slave!

The Days Seem Lank and Long

A voyage on *Lord Nelson* as a watch leader.

member. We organised rallies to various ports in the Solent and several to France and the Channel Islands. Unfortunately, pressure of work meant that Ellis became less and less available and I had to find competent crew members to join me on the various voyages and I joined other Southerly owners on their yachts – which wasn't the same.

Alice was never very keen on sailing but she managed several trips in the waters of the harbour and had an excellent reputation as a galley slave. Everyone loved her scones. It was always easy for me to find a crew when they knew that Alice would be providing the food.

Having sung for many years in the St Helier Opera House, Jersey, it was a great thrill for me to sail into St Helier marina and realise my ambition to make that exciting voyage.

I applied to be, and was accepted as, a 'Watch Leader' on *The Lord Nelson*, a three-masted barque, specially adapted to take disabled personnel to sea. I did a seven-day cruise, visiting ports in the Solent, Jersey and France. I was in charge of a crew of ten, both male and female, including two in wheel-chairs. There was also a crew of ten professionals, including the Captain and Bo'sun. We had eight years sailing up and down the Solent, around the Isle of Wight and across the Channel to the Channel Islands and to France.

Whereas I was finding more and more time to sail, Ellis was spending more and more time trying to make a living.

When we moved up north in December 1988, I decided to sell *Minuet*. However, Alice and Ellis persuaded me not to do so, and I had the yacht transported to Lake Windermere; I'm so glad I did because I have thoroughly enjoyed sailing the ten and a half-mile long lake, amid the most wonderful of scenery.

Also, I learned to handle *Minuet* single-handed, which I would never have done on the sea. Of course I chose the days when I sailed alone; I never took unnecessary risks.

In the spring of 1997 I decided to sell *Minuet* – I'd had a good innings of seventeen years' sailing – and I thought that it would take at least until the end of that season to find a buyer and so I could still look forward to another summer of sailing.

I rang Northshore and put the sale in their hands. What a shock

I had – within a week a family from Hull came over, liked *Minuet*, liked the price and it was all over. A few days later I had to say a sad goodbye to my yacht as she was lifted out of the water and transported to Hull for another life on the North Sea.

'And They'll Set the Thames on Fire Very Soon'

I mentioned earlier that our company had made films of the highlights of eight of the G & S operas, with a narration linking the various scenes, and that the soundtracks were issued by BASF Records and then by Pye Records. We were receiving a steady flow of royalties, but only small amounts, which, when divided on the system we had adopted, was hardly worth the trouble on Alice's part.

However, one day, Richard Warren of Anvil Films, where we had made the soundtracks, invited Don and I to lunch to discuss the royalty situation. The result was that for a lump sum we sold out the UK and world rights to the records.

Three or four weeks later, John Cartier rang us from the HMV record shop in Oxford Street in London, to inform us that our soundtracks were on sale on cassette tapes. So, instead of dying out, as we had been informed, they had now been given a new lease of life. Don and I felt that we had been out-smarted.

That was not to be the end of our 'film story' – since we moved up to our present home, I had occasion to want to see four of the eight films that I'd had in my possession since they were produced.

I spoke to a friend of mine who was in charge of the Sound Music Department at St Martin's College, Lancaster and asked him if he had the facilities at the college to project 15mm films. He said that he had and what did I want to show? I told him that I had four films that our company had made. He completely staggered me by saying, 'Why bother with a projector? They are all now on video tape.'

He also said that he had a copy of 'Ruddigore' in his possession, which he produced and put into his VCR and immediately, I was seeing a film I hadn't seen for thirty years. He also said that he could obtain the eight films we had made if I would like them. Of course, I said, get them, and two or three weeks later, I had them in my possession. I thanked my friend Ian Birnie very much, because I am sure I would never have found out about the videos if I had never approached him about the films.

It was marvellous to be able to see all the films our company had made so long ago, and really they are good to see, apart from 'The

Pirates' and 'Pinafore' which have suffered colour problems. Don and I were completely mystified as to how they had been produced on video without us hearing about it.

I must mention the Buxton International Gilbert & Sullivan Festival which Ian Smith and his son, Neil, have presented for a period of two to three weeks at the Buxton Opera House every year since 1994.

Briefly, Ian and Neil, who have a marketing business in Halifax, Yorkshire, and are Gilbert & Sullivan fanatics, invited amateur companies throughout the UK and the USA and Canada to come to Buxton and present their own productions of the G & S operas in the famous Buxton Opera House. The response was tremendous and fourteen operas were presented during those first two weeks. In addition, he engaged a dozen or more ex-D'Oyly Carte stars to present an opening concert to the Festival – also to hold master classes, to give informal talks and generally to be on show during the two weeks.

The Festivals have grown in popularity and have included two in Philadelphia and one in San Francisco, and this year will see the eighth Festival in both Eastbourne and in Buxton.

At last year's Festival, I mentioned to Ian and Neil that I was in possession of eight films made by Gilbert & Sullivan for All. Ian asked me if I had the address of the company issuing them. I provided not only the address of the company but also a brochure with the full particulars of the videos. A few weeks later Ian Smith informed me that he had bought the full distribution rights of the films and that he planned to re-market them. He also surprised me by stating that he wanted to replace the two narrators of the films and requested that I supply the narration for them instead. This has now taken place.

I now present several 'One Man Shows', telling of my life in the musical theatre, with the D'Oyly Carte Opera Company and of my broadcasting career.

Donald Adams, my friend and business partner for forty-three years, died four years ago and he is still badly missed. John Cartier, who sang with us for many years and was involved on all our tours, has also died.

Naturally, I have mentioned my wife Alice several times in this story but without her love and support through all these years, I would never have succeeded in my chosen career. Even our friends and colleagues tied our names together and it was always 'Tom and Alice'.

In this year of 2002, we are in our sixty-fourth year of marriage, but we have known each other since we were four years of age.

Since we were married in August 1938, we have spent many long years apart because of the war and the demands of my profession, and Alice has had to cope alone to attend to the everyday business of running our house and looking after our son, Ellis. We always

The last picture of Don and me at the Buxton Festival in 1997, six months before his death.

discussed any major decisions, but she never allowed her own needs to stand in the way of my career, and on the contrary, encouraged me to accept contracts which would mean great sacrifices on her part.

Alice was the personal secretary to the owner of an engineering firm in Barrow-in-Furness, a job which included bookkeeping, and so one of her tasks has been, and still is, keeping me on the straight and narrow with regard to my finances. Even our several accountants throughout the years have praised her presentation of my yearly accounts.

I have been fortunate indeed to have had Alice by my side all these years and I have finally decided to make our relationship a permanent one!

Earlier in this narrative, I mentioned Isidore Godfrey getting up from the piano, stating that he could not play for my first audition because I had not got any music with me. In other words, he would not try to play anything 'by ear'.

I was listening to a very interesting talk at the Buxton Festival last year, given by Peter Parker, the son of Stanley Parker, the private secretary to Miss Bridget D'Oyly Carte. He mentioned this fact about Isidore and it jogged my memory. In September 1948, when the D'Oyly Cartes were playing at the Theatre Royal, Glasgow and Godfrey and I were sharing the same digs in Hill Street, I had several sessions

The Days Seem Lank and Long

of practising new songs with Godfrey accompanying me on the piano. I remembered that I had three ten-inch 78 rpm records, which he and I recorded.

When I got home from Buxton, I searched for, and finally found, the three records and what a thrill it was to hear them again after all those years. I cannot remember how we came to choose the songs or where we went in Glasgow to record them. I know we could not have cut the records at our digs, but it's a complete mystery to me where we made them. Anyway, they are a treasured possession, which I hope will end up in a G & S museum sometime in the future.

'Ah – here it is at last – I thought it would come sooner or later.' (Act One quote from 'The Mikado.')

I'm sure every principal of the D'Oyly Carte Company has been asked this question many times – I know I have – 'Which is your favourite Gilbert & Sullivan opera?' The stock reply is, 'The one I am performing this evening.' When Donald Adams was asked this question, he invariably replied, 'The Gondoliers'.

'But you're not in 'The Gondoliers',' was always the surprised response.

'That's right,' was Don's answer.

My own reply was always 'Ruddigore', followed by 'The Yeomen of the Guard'. I know I should say 'The Mikado', because it was the first G & S opera I ever saw on stage, it was the first recording I ever made, it was the first opera I sang as a principal tenor in the company and it was during the recording of 'The Mikado' that I first met Donald Adams. Four good reasons why I should say that it is my favourite G & S opera. Of course I like it very much, as I do all the operas – but let me explain.

The juvenile leads or the romantic roles – this applies to the soprano leads too – are, in my opinion, the most difficult parts to put across to an audience; whereas the 'patter' roles, and those such as the Mikado and Pooh-Bah are, in several ways, a gift. They are usually in flamboyant costumes, with equally flamboyant make-up and so the characters make an immediate impact on the audience before they have even uttered a word.

Their dialogue is usually full of ready-made funny, sardonic, pompous or domineering speeches and as Gilbert said years ago, 'I only want you to able to be able to speak my lines intelligently.' What do they say in grand opera? – 'Put a hump on your back and there you are' – Rigoletto. Not so with the juvenile roles; nice costumes, of course, not flamboyant, plus a completely straightforward make-up – usually a light covering of a No. 9 Pancake!

In my case, in every role I played, I couldn't disguise the fact that it was Thomas Round on stage. My dialogue was always nice, sometimes a bit silly, as in 'The Pirates' and so the only way to register with the audience was to be completely sincere, not only with the dialogue, but with stage manner also; and to try to convince the audience that it wasn't Thomas Round they were watching, but Nanki-Poo, Marco, Ralph or whoever, with Thomas Round's face, with no hideous or outrageous make-up to hide behind. If, under those conditions, you were able to win over an audience, then I should say you were a very good actor or actress.

I always remember an interview with Mr Rupert D'Oyly Carte when we were discussing my contract for a coming tour. With great trepidation, I asked him if he would please consider relieving me of the role of Luiz in 'The Gondoliers', and allow me to play Marco instead. His reply was that during the past few years, the scenes with Casilda had become – in the audience's eyes – just a means of giving the other principals a rest between their scenes.

Now, they were being portrayed as real love scenes and so, for the time being, I would have to continue playing Luiz! By the way, the Casilda at that time was Margaret Mitchell.

I am not decrying the character roles in any way; I am just defending the love interest roles in the operas and why my favourite roles are Dick Dauntless, Colonel Fairfax and Cyril, because they are sometimes more demanding.

With Dick Dauntless I could relax from the ever-smiling or sometimes lovesick swain and do a bit of swashing and buckling, especially with the hornpipe, which was always a showstopper. When I took over the role of Dauntless, I asked Philippe Perotte (who was the ballet master with the Sadler's Wells Opera Ballet at that time) if he could teach me how to dance a good hornpipe.

I don't remember Leonard Osborn's hornpipe or who taught him, but I know he was very successful playing Dick Dauntless and that his hornpipe was excellent. Philippe agreed to teach me and I spent a number of sessions in the ballet rehearsal room at Sadler's Wells – where I had spent so many hours in the past, rehearsing various operas – working on the various step sequences of the hornpipe. It has often been suggested that I should write the sequence of steps down for future players of Dick Dauntless: well, here it is, just as Philippe typed it for me so that I wouldn't forget the sequence, and also a couple of shots of me in action.

'The Hornpipe'

1st half – Hornpipe dance around – arms akimbo
8 bars (1, 2, 3–1, 2, 3)
Last four bars – skip backwards

2nd half – Sailor Hitch to right and left – one each bar
Skip back last two bars
1st half – Scissors Step (wiggle). Cross feet every bar
Hands down in front of body – clasped, with palms down
Last four bars – skip back

2nd half – Heel and toe step round in a circle
8 bars scanning horizon at same time
1st half – Pull ropes down in front of body – on own ground
1–2–3 with feet alternately

2nd half – 1–2 stamp, 1–2 stamp – Right and left
8 bars. Run back on heels – rolling forearms towards body – last
two bars

1st half – toe – heel – toe step, right foot – left foot
8 bars. 4 bars.

Heave Ho – Heave Ho – Step
Pull rope and kick right foot
Pull rope and kick left foot

4 bars. Pull rope and move down with Charleston Step
Hat off and cheer on last note

Encore
8 bars Skip round with two girls
Skip back on heels with them
8 bars   With arms folded – right leg over left – left leg over right
4 bars
Pull rope and move down with Charleston step
Hat off and cheer on last note.

'There, thou hast it all … make the most of it.'

I introduced my grandson, Mark, to the delights of G & S by persuading him to appear with me in 'HMS Pinafore' at the Opera House, St Helier, in the small part of the Midshipmite. He was only ten years old and so I had to make all sorts of applications and fill out several forms before he was allowed to perform with us. His mother, Margaret – my daughter-in-law – had to be in attendance, in the wings, at every performance.

During our Holland Park Productions, he again played this part and also Ko-Ko's axe boy in 'The Mikado'. My granddaughter, Susannah, also joined us at Holland Park as a little make-up girl, holding the mirror while Pitti Sing and Peep-Bo helped Yum-Yum prepare for her marriage to Nanki-Poo. Susie also appeared as a little flower girl in 'The Gondoliers'.

He can dance as well!

In 1950, I was proposed and seconded for membership of the famous Savage Club in London by David Ghilchik, a well-known painter and Dr Charles Budd, a Nobel Prize winner. I was truly surprised that I should qualify for such a club because membership was only open to those who had virtually reached the top of their profession in either music, literature, science or art and I had only been singing as a professional for four years.

However, I was accepted, and now I was able to be in the company of singers and actors such as Donald Wolffit, Jack Hawkins, Norman Allin, Owen Brannigan, Harold Williams, Stanley Clarkson, William Herbert, Trevor Jones, Parry Jones, John Lewis and others. There were great characters such as Gilbert Harding and George Baker, painters like David Ghilchik and Harry Riley, and on the science side, Dr Charles Budd.

If some of the members thought I was rather young to be a member, I was soon accepted after singing at several of the Friday Night Dinners for which the club was famous. David Ghilchik also introduced me to the London Sketch Club and I rubbed shoulders with many well-known artists and sketchers. After singing at a few of their well-known Bohemian Evenings, I was made an Honorary Member of the Club – I still am to this day.

After thirty years' membership of the Savage Club and when we decided to move back to the north-west, I resigned from the club.

Again in October 1951, David Ghilchik aroused my interest in Free-masonry and he proposed me as a member of the Savage Club Lodge – seconded by John Young (night editor of the *Daily Express*). Having moved to Bolton-le-Sands at the end of 1988, I joined a Masonic Lodge in the nearby town of Milnthorpe and was made an honorary member

'The Mikado' and 'HMS Pinafore' at Holland Park, London, with my grandchildren Mark and Susannah, and Angela Jenkins as Yum-Yum (left).

of the Savage Club Lodge. In October 2001 I celebrated fifty years as a Freemason.

Still on the subject of club membership, I am an Honorary Member of the Gerrards Cross Sailing Association, and also a Founder and Honorary Member of the Southerly Yacht Owners Association.

'The Final Curtain'

Many years ago when I was on tour, Alice and Ellis were at home. From what Alice has told me, they had gone to bed in their adjoining bedrooms and one or the other of them had started to sing Sir Joseph Porter's song from 'HMS Pinafore', substituting words about my life. They managed to compile three verses and then gave up.

Those three verses have only come to light in recent months – I have now compiled a further four verses. (DCC, of course, refers to the D'Oyly Carte Company!)

Here is my final curtain call:

1. When I was a lad, I served a term,
    As an apprentice joiner in a steel works firm.
    I swept up the shavings and I brewed the tea,
    And I thought I'd never sing a high top C.
    I brewed that tea so carefully,
    That now I am a singer in the DCC.

2. After several years I became a PC,
    And tramped the streets in Lancaster city.
    I sang my songs walking round my beat
    And never thought another kind of beat I'd meet.

I sang those songs so well you see,
That now I am a singer in the DCC.

3. The war began and I soon became,
A fighter pilot in an aeroplane.
In Terrell, Texas, I received my Wings
And was known in Dallas, as the pilot who sings.
I flew my plane so effectively,
And lived to be a singer in the DCC.

4. I then decided to leave the DCC
And try my hand at operetta you see.
I toured for a year as Schani Strauss,
I also sang for Broadcasting House.
I gave recitals and sang so well,
And soon I was singing on 'Grand Hotel'.

5. Grand Opera called and so I tried
My hand at singing in the 'Bartered Bride'.
I followed this with 'Die Fledermaus'
And signed a contract with an Opera House.
I enjoyed my years, as well you know
My contract ended with 'The Merry Widow'.

6. Now all you people who do aspire,
To sing G & S in the local choir,
Brush up the shavings and tramp the beat,
And fly your plane in aerobatics so neat.
Take my advice, and you all might be,
Singing right beside me in the DCC.

7. Through all those years as you can guess,
I never lost my pleasure in G & S.
I still love singing about Sparkling Eyes
And will keep on singing it until I dies.
So thank you all, whoever you may be,
For all the years you have supported me.

'A Wand'ring
Minstrel, J'

CHAPTER FOURTEEN

The Epilogue

*T*HIS YEAR I AM PRESENTING CONCERTS of Gilbert & Sullivan for All, and I have also been invited to present two programmes at the Eighth Gilbert & Sullivan International Festival at Eastbourne – one about my life in the D'Oyly Carte Company, and one on my life in grand opera and operetta. I have performed in all eight of these Festivals, organised by Ian and Neil Smith, mentioned earlier – two avid devotees of Gilbert & Sullivan and musicals in general.

I practise nearly every day and every Monday morning, emergencies excepted, Gillian Allen, a friend and very busy music teacher, comes to my house where we sing for an hour and a half. Gill keeps me on my toes musically and will not allow me to get away with even the slightest deviation of time – a dotted quaver means a dotted quaver and not just a quaver. If a note is written to be held for four beats, then four beats it is. I suppose it is good for me!

Some mornings we sing opera arias; others, songs and ballads; and others, oratorios and sacred songs. Gill has also accompanied me in several concerts locally.

I am President or Vice President of several Gilbert & Sullivan and Operatic Societies in the country and I try to attend their annual productions each year.

It will be fifty-six years in February 2002 since I walked into the Savoy Hotel in London and started my career as a professional singer. It is wonderful how, in the most unexpected of places, I am approached by people saying how much they have enjoyed my performances on stage or on the radio or television, and how they can often recall performances of thirty or forty years ago. These occasions give me great pleasure and I can look back on a career that has not only been a pleasure for me, but has brought pleasure to many people world-wide.

I have often wondered what will happen to the dozens of reel to reel, cassette and video tapes and all my sheet music and operatic scores when I arrive at the end of my life.

Some articles of my memorabilia are housed in a wonderful Gilbert & Sullivan Museum in Oak Hall on Lord Sheffield's Estate, owned and presented by Melvyn Tarran. I am sure he cannot absorb all my material – he recently received a box of forty-two scrapbooks from a lady who has followed my career for at least fifty of my fifty-six years on the stage.

My son, Ellis, has also followed my career closely but he could not hope to take over all my memorabilia. Alice and I are already trying to shred lots of papers, but we seem to make little impression on the stacks of newspapers and magazines. I am quite embarrassed when I read some of the reviews and interviews – but despite this I have dared to include some in this book. As they say, 'You must stir it, and stump it and blow your own trumpet, or trust me you haven't a chance'.

Why not – it makes me feel good to read them! Some of the best are in magazines like *Opera* and *Music and Musicians* and newspapers like *The Times* and *The Telegraph*, as well as London and regional papers.

Of course I have had some bad reviews, like Lord Harwood's dismissing my performance in 'Die Fledermaus' with one short phrase – I quote: 'As Eisenstein, Thomas Round wasn't even in the picture.' That's what I call a destructive – not a constructive – criticism.

Now in my eighty-eighth year, I am still quite active and in demand as a singer and entertainer. I present programmes of my life as an opera singer, with cassette tapes of broadcasts, and computer-projected photographs of some of the operas and operettas in which I have appeared.

Looking back, I have had a wonderful life in my chosen career and have met countless numbers of marvellous people. Once again, Gilbert provides the perfect ending:

'SPRING AND SUMMER PLEASURE YOU
AUTUMN, AYE, AND WINTER TOO
EVERY SEASON HAS ITS CHEER
LIFE IS LOVELY ALL THE YEAR.'